THE FUTURE OF GOVERNMENT

BY THE SAME AUTHOR

FOREIGN GOVERNMENTS AT WORK
(Oxford University Press, 1921. *Out of Print)*

REPRESENTATIVE GOVERNMENT AND A PARLIAMENT OF INDUSTRY
(Allen & Unwin, 1923)

THE BRITISH CIVIL SERVICE
(Allen & Unwin, 1927)

THE THEORY AND PRACTICE OF MODERN GOVERNMENT
(Methuen, 1932)

ENGLISH LOCAL GOVERNMENT
(Methuen, 1933)

THE FUTURE
OF GOVERNMENT

BEING A CONTINUATION OF THE 'THEORY AND
PRACTICE OF MODERN GOVERNMENT'

BY

HERMAN FINER

METHUEN & CO. LTD. LONDON
36 Essex Street, Strand, W.C.2

First published in 1946

BOOK
PRODUCTION
WAR ECONOMY
STANDARD

THIS BOOK IS PRODUCED IN
COMPLETE CONFORMITY WITH THE
AUTHORIZED ECONOMY STANDARDS

PRINTED IN GREAT BRITAIN

To the Memory of My
MOTHER AND FATHER
THEIR VALOUR, WISDOM, LOVE, AND GAIETY
KILLED, JANUARY, 1945
BY V-2 ROCKETS IN LONDON

PREFACE

THE following pages were written to accompany a reprint of *The Theory and Practice of Modern Government*, and so to carry its themes forward to the present day. It was then realized that the reprinting must be deferred for some time by reason of the paper shortage. However, it was believed the new introduction, or sequel, whichever one likes to call it, might well be published as a separate work. As such, it is complete in itself. Yet it is also a supplement to *The Theory and Practice of Modern Government*; and from time to time the text of this volume refers back to the original work.

War-time obstacles have imposed an interval between the completion and the appearance of the work. It is most gratifying to find that the analysis of the problems of government between 1932 and the outbreak of World War II— which might be called the War of Democratic Deliverance— has been justified by subsequent events; it is hoped that the indications and predictions of tendencies and problems will be equally supported. Above all, it is hoped that the citizens of free societies can attain to the self-mastery required to keep their societies free while they pursue and achieve their happiness, always so poised in themselves and their principles of government that the way back may always be as negotiable as the way forward. Their hands to-day are certainly heavy with a mighty power, and their brows illumined with a greater comprehension than ever before in human history. Can they master their Will and vanquish their Fears ?

HERMAN FINER

HARVARD UNIVERSITY

CONTENTS

CHAPTER I

THE PROBLEMS OF 1932–39

WHEN *The Theory and Practice of Modern Government* was first published in 1932, a critic pronounced its conclusions to be too pessimistic, ' more pessimistic,' he added, ' than the conclusions of Bryce's *Modern Democracies* '. He then sat back and refilled his pipe. But, alas, there followed the dreadful decade when all we learned was agony and all we reaped was war. Time after time in those years of moral bereavement and economic distress, I felt like confessing to my students : ' Close your books on political institutions : you will not need them for a quarter of a century.' For in the richest country in the world, starving millions were crying, ' Mister, can you spare a dime ? ' In another, a political song ran, ' The future lies hidden in the barrel of a gun '. In still a third, to the utterly desperate question, ' Little man, what now ? ' the corruptor was preparing the sinister response, ' We spit on liberty ! ' In every democratic State the themes mingled and fermented.

War was the last thing anybody except the Nazi Party in Germany wanted ; but it was the necessary consequence of the first things that everybody demanded, and everywhere of the moral lassitude of large majorities of leaders and masses. The Concluding Observations of *Theory and Practice* suggested, ' Yet a single new force, *one louder voice*, a question, stupid no less than clever, a trifling discovery in technique may be uncontrollably disturbing (to the laboriously achieved democratic system) . . . there is always the danger that something will boil over, or crack or catch fire '.

In spite of all, the impulse of despair could not bear away the victory. For, if the calamity of 1939 was inevitable, it was as certain that some day the world would return to peace. Then the sifted body of teachings regarding the millennial experience of human nature in government would still be an essential guide.

Of the four great democratic polities those volumes described, one destroyed itself and nearly destroyed the others, though a few yet defended the seed of the spirit against the breath of Nazi corruption. Another stumbled towards the pole-axe, the integrity of its national character destroyed by the sight of the dreadful weapon lifted against it. The third nation, set in the defensive sea, avoided extinction by a minute margin of luck, and in that breathing spell redeemed its political virtue. The fourth, the mighty giant, with inarticulated framework, learned just in time, that where moral responsibilities and conflicts are concerned, out of sight is never out of mind, and 3,000

N.B.—The Notes to this Chapter begin on p. 171.

miles away is not even out of sight in a unified world economy served by electrical science and motor-fuel.

It is worth reflecting on the governmental problems of the decade 1932–42, though it is here impossible to do more than sketch them. Victory will not solve the world's problems of government but will merely retrieve the chance to solve them. This brief review is not an arraignment; there has been violence enough already. Within the small space available in this volume the attempt is made to suggest the character of the governmental problems of our time by looking at them, first, in a general survey, then secondly, by presenting the more significant phenomena in each country, and finally, by offering some reflections on the contemporary tasks of democratic government. This will give the opportunity, incidentally, for furnishing a bibliography which the student may wish to consult for further discussion on the subjects presented in the text.

*   *   *   *   *   *   *

It is tempting to group the governmental problems of the four democracies under two heads, the Economic and the Warlike, but this is really too narrow a classification, and at least as regards the first, would give rise to a misunderstanding of the author's judgment that economic factors, looming large as they did and do, meant much less as the primary cause of social disturbance and movement than it has become the easy fashion to claim. Yet, if we commence with the effect of the Economic Depression, beginning in 1929, and the preparation for Offensive or Defensive War beginning in 1933, we have two conspicuous pivots of discussion which may be later qualified and adjusted as the discussion proceeds. These two themes intermingle, the facts of each affect the other, and sometimes indeed are only another aspect of the same thing. The Economic Depression hit the countries at slightly different times; the Menace of War came clearly from 1933 onwards, with the Chancellorship of Adolf Hitler in Germany.

Now, the problems of contemporary government, as they were expounded in 1932, are the problems, still, of the present time. But the two agonizing anxieties just mentioned, and presently to be developed, did much more than intensify the existent issues. So severe did these become that they projected another of ultimate significance. Could the Democratic form of government, that is, the peaceful and progressive and tolerant rule by freely elected majorities, be maintained? Or must democracies succumb to internal convulsion; or perhaps retreat into suicide by the surrender of their basic principle; or through domestic disruption, general moral debility, or subversion of a united national will and virility due to internal social antagonisms, lay themselves open to destruction by dictatorial powers ?　Can democracies survive, or must they disintegrate ; and if they disintegrated, what were the terms of a new integration of the great masses of mankind, living in their ancient homelands ? Or, is the only other alternative that nations shall pay their respects to a façade of democratic forms, while actually living a social and political life at the gross, shabby level of material traffick and bargains, with the Commodity of the Bastard of King John as their moral standard, so that life may be nasty, brutish, and *long*.　Some observations on this grave subject are offered in Chapter 7 of this Introduction.　For, first it is essential to survey the consequences of the Economic Depression and the Menace of War, and then to consider the march of events in the different countries.

The Economic Depression raised the question whether democratic government could cope with the problem of Mass Unemployment. The Italian Dictator was early to ask : Was it a crisis in the capitalist system or a crisis *of* the system ? [1]　Was it a wound or an organic disease ?　Were modifications possible or total change necessary ? This again recalled and emphasized the governmental problems of Planning, of Bureaucracy, and the relationship of diverse economic groups in social change.　The resultant controversy led to, and was much sharpened by, agitated interest in the system of government of the Union of Soviet Socialist Republics, its objects, spirit and structure, and the government of Fascist Italy and Nazi Germany.　It was argued that certain chronic maladjustments, like long-term economic and social inequalities founded on inherited position and property, and more acutely unemployment, could apparently be solved much more quickly by these systems than by democratic machinery, even assuming that the latter could do so at all.　Yet it was appreciated that a choice might have to be made between delicately measured and adjusted degrees of political freedom and degrees of economic welfare.　For the provision of full employment must depend upon the enhanced powers of the State in the direction of public enterprise (public works, development works and even nationalized production in competition with private enterprise) ; the public provision of credit facilities, as for example by the Reconstruction Finance Corporation in the U.S.A. ; the maintenance of stable wages and prices, the organized retraining and transfer of workers from declining occupations, and so on.[2]　There was a clash between the notion of government which was responsible to a free electorate and the kind of government which might possibly act with benevolence but which provided no guarantees (which begs the question) for its action.

Another challenge to government came from warlike preparation. This came chiefly from Germany.　The challenge involved a number of consequences.　For the aggressors it was necessary to organize the economy of the nation for ' total war ', that is, to make all economic operations serve a military goal. As the total war of our age requires pervasive as well as extensive control, it meant an immense plan in which everybody, in all things, was altogether in servitude.[3] The extinction of all opposition was essential; and this reinforced the need, connected with unemployment measures, for governments not answerable to the people, to suppress dissent and enforce obedience to totalitarian commands. Now, it is far from the present intention to attribute the origin and action of dictatorships to purposes of war alone, though it is arguable that the Fascist and Nazi leaders, being from their outset bent on war, became dictatorships. Yet, whether from non-military dictatorial aims or for deliberate war ends, the dictatorial systems had to forge an apparatus out of the regular machinery of the State and a single monopolistic political Party, to organize and manufacture obedience and at least a show of loyalty, and to choke signs of opposition at birth.

Dictatorial practices attracted many in the middle and wealthy classes in democratic countries (though there were also many vehement dissenters in these groups) for economic reasons, for reasons of their own prestige and status in society, for the continuance of their traditional domination of politics, and as philosophies of life, ' the wave of the future '. Other groups, not of these classes, shared these or similar interests—some for non-economic, romantic, nationalistic motives; others, like shopkeepers and salaried employees, because they could not stand their economic insecurity in time of depression and because, normally, they were jealous of their snobbish status threatened by the rising working class. Others, again, of all classes, lusted for power over their fellows. Many were eager to flee from the effort required to uphold their freedom, or did not want it, even if they understood its value. It is difficult to sever the motives, and it is scientifically and politically dangerous, to put the consequences down entirely, even substantially, to the economic. If some simplify the crisis of our time down to a mere consequence of something they call ' capitalism in a phase of contraction ' and of ' class conflict ', it may at once be said that such explanations would make governmental progress far too easy compared with the tough problems that actually have to be solved. The real state of affairs is (a) a class conflict where ' class ' is ambiguous in theory and seriously incompatible with observed election results; (b) universal economic acquisitiveness; (c) a conflict among the many occupations cutting vertically down through ' class ' groupings for a share of the available economic benefits or avoidance of economic hardship; (d) the malaise of all occupational groups and of classes as such in a time of rapid and vast scientific and technological change; (e) the anxieties of the individual in relation to his occupation and to society as a whole; (f) deep individual perplexities and insecurity regarding spiritual values.

More will emerge to clarify even this rather more complex but still simple analysis as the discussion proceeds. At this point, at least, this must be said. The simpler class explanation would not account for the fact that, in Germany at any rate, a mass movement was behind the Nazi leaders, necessarily including millions of working class recruits *before* the peak of the economic crisis. Nor would it tell us why in democratic countries millions of the working classes steadily vote for conservative or liberal parties, why millions more do not belong to working class organizations, such as trade unions, but sometimes even express contempt for them. Much of this can be explained by illiteracy and ignorance and confusion spread by opponents ; but many of the literate and knowledgeable members are fiercer in their aloofness or hostility than the rest. If the explanation is (as a fault) shifted to denial of education, an even more serious misgiving arises, namely : why millions of people who have everything to gain by education do not take it for themselves ? If so many working class leaders have, in the teeth of the most difficult circumstances of job and home, managed to educate themselves, why not the rest of the workers ? Nobody can stop a man reading a book. The workers themselves know better their own weakness than do some of their non-working-class champions : ' Men who suffer an injustice with the power to remove it deserve not compassion but contempt ', is the motto of a British trade union, though the present author does not subscribe to ' contempt '.

May we expect that, as a result of a number of future successive elections and parliamentary terms, stretching over the next twenty-five years, and with the quickening in social consciousness and feeling generated by the present War, a fuller and clearer class confrontation will decisively appear in democratic politics ? That will be the test of the veracity of the Marxist exercise in division by two, and an answer to the question whether men and women suffer their politics to be dominated by the dictates of their occupation. If there is any excuse for deviation from the strict pursuit of occupational politics to-day, by reference to still existent ignorance of the meaning of politics and government, then with another quarter of a century's experience and education at school and by the Press, there ought to be no excuse that ignorance is the only reason for existent political choices and voting. The explanation will have to be sought either in coercion (which looks like nonsense) or in fairly deliberate preference for the non-class votes that are cast. We have yet to see.

Many among the upper-middle and wealthy classes applauded and were zealous to import the ideological outlook and ceremonial as a prelude to the whole governmental apparatus and method of the Fascist dictatorships. Thus, challenging democracy as well as Communism, and often democracy under pretence of Communism, they set up a domestic reaction and conflict which intensified the rift in national unity already opened by the competing blocs and interests in each country in their sectional endeavour to avoid suffering from the decline in the national economy or from adapting themselves to meet industrial, commercial and agricultural vicissitudes resulting from inventions and changes in the demand and markets. This domestic dissension presented the dictatorial nations with the opportunity of intervention by propaganda, world uproar, and incitement, less for the sake of their ideology as such (for both Hitler and Mussolini were far too cynical to believe in the universal value of the ideologies they shouted) than for fomenting discord in other countries. A humanist may walk alone ; an honest man may seek disciples ; but the dictators searched only for Quislings.

Foreign intervention by propaganda in the government of peaceful democratic neighbours provoked the question implied in *Theory and Practice* (Vol. I, p. 26), namely : ' If one powerful teaching body were able to operate unhindered and uncontradicted for a couple of generations with an attractive creed, effective forms, as yet inconceivable, could be provided for the State.' In England, France, and the United States the question arose whether life had not departed from the democratic faith, whether liberty was not, as Mussolini alleged, merely a ' putrid corpse ' ; in Germany it was answered. From this question sprang at least four problems to trouble governments and governed, namely : (1) the virtue and strength of the moral basis of liberty, equality and fraternity ; (2) the most efficacious means of inculcating this in mass democracies clotted around interests and social ideals which fracture the unity of the State ; (3) the conditions of successful propaganda ; and (4) the social and economic changes necessary to meet the charge that existent social inequalities are at once, in themselves, so unjust as to destroy belief in the equality among men and women assumed by the democratic faith, and a practical reduction of the value of the political franchise in its various forms.

The spiritual, economic and military challenge of dictatorial governments raised a question even more vital, that is, the problem of Leadership in democratic government, leadership which always implies a free following which freely selects its leaders. That there was a breakdown of leadership in Great Britain and France between 1932 and 1939 was clear to many in those years and must be clear to all by now ; and similarly, that in the United States of America there was bitter opposition to it. But, that there was a collapse of democratic citizenship is just as obvious and even more troubling. In its primary form the essential trouble was the relationship of the individual and leadership in a free society. It involved the question of the degree of responsibility attributable to any people which tolerates a government that steadily pursues a manifestly disastrous course. For there are domestic and foreign policies the consequences of which are irrevocable even when the minority in opposition becomes the majority in office. This same question has had to be asked above all of the Nazi and the Fascist states, for they were not secular dictatorships but had sprung from democratic systems. But in the long run it is a graver question for the democracies—they could have avoided the Second World War by right policy, pursued not by their leaders only, but by their sovereign voters.

It is necessary now to return to the beginning and amplify some parts of the outline already sketched.

The Economic Depression caused a shocking fall in the general prosperity, but for some—the working population, without property and little savings and no credit—it was a mortal affliction. In Great Britain, and in the U.S.A. and Germany, about one person in every five of the occupied population was without work at the depth of the trough.[4] The trouble came later to France. Everywhere it lasted a long time. The national income shrank (in U.S.A. from 100 billion dollars in 1929 to 40 billion in 1932), savings were lost, homes had to be abandoned, health was undermined, families starved. Yet, for individuals, the most harrowing effect was the sense of not being wanted by society, the insecurity of all the to-morrows, the submission to a test of means or need by those who dispensed public or private relief, and the loss of social esteem. The rich could not understand this; they could only believe that the dole would continue to encourage malingering or ' boondoggling '.[5] This disaster came in an era when the standard of living had been established (as suggested in Vol. I, Chap. III, of *Theory and Practice*) as god, when dietetics and nutritionism had become the monitors of public ethics, when science and technology allowed the reasonable promise of ' an age of plenty '. The slogan ' poverty in the midst of plenty ' embodied the bitterness of gall, for side by side with misery and starvation, there were supplies in some places so in excess of effective demand that they had to be destroyed,[6] and in some countries government itself, or monopolies not discouraged by government, instituted schemes to destroy productive capacity.

What could again set going the process of full production and exchange, but a centrally-organized arrangement whereby men without work were given it, in order to buy the excessive supplies at prices which would not be (as they were) ruinous to the producers, and an organization to buy the surplus goods and sell or give them to those who could not afford to buy them because they were temporarily non-producers ? From 1933, the answer of the U.S.A. was the policy known as the ' New Deal ' to give work, to buy up supplies and restrict the production of others ;[7] in Great Britain it was an exceptionally timid attempt to find work, with excessive reliance therefore on the 'dole' and the means test.[8]   Russia had no unemployment (but she was very poor) ; [9] Nazi Germany, which pretended that only Hitlerism could solve unemployment, shelved, but *did not solve*, the problem by public works directly connected with the attainment of military strength.[10]   All countries (even including France, which had less a problem of unemployment but more a problem of disastrously unstable agricultural crises and intermittent flights of capital, with therefore continual pressure on the national budget) expanded their State activities and State control over private enterprise.   This took the form of direct departmental controls (for example, the agricultural schemes of U.S.A., the Works Progress Administration, control over credit facilities, the marketing schemes in Great Britain, the Wheat Board in France), or in that of public corporations [11] (for example, the L.P.T.B. in England, the Reconstruction Finance Corporation and the Tennessee Valley Authority in America, the Bank of France) designed to carry on works of economic development in a shape free from 'red tape', or, as President F. D. Roosevelt expressed it in his message on the Tennessee Valley Authority (a regional development works project of immense scope), 'clothed with the flexibility of private business'.   In the dictatorial countries the dictatorial form, the military purposes and the economic planning required for anti-depression measures, led to the establishment of the corporate system in Italy, and a highly centralized and authoritarian system in Germany [12] which unified the whole State, and then, for political and economic purposes, allowed some sectionalization the better to secure obedience and devolve detailed and intricate technical responsibilities.

In the democratic countries grave clashes occurred between big business and the governments, the former seeking to escape from government interference and control, the latter not necessarily pressing big business but being continually harassed by the opposition parties to control or collectivize it.

How to secure men against mass unemployment ?   The problem was not solved, when war preparations or war itself began.   Indeed, its solution would require a tremendous leap towards State regulation of economic life and the actual ownership and management in a decisive sense of some of its units.   At least one of the required factors, namely, currency, credit and securities, was in the U.S.A., Great Britain and France subjected to extremely firm and increasingly thorough control, the easy beginning, perhaps, of a wider control of all economic processes.

Underlying this development, another of earlier origin and more permanent significance took hold of the public mind : Economic planning.   Planning (Vol. I, Chap. III) has either of two general motive forces—increased production, or more equitable distribution and consumption, and both require a high degree of government control of economic processes. The first motive implies the use of the natural resources, labour, skill, science and organization to the maximum degree and kind of productivity, that degree and kind being established at a central and upon a unified point of view in the belief that an immense increase of production and a lightening of human toil can be so secured. One aspect of this order of thought is ' Technocracy ', the government of society by technical experts.[13] The most extreme views of this kind, extreme to the point of political impossibility, even perhaps in the dictatorships we already know, ignore the free expression of citizens' preferences, and neglect the consequences to civic liberties and the rights of opposition. But more sensible views look to production planned for maximum consumption with an earnest and preventive eye upon the possible loss of freedom. Indeed, this is the crucial problem of modern democratic government, to discover how to plan maximum production, and distribution which will promote the maximum welfare, while preserving liberty of political dissent and vigorous economic experimentation.[14]

The other motive force towards planned production begins with the idea of more equitable distribution. This means, not distribution according to a man's capacity to produce, and especially not the capacity to produce in the present rather haphazard economic process, but distribution according to need, consumption needs being the governor of the programme of production, not profit-making, which follows the indicator of effective demand. It includes also a wish for ' justice ' in the human relationships of production, of labour standards, workshop management, and so forth, and of a better share of the employees in the process as well as the product of industry, the process itself being a contribution to the latter. But any considerable intervention in distribution can only be implemented by control of production : that is the lesson of Soviet experience [15] as well as the plain twice-told lesson of the war economies of all the belligerents.[16] The movement for planning has its origins in the war of 1914–18. The chief impetus came when the German Generals suddenly saw the war was not to be won quickly and that all resources, human, material and scientific, must be mobilized for a single purpose.[17] Little as the post-war fulfilment was, relative to the promise of a better world made during the war of 1914–18, something of the promise was kept. Moreover, there remained a mental and moral sense that certain social changes could no longer be denied in modern states simply on the ground that they were administratively impossible : what had been done for war, could be done for welfare.

Planning had its immense difficulties even in war-time when aggressive or defensive emotions unified great multitudes of men and women as to the purpose of the State. For the millions of individuals were not absolutely like-minded, nor by any means identical in the degree of sacrificial determination, nor in their endurance, or toleration of socially imposed hardships, for the purposes of victory.[18] There-fore, the observer must ask himelf questions about the effectiveness of governmental planning not merely in terms of administrative techniques and institutions, but above all in the context of the diverse and changing aims of individuals and groups. Can a plan, far-reaching and taut, be arrived at by free discussion and agreement, which will not only satisfy a vast majority, but continue to satisfy a majority ; and is society to permit the usual free right of opposition to and criticism of that plan and its administration with the possible result of its piecemeal dismantlement or total subversion ? Furthermore, there is the question whether those who plan can limit their influence to what is consciously planned only, or whether the plan will not have *indirect* consequences of control over the rest of individual activity. Have governments the psychological and technical ability for self-limitation in their planning activity, or must they become absolute ?

Yet in various ways, as a consequence of the productive and dis-tributive motives referred to above, and side by side with the need to take planned anti-depression measures, unmistakably important advances were made in all countries, democratic and otherwise, along the lines indicated. Here and there, in the various sectors of economy, a number of public corporations arose for production purposes, while simultaneously more and more comprehensive social security schemes, that is, schemes for the maintenance of the income of the unemployed and those distressed by accident, invalidity, sickness, old age, widow-hood, orphanhood, &c., were established.[19] Along the distributive line, World War II aroused sentiments of social equity, based upon the notion of the justice of equality of sacrifice of all classes and occu-pations in a community at war for common survival. This culminated in such instruments as the Atlantic Charter, with the declared objective of ' securing for all, improved labour standards, economic advance-ment and social security ', and so that ' all the men in all the lands may live out their lives in freedom from fear and want '. Another such pronouncement of political intention was the declaration made by President F. D. Roosevelt in January 1942 of the Four Freedoms : Freedom from Fear, Freedom from Want, Freedom of Religion and Freedom of Opinion.

As piece by piece was added, in the inter-war years, to its specific organs of planning of production and social security and assistance, each nation established an agency of comprehensive planning, that is of plan-making and studies and investigations to that end. In the original edition of this book, it was possible already to analyse the nature and effectiveness of the German Economic Council ; [20] the Economic Advisory Council in Great Britain and British Royal Commissions and Advisory Bodies ; [21] the Conseil National Economique of France ; and since then the United States Government established and abolished the National Resources Planning Board.[22] All of these institutions fulfil one or both of two functions, namely, they bring together representatives of the main economic groups in the hope of securing from them both intimate and expert expression of their special views and desires (essential to the education of public administrators whether as executives or draftsmen of laws), and a mutual arrangement of policy based on this. Or, they make scientific and long-term analysis of trends requiring governmental intervention, if a particular economic or social result were desired by the government rather than a fortuitous result growing from the undirected operation of those trends. The Economic Advisory Council [23] in the United Kingdom and the National Resources Planning Board in the United States were more particularly adapted to this latter objective ; and of the two, the wide vision and scope of the National Resources Planning Board, its uncurbed status as an organ of insight and foresight, its independence of immediate politics and politicians, resulted in a considerable contribution to social prescience, if not to the adoption of executive plans.[24]

The work of these comprehensive planning bodies achieved little, because over-all planning, as suggested previously, is a political act on the highest level. It is a matter for the supreme executive and the parliamentary assembly, with the assent of the people. Any planning body of the kind mentioned, whether exclusively advisory, or whether fitted into the governmental machinery like the *Reichswirtschaftsrat* or the *Conseil National Economique*, cannot but be an adjunct, a subservient if useful and even indispensable organ, to the process of planning which goes on continuously in every state in the form of the more thoughtfully predictive and concerted progress of government policy. It is, indeed, a mistake to place exclusive hopes in democratic countries in one single organ of planning of the character indicated. Democratic governmental systems are served, as it is, by a planning process which looks something like this. In the centre are the Cabinet or the President and the parliamentary bodies upon whom falls the first as well as the final responsibility for results. They ultimately decide ; and their decisions become not merely a plan, but a special form of plan, namely a law, which is normally followed by application in detail. Before, however, the matter comes to the summit point of decision, there is a twofold process, one commencing at the Cabinet or Presidential stage, while the other finds its destination there, but emanates from the distance outside. In the first process, the Cabinet or the executive or a parliamentary steering body develops a policy, that is a plan : a considered pattern of desires and the will to their attainment. Through its offices it then marshals the information, the suggestions, the favourable or unfavourable reactions of, it may be, hundreds of social organizations and individuals, in order to make that plan workable, to fit it to the hard and the soft contours, and perhaps modify it when analysis proves that ambition or ideals have outstripped national capacity to fulfil it.

Simultaneously, in any highly developed society, a second process is going on. Various societies of interested people, some occupational, some social, some religious, some anxious to give, others to receive or be protected, have their plans, that is to say, desires that government shall make universal certain rules of civil conduct. Universities, for example, are not only concerned with teaching, but with research in economic and social matters, with the possibilities laid open by natural science. Enjoying relative independence of thought, they are able to suggest long- and short-term directions and recommend ways and means. Besides, in the last quarter of a century there have come into existence various Institutes of Social Research—historical, economic, statistical, for political and economic planning, and so on. Usually these are without a political party bias, though they may have very definite corporate convictions regarding the plasticity of human nature, social organization, and the shape in which these ought to be moulded. In the end, however, whether there is a special all-comprehensive governmental organ at the top of this congeries of free planning bodies or not, the sifting of the plans suggested comes into the hands of the trusted professional civil servants, or career public employees. These are the professional advisors of political ministers and legislators, the draughtsmen of plans. In the end, to these is assigned the responsibility of converting the plans which receive the imprimatur of the sovereign political bodies, into the behaviour of the citizen. In the planning process the chief service is rendered by these civil servants. For, though they may not create or originate the laws, they hold a strategic position for sifting and collating, for the discovery of administrative and technical ways, and machinery, the adjustment of plan and plan, not to mention the everyday execution of the result. Hence, all importance ought to be attributed to their role, no matter how well organized the especially established private or political organs of planning. The final planners (if not the inventors or discoverers), before the plans reach the stage of enactment, are the civil servants, and nothing should be allowed to obscure the view that the making of the plan and its achievements are a direct function of the quality of the civil servants. For the recognition of this proposition has a decisive bearing upon the problem of education and recruitment of public officials.

In this and other ways, the development of intervention by the State made progressively more acute the problem of 'bureaucracy' (Cf. *Theory and Practice*, Vol. II, Chap. XXVII), by increasing the number of officials, by the grant to them of discretion in the interpretation and application of the law, and in the determination of cases by quasi-judicial procedure [25] brought by officials against citizens, or on appeals by the latter against their orders. Perhaps superior in importance was the fact that economic regulation increasingly demands that public officials shall directly initiate and conduct industry—going out to get business—rather than merely maintain a more remote if profound control from official points of strategic leverage. World War II raised the administrative problem with even more marked force ; and war plans, involving a special degree of State intervention, combined with extensive plans for social reform, to precipitate extremely important debates, [26] and in England proposals for reform. [27] Briefly, these specific problems are : the recruitment of public employees suitable for more dynamic and positive enterprise in economic and social matters ; [28] whether public employees should be recruited in youth or at a later age, to take advantage of acquired experience ; the comprehensive provision of education to all classes, in order to overcome narrowness in the class selection of the public services (more a British [29] and European than an American problem), thus increasing their range of understanding and sympathy ; the technique of discovering able recruits, or those who ought to be promoted, and of giving them special tuition to fit them for higher duties ; the nature of the process of weighing the merits of one candidate against another, that is by examination, competitive interview, selection for character as well as for knowledge and intellectual proficiency ; post-entry training, to maintain freshness of mind ; and the relationship of the various departments of government to a central agency thereof (like the British Treasury or the U.S. Bureau of the Budget) which exercises or should exercise an all-round control over establishments, organization, procedure, and method. [30] The subservience of nearly all public officials to Nazi authority and the obedience of most French civil servants to the Vichy régime questioned the limits within which civil servants ought to be neutral and impartial agents and expert advisers of no matter what party was in office, no matter how it arrived there, or what it intended to do to society.

Movements for social change in the inter-war years and since—to secure more equitable economic distribution, greater equality of economic and social opportunity, and, through more collectivized and authoritative direction of economic processes, a rise in the total production available for distribution—produced a political strain in more than one phase of government. The most important, though by no means the only one, was the sharpening of class and group conflict in democratic countries, where expression was free. For changes adverse to the wealth and the governmental and social status of the propertied groups were clearly involved. In an age when material possession had come to be the first mark of social distinction and the principal object of industry, the threat of their loss was an insupportable injury to those who had something to lose. They feared insecurity, the insecurity of competition by lower level social groups whose claims could not but be privately admitted—though with a curse—and which therefore had been deliberately restrained by the governmental defences erected by those threatened. The ploughing-under of crops and destruction of surplus commodities during the acute stages of the Great Depression, were nothing compared with the secular ploughing-under of the brains of the masses by those in traditional control. This ploughing-under was more steadily pursued in Great Britain, France and Germany (which believed in education, not always for itself) than the U.S.A., the salvation of which nation from many political and economic flaws lies in its belief in wide-open educational opportunities.[31]

Tension and hatred became ever more acute and caused bitter clefts in national politics. It became almost impossible to make progress by the normal, patient and friendly Parliamentary procedures, and demands were heard for emergency legislative short circuits [32] for *pleins pouvoirs*. From one side came outbursts against ' economic royalists ' and ' Fascists '; from the other, the mildest liberal was denounced as ' dictator ' or ' bolshevist ' or ' bureaucrat ' or ' warmonger '. All this envenomed political activity. The first principle of election tactics became the provocation of panic and alarms; and some political parties, like the British Union of Fascists and the *Croix de Feu* in France, became militarized. As governments ceased to be candid because candour opened the door to Opposition reproaches, their prevarication aroused the contempt and compelled the cynicism of humble men of conscience. Democratic nations which, by their very principle, rested on the right of dissent became hardly able to act as a unity towards aggressive nations.

Nevertheless, it would be a supreme mistake to imagine that the excitement and disorders arose from a ' revolutionary ' feeling on the part of ' the masses '.[33] Occasional outbursts of feeling, claims for improvements in wages and labour conditions, are not to be mistaken for a great persistent ground swell of resolution to make a wholesale social change, the pattern of which is discerned and supremely avowed. Nor, in modern societies, *are* there any substantial undifferentiated masses. Rather there is a series of groups graded in income, of a social outlook and aspiration related to the character of the profession or occupation more than the size of the income. Thus the white-collared or black-coated workers may earn less than artisans in overalls and caps, but their social habits and ambitions are distinctly diverse. There are occupations which have a solidarity of interests against other occupations, manifested by the combination of labour and management to fight for their own sectional share in the national income at the expense of other occupations and consumers, and by the inability of trade unions to maintain a united front in a general strike for any length of time.

The Marxian division of society into two solid groups, bourgeois and proletariat, with progressive accumulation of wealth on one side and ever more crushing misery on the other, is *not* the most serious problem facing modern government.[34] For, as we have already observed, there are many intermediary groups, and within each group there are material and cultural differences among sub-groups. What truth the Marxian cleavage has is less as a division of society into two camps than as the indicator of social divisions as such, and far more graduated than two. It has, in addition, more significance as a recognition of universal economic acquisitiveness than as war between classes for political domination. But even more than the division of interests and outlook on civilization discernible in the groupings mentioned, is the vertical division of interests among individuals. Individuals compose these groups, which are not so coherent as to reassure their anxious leaders and officials, who are always fearfully looking over their shoulders to see if they are being followed. Thus, contemporary publicists who win spectacular games by playing literary chess with a set of simple Marxian counters have done so only by neglecting what is a far more important and difficult problem than that of class division : the problem, that is to say, of discovering the conditions integrating the individuals and their manifold vertical groupings and sub-groupings within the State as a unity, and beyond the State, the world. There are many strata and many gulfs. All evidence goes to show that Stalin has found Karl Marx much more useful as a disintegrating critic of an unwanted society than as a guide to the building and government of a durable and developing community. And Stalin's successors are likely to find, even more than he, that Engels' carefree forecast that the State will wither away, is of less use [35] still, even when the bourgeois groups have been altogether liquidated. They, as well as we, still have the individual on our hands.

Have Western societies in our time been the scene of class struggle, or not ? The answer is that there has been political tension, even struggle, and sometimes riots, and the aim has been more wealth and freedom on the part of the poor. And on the side of the richer part of the people, there has been tension, struggle, sometimes chicanery and violence and inert force, but also substantial concessions (consider the remarkably large proportion of the national income transferred from the richer to the poorer in the form of social services by peaceful legislative process) and they also have sought for wealth and the continued power to govern others. Has the struggle been conducted by 'classes'? The answer is No; not as a clearcut twofold class division, but as a confused, intermixed struggle of men and groups of all sizes, with much crossing of interests, loyalties, voting and fighting. Does the majority in the various democratic countries want the 'struggle' to be 'war'? The answer is No. Do the industrial workers, the manual working groups and their families want the struggle of groups to be war? Observation of their activity and declarations offers the answer, No.

What, then, is the struggle about? In our own time the heavy emphasis of all the contenders is upon the acquisition of wealth. Most would like to be richer and work less and in more agreeable occupations. But how much do the contending groups and individuals press for greater wealth? And, again, how much in comparison with other values? No one can be dogmatic on this score, if only that we have no yardstick by which to be guided. Then, it would seem that no one has the right to be intransigently, still less revolutionarily, dogmatic about the drift or necessity or character of the 'class struggle', if he pretends to found himself on observed facts, and to be a friend to mankind.

We only know that it appears that the values of liberty, humanity, toleration, and mutual help are demanded by the political contenders of all kinds, as well as wealth, and that the strength of these desires varies from land to land and *person to person*. Man does not die for bread alone. If all were for riches, and for nothing else; and if the determination in its pursuit were universally intense, then the present state of economic scarcity would result in a state of continuous murder. Indeed, the state would have withered away! 'Class' is far too easy as a definition of the problem of government, even as short-run politics, and it is crassly irresponsible, viewed as the long-term formula for the tasks of government. But in the politics of democracy anyone may intervene and talk; and since the passions must be whipped up, politics provokes extreme talk. And so, the myth of the class struggle, consciously recommended by some for this very purpose, and to some extent valid as a theory, and to others acceptable as a principle because they are by nature one-idea men (at any rate, one idea at a time), is paraded for its qualities of incitement. But it appears to the present author that the extreme of incitement often goes far beyond what party leaders know their modest followers are asking for, or what they themselves would recommend or claim. Smart men use the myth tactically—ask a lot and you will *frighten* opponents into giving up something. Thus, the theory obscures the tough bitter secular problems of government, both by its opaque simplicities, and its suggestion that a day will come abruptly after which all will be well; whereas we are entitled to believe that classes may go, if they exist, but the individual will remain, and severally and in associations cloven vertically men will still ask for and need government. For Adam lived before Marx and will even go on living after Stalin.

Now that the majority, that is to say, the poorer members of democratic nations, are on the threshold of power after centuries of struggle, we have still to see whether they will not deliberately reject the total socialism towards which Marx proclaimed they were or should be striving. Before instituting it ; or, ruefully, after seeing it in practice. As men do and must continue to differ in their material and spiritual needs, in their preferences regarding general equality, personal wealth, and distinction, they must call in the services of government just as they have always done, to adjust and moderate the differences among those inveterately stubborn units, individual persons, millions and millions of them, in order to preserve the general liberty and order.

CHAPTER II

EXPERIENCE OF DICTATORSHIPS

SOON, as soon is reckoned even in a man's lifetime, the Nazi and Fascist dictatorships will be but smarting scars, and the Soviet system will have softened its grinding, despotic arrangements as it attains its chief productive and distributive objectives. In order that the democratic way may be the better understood, and therefore, perhaps, more faithfully applied, it is as well that the chief features of its opposites be remembered. In two fundamentals, one of principle and the other the application of principle, the dictatorial systems stand the world apart from the democratic ; that is, in their non-responsible basis, and in the exercise of the monopoly of power and propaganda by a single political party. Each of these requires some examination.

The meaning of the institutional arrangements differentiating the democratic and dictatorial systems of government is best clarified by distinguishing the responsible character of the former and the non-responsible character of the latter.

Now, there are two principal meanings of the word ' responsibility '. ' Responsibility ' may mean answerability or accountability *to* another person or institution *for* some duty. It stresses liability to be called to account by an external body. Responsibility in this sense requires an apparatus to secure it ; and such a controlling body would require authority to operate even *against* the wishes of a government, that is, the government organ which is responsible. There is another meaning to ' responsibility '. It is to be merely accountable for one's actions to one's own conscience on self-made or self-accepted standards. In a democratic system of government both these meanings of responsibility are invoked ; but it is the former, that is, accountability to an external agency and ultimately the people, that has the power of discipline and correction which is the true distinctive nature and merit of democratic government. In autocratic countries this conception of responsibility is deliberately, even contemptuously, repudiated. Instead, there reigns the idea of ' leadership ' or ' trusteeship ' founded upon this second meaning of responsibility only. (For further development of the theme see the author's article, ' Administrative Responsibility in Democratic Government ', *Public Administration Review*, Autumn 1941.)

Thus, the Nazi dictatorship is founded upon the notion of responsibility so expressed by Hans Frick : ' All powers of government are concentrated in his (the Fuehrer's) person, while he himself is respons-

N.B.—The Notes to this Chapter begin on page 173.

18

ible only to the nation '; while Hitler himself says (*Mein Kampf*):
' The principle of the establishment of a whole State constitution must
be the authority of every leader to those below and his responsibility
upwards.' [1] This provides for a responsibility which goes upwards
and upwards, from sub-leader to sub-leader; but once it gets to the
leader himself, responsibility, in the sense of answerability and the
liability to be called to account, goes outward only to the dictator's
looking-glass. Nobody in such a system can call the leader to account
for his distribution of authority to those below him, or his activity
or remissness in calling them to account for their use of that authority.
Beyond the leader there is no appeal; and he denies the validity of
opposition, contradiction and challenge by the aristocratic doctrine
(*Mein Kampf*): ' To give this earth the best people . . . it is necessary
to assure to the best minds the leadership and highest influence within
the nation. Thus it is founded not on the idea of majority government but on personality.' Then the Leader's constitutional jurist will
chant :

' The Fuehrer unites in himself all the sovereign authority of the Reich ;
all public authority of the State as well as in the movement is derived from the
authority of the Fuehrer. We must speak not of the State's authority but of
the Fuehrer's authority if we wish to designate the character of the political
authority within the Reich correctly. . . . It is not limited by checks and
controls, by special autonomous bodies or individual rights, that it is free and
independent, all inclusive and unlimited . . . it is free of all outward ties because
it is in its innermost nature firmly bound up with the fate, the welfare, the
mission and the honour of the people.' [2]

Mussolini's essay on Fascism says the same.[3] Here it is declared
that one man may represent, better than any other, the real needs of
the nation, and this is supported by the denial to all others of the
appropriate knowledge of government and also the rectitude of their
inspiration; and so there is no ground for the responsibility of the
Leader or Duce or dictator to any other institution or person.

In their work on Soviet Russia, the Webbs [4] are at much pains
to deny that the Russian system is a dictatorship, or as we should say,
a non-responsible system of government. They labour the case that
it is a democracy, in a sense even more vital than Great Britain, U.S.A.,
France, and the like. This rests on the admittedly multifarious means
whereby the Russian people may express their opinion, the many
channels through which they are deliberately consulted, and the ener-
getically recommended system of so-called ' auto-criticism '. All this
is true; consultation is rich and genuine and sufficient to distinguish
the Russian from the Nazi and Fascist States. But the most diag-
nostic mark distinguishing between responsible and non-responsible,
or democratic and dictatorial States, is not the ability of citizens
to represent their point of view, but in their ability to influence the

actions of their government even against that government's will to the point of changing or removing that government when it does not respond to the popular will.   All respect may be rendered to the famous speeches of Stalin and Molotoff at the Constitutional Congress of 1936,[5] arguing that the national ownership of all productive and distributive property made Russia a democracy more genuine than any of those so-called.   But this argument, far from being conclusive, merely raises one of the gravest questions of all in the conduct of States ; the question, namely, not in whom is the property vested, but who actually manages and has disposition of the property, by what authority and subject to what popular impulses of control ? Every particle of property might belong to all the people as a community, and yet no single part of it might be utilized as any single person would wish.   Indeed, all of it may be employed in ways considered to be good by its managers, men who might be self-appointed, and in any case not under the responsible control of the masses.[6] Abundant social and economic benefits may be rendered by this system, and evidently have been rendered in Russia : but the question at issue here is the nature of responsible or non-responsible government.   Trusteeship for the people may be socially beneficial, especially in the short run, but much less certainly in the long run.   For where is the guarantee ?   Such a government is not, when seeking what it non-accountably decides to be the ' real ' interests of the people, a responsible system, in other words, a democracy.

Expressions from the constitutional experience of the responsible governments make clear, beyond a doubt, the distinction between the two systems.   Since there is no written constitution for Great Britain, we must rely upon another source.   Thus, in the Report of the Committee on Indian Reforms of 1934 (Vol. I, part 1, p. 5), reference was made to ' two familiar British conceptions ; that good government is not an acceptable substitute for self-government through ministers responsible to an elected legislature '.   Again, the American political process has crystallized itself in such expressions as : ' Government by consent of the governed ' ; ' Where annual election ends, tyranny begins ' ; and ' Government of the people, by the people, for the people '.   In the German Constitution of 1919, sovereignty was declared to issue from the people, not from the government ; it was exercisable through organs of government, and the resignation of the principal organ, namely, the Cabinet, when the confidence of the Reichstag, elected by the people, was expressly withdrawn from it, was established by an article of the Constitution.

The non-responsible or dictatorial systems of government differ, however, from the old autocracies by the establishment of mechanisms for the permeation of the whole body of the people, or as a Fascist political theorist has put it, by ' the identification of people and government '. The dictatorial systems of our own time have shown that such identification has been more concerned with contriving that the views of the people become identical with those of the government than to identify the government's views with those of the people. There is, therefore, created a machinery for the discovery of opinion, for the destruction of opposition at the earliest moment of exposure, and then for the deliberate manufacture of opinion in order to secure civic obedience. This implies a permanent need for a political party enjoying the monopoly of power to the exclusion of all others, and an arrangement of propaganda or political education, strong, calculated, incessant—a matter to which we return later.

Systems of government as far apart as the democratic and dictatorial, the responsible and non-responsible, often retain the same words to represent functions of government which differ remarkably from each other. Thus, particularly, the words ' party ', ' parliament ', or ' congress ', and ' elections '—terms which still obtain in the constitutions of the dictatorial governments—actually hide (as intentional deception, frequently) an enormous gulf in the meaning and part played by these institutions as compared with democratic government.

The difference of function is a product of the difference in basic philosophy, and it is proper at this stage to point to the two chief elements that differentiate the general outlook of the responsible from the non-responsible systems of government. The democratic systems acknowledge (1) political equality, and (2) the advantages of freedom. By the convention of political equality they do not mean and have never meant that all men and women are in fact equal in physique, spiritual and intellectual qualities, dispositions of character, experience, learning and the rest. They mean that since there is no external objective standard of the ultimate good, society perhaps may arrive at a notion of it if each and all are allowed the equal expression of their conception of it. There is no way, they believe, of disproving a priori the equality of one person's ultimate conscience and insight into the ultimate good and social values compared with another's. Therefore, the attainment of the maximum political good—which is the discovery of our social duty by the discernment of our individual nature and destiny—can come best only from the free interplay of opinion and utterance of what is believed to be the truth, and, consequently, the contest of truth with error. But to attain this freedom, it is essential to stand upon the basis of equality, for without such equality there is no encouragement to speak forthrightly with any hope of being listened to, or to speak with courage should a struggle be necessary, nor is there ground why the sanguine and arrogant official or political leader should listen and be influenced by ordinary men and women.

Knowledge of the facts is, of course, indispensable to right political decisions; but the *valuation* of these facts and their relationship to a sense of the ultimate good and the nature of human destiny may come as well from any man as from any other, whether high-born or low-born, rich or poor, educated or uneducated, literate or illiterate. The facts can always be supplied by books, civil servants, teachers, politicians. In the discernment and appreciation of man's destiny and in the consequential principles and conviction of duty, all men are equal. The issue is not intellectual, it is spiritual; not facts, but values; not techniques, but purpose. On this ground ordinary men have been as wise, indeed wiser, than many kings, statesmen, philosophers, dictators, generals, and churchmen. By how much, indeed, has the spirit of man been enriched by the life of a certain carpenter's son, of a humble lens-grinder, and a small country-town lawyer!

These things dictators deny. Their doctrine is plainly aristocratic, as in the case of Mussolini, where Nature arranges from time to time for great representative men to impose themselves on the people. Or, as in the case of Hitler, it may additionally take the form of a doctrine of the superiority of one race to all others, of the superiority of an élite or group within that race, and finally of one man—himself— as the hero responsible to destiny alone, knowing destiny more vividly ꞏꞏꞏ in its reality than anybody else, and therefore with both the ꞏꞏꞏ nal right and the personal pathos of supreme government. In part, this echoes the notion of the Hero in history as developed by Hegel and Nietzsche among others—that is to say, a leader imposed by destiny; a destiny which is inscrutable; a leader and a destiny, therefore, which owe nothing to the people's will; a leader and a destiny, finally, which admit and can admit no responsibility, since all is settled by Fate. If there is a right of judgment at all, it belongs not to the people here and now, but to the philosophic historian some generations, perhaps some aeons, distant![7]

The second phase of the difference in basic philosophy between non-responsible and responsible systems concerns the advantages of political and social freedom. Dictatorial systems are afraid of the consequences of freedom. They are convinced, or at any rate claim, that the final pattern of social perfection has already been revealed to man, whether it lies in the personal doctrine of a Mussolini and a Hitler, or in a philosophy of history (bits and pieces of which may be part of a personal doctrine) such as the Marxian, adopted as the basis of the Soviet State. There are differences arising from the fact that in the first the personal element dominates that of doctrine, although it might be argued that the doctrine itself sets personal leadership in the centre of the system; while in the second, the leaders acknowledge the over-ruling monition of the doctrine. And yet, in the case of the Soviets this cannot be carried too far, for, as we have already observed, Marx's criticism of society, while offering a perfect armory of weapons for the destruction of the bourgeois state, offers nothing but the faintest clue, if that, to mankind's task of self-government. In the present context, the question is secondary whether the dictators' claim to an ideal is honest, or merely a cynical trick to gain irresponsible power.

Postulating that the pattern of social perfection has been discovered, there follow, for dictatorships, certain consequences for public education, the regimentation of opinion and action, and the centralization of leadership. In democracies—and it may be suggested once and for all that the present author is fully aware of the economic, administrative and political imperfections of actual democracies—there is inherent a sense that the pattern of perfect policy has not yet been found, that it is still to be searched for in an ever-developing world, that indeed, it may never be found in all matters on a single occasion, but will be revealed by humanity in part by stages and at different times. Hence, whereas the dictatorial systems look to a unique leadership, the essence of democratic government is the diffusion of leadership. The purpose of its diffusion is its increase, not its diminution, in the numbers sharing it and in vigour. The democratic doctrine denies the centralization of leadership, not in order that there may be no leadership but in order that leadership may be more abundant. It is, therefore, not a doctrine of passivity or lassitude, but of a combination of reforming energy with patience and tolerance, and let it again be repeated, of reforming energy. It is not intended to limit, but to release. The old autocracies and feudalism were overthrown not in the name of social passivity, but precisely to secure the permanent liberation of social energies for the purpose of moving towards, even if one could never attain, perfection. A belief in perfectibility and progress is its animating force, not, as with dictatorships, a final perfection already found and dictated here and now. Democracy is, therefore, a principle which takes risks, and chiefly the risk that its citizens will not rise to the height of their opportunities and the personal and public obligations which sustain them. Dictatorships, being misanthropic, take no risks ; the dice of the dictator are thrown against his subjects, loaded with lead. The development of all modern technology makes non-responsible government easy, for it favours mechanized repression ; [8] and responsible government very difficult, for it encourages social differentiation and groupings which beat strongly against the framework of unity.

Between the responsible and the non-responsible systems a wide gulf therefore yawns, each having its own particular technique ; and yet in each of these categories the differences of tradition, history, economic system, and the geographical extent of the country cause a national differentiation.

The foregoing discussion of principle, on which the differences

3

between democratic and dictatorial government rest, leads now to a consideration of two major differences in institutions : the monopoly of political activity in a single party, and the character of propaganda. We consider, first, the nature of parties in dictatorial States.

In democratic systems, as *Theory and Practice* has shown (Vol. I, Chaps. XI ff.), the animators and directors of political thought and action are the political parties. They are the link between the individual voters and the community as a whole ; they are the integrating factor among the interests, social groups and the State. But the parliamentary bodies in these communities are always singled out for minute analysis because the confrontation of opinion and the accommodation of interests, spiritual and otherwise, occurs in this final instance which converts the accommodation arrived at into law. In particular, emphasis is laid upon the procedure for safeguarding the minority, but also on the rules which permit the majority in the end to have its own way. No such emphasis on the parliamentary stage would correspond to the reality of political dynamics in a system of non-responsible government. The dictatorships place all the emphasis upon the political party, though they may pay lip service to their parliaments or congresses—I had almost said ' legislative assemblies ', but to call them this would be to beg the question whether they legislate. In fact, they are not. Some other organ in the State makes law ; but this formal organ itself is dominated, directly or indirectly, by one single political party without the possibility of debate, or amendment, or even dissent, because all other parties have been dispersed, suppressed and prohibited on pain of death. A German commentator says : ' Future political science will, in the study and in the shaping of the Constitution, start with the Party and proceeding from it determine the rank and frontiers of the State.' [9] Dictatorial countries have no political parties in the original sense of the word, namely, that they are parts of the State, for to be a part of the State would be to imply that there are other parts. The dictatorial party has attained its monopoly by the exclusion of other parties, either by positive law as under the Nazi and Fascist systems, together with a simultaneous liquidation and prohibition of others, or as in Russia, without the formal gift of monopoly to a Party but its *de facto* assumption by the Communist Party preceded and accompanied by the forceful liquidation of all opponents of its leadership. Both in Germany and Italy, the parties were given a special status as regards their property and the dignity and physical safety of their membership. By being made public corporations they were assured that the use of their property, if challenged, would be given a special consideration in relation to the ends the Party performs ; and Party members, and especially functionaries of the parties, were granted various immunities from arrest, the capacity to apply force, and protection by the law against insults.

In Russia, ' anti-national ' (which can have a wide meaning) associations are not permitted, and since political parties are associations, the domination of the Communist Party is assured. Further, Article 126 of the Soviet Constitution which enumerates the organizations that may be established by citizens, sets up the Communist Party as that in which ' the most active and politically conscious citizens associate '.

In contradistinction to democratic political parties, dictatorial parties are characterized by a sanguine doctrine. (From the sanguine to the sanguinary, the step is short and natural.) This faith springs either from a philosophy of history, expressing itself through a collective party leadership, or, as in Fascist Italy and Nazi Germany, from the dicta of a leader. There is a significant difference, as will be appreciated later, between the two. Since the leaders in either case are the repository of this faith, they claim and normally obtain unquestioning obedience. Perhaps the best psychological analysis of such bonds is Arthur Koestler's novel, *Darkness at Noon*, on the theme of loyalty to Communism. For Naziism, one among many illustrations is Dr. Ley's avowal, ' The National Socialist Party is Hitler and Hitler is the Party '. The Party Organization Book contains the oath of loyalty to the Fuehrer which runs : ' I pledge allegiance to my Fuehrer, Adolf Hitler ; I promise at all times to respect and obey him and the leaders whom he appoints over me.' It is a regular pleasure for Nazi leaders to declare that they have no conscience but Hitler. Italian Fascism shows a like absoluteness of declared submission.

In a democracy each party has every interest in securing for itself the largest possible membership and makes desperate efforts for success, for the size of its membership will directly or indirectly determine the extent of its control of the parliamentary and executive machine. The dictatorships deliberately practise the limitation of the membership of the dictatorial party, especially after they have achieved power. Thus, the Communist Party of Russia probably has no more than five million members. The Fascist Party in Italy had something like three million members. The Nazi Party has nearly three million members. The restriction of membership is intentional, with various objects. First, they aim at maintaining militancy of the organization. With excessive numbers, a dilution of doctrine would arise as the chances of internal dissent increase with every additional person recruited—he brings his individuality with him. Also, closeness of organization, discipline, a feeling of community are attained with smaller numbers. Nor can it be forgotten that a dictatorial régime founded on the will of a minority must rely—especially in times of domestic or foreign critical challenge—upon especially intense feeling, ' fanaticism ', as the dictators say. But this needs activation by the leaders, and this cannot be successful except among a small number, and except that these do not move outside their artificial seclusion. Secondly, it is desired to maintain a sense, both in the public at large and among the members of the organization, that the members of the Party are an *élite*, selected for their superior quality in comparison with the rest of the population. This serves to give them self-respect, to feed their confidence and pride, not to say their arrogance, and ultimately to supply that feeling of alienation from others necessary to ensure the consistent and successful practice of hot persecution and cold brutality. Thirdly, the restriction of numbers makes it possible to claim that admission into the Party is a privilege and a reward. Fourthly, none of the dictatorial parties offers membership as a pleasure, excepting that of a duty properly performed ; candidates join as members of a vocation, and indeed, especially in the Russian system, there is emphasis on the sacrifices they must make by voluntary unpaid work in the task of government and leadership.

It is important to re-emphasize the austerity of the vocation of Party membership. On this the Party documents are clear. ' Any one who becomes a Party member does not merely join an organization but he becomes a soldier in the German freedom movement, and that means much more than just paying his dues and attending the members' meetings. He puts himself under the obligation of subordinating his own ego and to place everything he has at the service of the people's cause . . . readiness to fight, readiness to sacrifice, and strength of character are required for a good National Socialist.' [10] The introduction to the Nazi Party Organization Book [11] stresses the conception of servanthood of the movement and people ; prohibits arrogance as between Party comrades ; demands that each member should be a leader and promoter while on duty, and while off, a good comrade ; prescribes simplicity and modesty of bearing ; inveighs against vanity ; applauds honesty and candour and constant solicitude for the humblest members of the people. Festivities, honours, gifts and drinking are deprecated for participators in ' the unspeakably hard work ' of constructing a better Germany.

The Communist Party in the Soviet Republics expresses the austerity of the life of a Party comrade all through its Rules. Its Preamble says : ' The Party is a unified militant organization held together by conscious, iron proletarian discipline. . . . The Party demands from all its members active and self-sacrificing work. . . .' There follows a heavy list of duties.

It is well to reflect on the austerity (at any rate, as commanded) of Party membership in the dictatorial as contrasted with the democratic countries. There is a considerable difference. In democratic systems, first, of course, almost any one can join any party subject to practically no test whatever by the party. The joining of political parties may, by some people, be regarded as dedication to a serious public purpose, but it is also regarded by very many simply as a diversion or hobby, with dues unpaid and meetings unattended, an association which can be casually relinquished at any moment. Furthermore, in contrast to unquestioning obedience in dictatorships to the dictatorial leader, the follower in a democratic party is free, within very broad limits, to criticize the personal character, ability, motives and policy of the leader. Indeed, in democracies the leadership is always on trial, and the displacement of the leader by some one more capable is the proper and the applauded object of political activity. In a dictatorship, the gain from discipline is militant strength and energy—for a time. But it is accompanied by the constant possibility of deadening the thoughtful and creative vital processes of both leader and follower, because there is no guarantee of mutual stimulation. Originality in the ranks is flattened by command from above. The creed that the leader is always right inhibits the movement of ideas upwards to him. Since his power to make or break political careers is absolute, and since any appeal against him is revolution and treason, he tends to become insulated from the views of the members of his own party who, paradoxically enough, have been commanded to keep in touch with the masses. In the democratic system, there is the open possibility of continued competition of ideas. There is no unbreakable, stereotyped hierarchy of value or opinion. And though the democratic leader is not endowed with an extraordinary status to summon up the political energy of the party members, the mere existence of free contestants for the prize of a sovereign power that is accessible to all, ensures the continuous renewal of the membership and, necessarily, as the continuing cost of success, of reasoning, reflection and the development of policies and programmes of action.

Since the doctrine of dictatorial parties is one of already conceived perfection, and since this is fanatically embraced, and, since also the focus of Party life and doctrine lies in a single person, the conditions are present for highly selective recruitment and for ' expulsions ' or ' purges ' or ' liquidation ' of those held to fall below the useful standard of mind, character and physique. In the early days of the Fascist and Nazi dictatorial parties, a process of personal selection was conducted by members already in the Party, careful account being taken of their general personal characteristics, readiness to assume responsibility, political dependability and firmness of character, their grasp of the Party doctrine, their willingness to fight and sacrifice, their absence of self-seeking and ability to fulfil the various technical tasks. The Party recruiting officials are enjoined to realize that this selection of members is a most serious responsibility. Russian Communist rules for ' cleansings ' of the Party indicate the positive qualities for retention of membership. Thus : ' Double dealers who deceive the Party . . . overt and covert violators of the iron discipline of the Party and of the State ; . . . careerists, self-seekers and bureaucratical elements ; morally degraded persons who by their improper conduct lower the dignity of the Party and besmirch its banner ; passive elements who do not fulfil the duties of Party members and who have not mastered the programme, the rules and the most important decisions of the Party.'

In their earlier days, these Parties recruited from among both old and young. After a time, graduation from the Youth Organizations became almost exclusively the source of recruitment. Choosing from organizations of school-children and youth, the Party has some guarantee founded upon several years of deliberate observation of the effect of its training upon the candidates.

The experience of these countries is far too short for conclusions regarding the efficiency of breeding a new political generation, except that they have been able to secure unconditional obedience and fanaticism within the fixed order from some, especially in Germany. Yet it has left or produced apathy in others, especially in Italy. Not a few remain untouched and rebellious, while such obedience as was achieved can be to an important extent ascribed to fear of force, and to enjoyment or promise of the spoils of office.

The only formal discussion—not merely exhortations by Party leaders—of the requisites of mind and character of Party members known to the present author is one which occurred at the 18th Congress of the Communist Party of the Soviet Union.[12] The inductions into the Communist Party in Russia are governed by a well-conceived set of rules, the principal of which are as follows : From one to two years of candidature, admission to which requires recommendations from several Party members of some years' good standing ; followed by mastery of the programme and rules of the Party ; or, proven worth in the groups of sympathizers and youth organizations, and the Soviets, trade unions, and co-operatives.

At the Congress the question was the introduction of more vigour and life into the Communist Party, and one of the principal issues was the intellectual preparation of candidates. Must the candidate be an adept at Marxian doctrine ? If so, the Party would become a Party of intellectuals and doctrinaires and filled with too large a proportion of university recruits. It was true that a mastery of doctrine was desirable on the part of some and perhaps of many ; but what was also necessary was a membership which would show proven goodwill and reliability. Stout and decent believers, not philosophers, made a sound party. The Congress abolished the rule that candidates must have thoroughly mastered the Party programme, and must be a real Marxist, a theoretically tried and trained Marxist. ' I do not know whether we have many members of the Party who have thoroughly mastered our programme, who have become real Marxists, theoretically trained and tried. If we continue farther along this path we should have to include only intellectuals and learned people generally in our Party. Who wants such a Party ? We have Lenin's thoroughly tried and tested formula defining a member of the Party. According to this formula, a member of the Party is one who *accepts* the programme of the Party, pays membership dues and works in one of its organizations. Please note : " Lenin's formula does not speak about *thoroughly mastering the programme* but about accepting the programme. These are two very different things." '

To assist those who accept the programme but cannot rise to a mastery of the theoretical basis, the ' short histories ' of the Communist Party of the Soviet Union are employed. The problem, however, still remains : without a *full mastery of the grounds* of the doctrine and their acceptance, how can the rulers believe in the reliability of their followers in the long-run evolution of their State ; how can they be sure that they are *followers* ? While if, indeed, many do master the elements as propounded by the prophet, they may become very inconvenient purists and proclaim the falseness of the leaders. Men have murdered kings out of royalism. In a sense, the simplest way to provoke a schism is to discuss fundamental principles. Burke warned against too searching an inquiry into society's foundations. For a democracy this is no problem, for, in a way, dissent is what it exists to produce. Yet *mastery of the grounds* is the only reliable and durable foundation of life in the State, the national or world order ; the democratic even more than the dictatorial. For if there is a gulf separating men, it ought to be seen, and then it might be bridged by voluntary conscious purpose ; if not, coercion will assume the task of unity.

There is one very important difference between recruitment in the Russian Communist Party and in the Nazi and Fascist Parties. In the former there is a process of free local election, in which, though direction is by no means lacking, there is more free discussion and choice at the local party headquarters than in the Fascist Parties which practise appointment by superior officials tempered by the collusion of favourites.

As for purges, these sometimes take the form of the expulsion, imprisonment and execution of large groups of Party members who, to use a Russian phrase, may have ' deviated ' to the right or left of the Party line as laid down by the central organ of the Party.[13] In Germany there was the Röhm massacre of 1934, when the Fuehrer claimed that he was the supreme judge of the well-being of the nation. But other than at revolutionary crises in the parties, the elimination of the infidels is not by such wholesale and therefore sometimes admittedly faulty treatment. In the Soviet Republics a return was made to the Leninist principle of ' individual approach to people ', especially because hostile elements could *en masse* cover their subversive activities by an outer show of agreement with the Party line and deceitful practices designed to persuade people that they were militantly loyal, ' creating an atmosphere of flattery, uttering solemn speeches, greetings, &c., in order to deceive and lull the vigilance of certain of our leading workers '. The ' individual approach ' was recommended also to stimulate Communist Party members to throw off an alleged unwillingness to investigate charges, to avoid hedging and considerations of personal safety, and especially to depart from the assumption that a Communist is a good or bad Communist, not according to his own personal deeds, but to the actions of his relatives, even back to the ' ideological stamina or social preference of a great grandmother '.

Naturally, all those in dictatorial parties who deviate are covered with infamy and stigmatized by a spate of the choicest invective. Calumny, indeed, is one of the well-tempered instruments of punishment, of undermining independence of mind, and of political destruction. If the Party doctrine were not clearcut and presented with intense emotional force (honestly or otherwise), there would be no grounds for the tactics of calumny, since there could be no deviation to which one could point as the mark of infamy.

It is a simple consequence of what has been said that dictatorial parties are highly centralized, and at the same time that their central organs are deeply penetrative of society through their local officials down to the last cell in a block of a city or the floor of a workshop, to the ' capillaries ', as the Fascists say. There is no space for portraying the numbers of the hierarchy, beginning with the Fuehrer, the Duce, or the Party Secretary at the very top of the pyramid, and then proceeding layer by layer, district by district, through the various governing bodies of the Party. The important thing is that even the most disciplined Party in the most democratic State does not begin to approach the intense centralization of dictatorial parties. Since there is such centralization, and since all movement must come from above, and since fidelity has to be maintained in all the ultimate organs of the Party, there is machinery at the top for inspections of the subordinate layers of the hierarchy, and at the same time for the appointment of the subordinate officials and trustees of the Party, going downwards.

In Russia, in characteristic contradistinction to the Nazi and Fascist Parties, democratic elections in the lower councils of the Party are permitted, but ratification by the Party organization immediately superior is necessary. Neither in Germany nor in Italy is a democratic choice of executives the principle or the practice ; the appointments are made from above by a process of delegation. In Russia—and this, let us re-emphasize, is a distinguishing mark of the régime—there is the principle and practice of so-called ' democratic centralism '. It arises mainly from the fact that a scientific (more or less) interpretation of history (more or less) dominates (more or less) the leaders, but also because those leaders govern an enormous area and have the good sense to know that achievement must depend upon local vitality. ' Democratic centralism ' means, according to the rules of the Communist Party, the application of the elective principle to all leading organs of the Party from the highest to the lowest and the periodic accountability of the Party organs to their respective organizations. That is the democratic side. But it also means the absolutely binding character of the decisions of the higher organs upon the lower and upon all Party members. That is the centralized aspect. The Party requires a free and businesslike discussion of Party policy in individual organizations or in the Party ; such discussion is declared to be the inalienable right of every Party member derived from ' internal Party democracy '. The declared purpose of this internal Party democracy is to develop self-criticism, that is, criticism within the Party itself, and to vitalize Party discipline which must be conscious and not mechanical. On this, the words of Lenin are always quoted : ' All revolutionary parties which have hitherto perished, did so because they *grew conceited*, failed to see where their strength lay, *and feared to speak of their weaknesses.*'

There is then a significant difference between the Communist and the Fascist Parties : in the former's tolerated self-criticism, indeed, the stimulated self-criticism, and even more, in the fact that it is regarded as a disloyalty to the Party to undertake any action which diminishes, or be remiss in any action which maintains, the freedom and liveliness of local Party life. We may refer again to the discussions at the 18th Congress, where it was re-emphasized that the work of the Party, which was the ' remoulding of the people's consciousness ', was frustrated by those who believed that all Communists were born free from prejudices and stood in no need of re-education. It was consequently necessary to restore the elective principle, to abolish the practice of co-option, to forbid voting by a list of candidates, to vote for individual candidatures, to guarantee all Party members the right of criticizing and rejecting candidatures ; to vote by secret ballot, and to guarantee periodical meetings of leading Party workers. The revival of the elective principle of criticism and self-criticism was sought, in order to heighten the responsibility of Party organizations to the Party membership, and to intensify the activity of the members of the Party. It was desired to develop and strengthen the feeling of contact between each Party member and the Party, and to enhance each member's sense of being a fully responsible unit. This was the meaning of 'inner Party democracy', and this would strengthen the unity of the Party and its 'conscious proletarian discipline'.

The democratic element in the Soviet Communist Party—a quality distinguishing it from the Italian and German dictatorships—has two sources : the liberating purpose of the Bolshevist Revolution and the tradition of the Party in its formative stage. In the first place, the Bolshevist movement was founded to overthrow the Tsarist régime, one of the most horrible tyrannies in the history of humanity, and to bring freedom to the Russian people. It had a dual purpose : not only to inaugurate a free system of government, but to establish an equalizing and socialized economy, each being enough to overtax the mind and energies of the mightiest statesmen. It proposed to progress from an inferior and practically primitive society of almost altogether illiterate members to a very highly civilized, most complicated and organized political and economic system. And it intended to progress with the greatest achievable rapidity in order to be able to withstand domestic and foreign hostility. Its animating force was liberty, equality and fraternity. But the Fascist and the Nazi systems were founded on the denial of freedom and equality, and were erected on the corrupt destruction of existent democratic government. They were movements of decline from a superior to an inferior kind of society, even if there were marked blemishes in democratic practice. In the second place, under Lenin, freedom of discussion in the Bolshevist Party was encouraged in order to stimulate vitality and to attract the sincere and the strong. Whatever Stalin may wish upon this score, and he may be a man of strong goodwill in this respect, he has to face the tradition of the Party, one of revolutionary ardour which still goes strongly on.

Side by side, however, with the democratic virility of the Russian Communist Party, there is the other aspect, namely, its centralism. The Party will punish such discussion on 'an all-Union scale' as would lead to the imposition of the will of an insignificant minority on the vast majority of the Party, or cause the disintegration of its unity by factional groupings and attempts to split it. It is only where the necessity of an all-Union scale discussion is recognized by several regional Party organizations, or if there is an insufficiently solid majority in the Central Committee on very important questions, or if a solid majority of the Central Committee wishes to test the quality of its policy by means of discussion, that such discussion would be permitted. These are the limits of internal Party democracy, beyond which internal Party democracy would be disintegrated. 'The maintenance of Party unity, the relentless struggle against the slightest attempt at a factional fight or a split and the strictest Party and Soviet discipline are the foremost duties of all Party members and of all Party organizations.'

It ought to be added, in order that the power of the central leader or leaders of the dictatorial Party may be fully comprehended, that since the dictatorial Party controls a totalitarian State, expulsion from the Party, as the leading officials openly declare, is a question of life and death for those expelled. For the key positions in society, economic and otherwise, are held by loyal Party members; and the conduct of the professions, and even ordinary occupations, can be made impossible on the mere fiat of the authorized Party official. Thus, the disciplinary force is tremendous.

Another mark of the dictatorial Party is its possession of a military organization. Within the Nazi Party, there are the Storm Troopers (S-A) and the Elite Guards (S-S), and the Gestapo or secret police; [14] within the Italian Fascist Party, the Militia and the O.V.R.A.; [15] within the Communist Party, the Red Guard and, acting with it, the N.K.V.D.[16] These organizations serve two purposes; first, of rooting out, as early as possible, the first faint stirrings of disagreement and opposition, and then, in the final resort, of defending the régime by force of arms. This organization of coercion is taken to the most minute point of detail, is well-equipped with all the best that technology and organization can offer, for investigation, record and torture, and makes revolt practically impossible. These organizations are safeguarded against legal action by citizens or members of the Party who have suffered maltreatment. They enjoy complete immunity from responsibility if their actions are in the interests of the Party, and beyond where Party comradeship and the maintenance of the power of the Party requires it.

Now, it may be that many thousands, even hundreds of thousands, of members of dictatorial parties accept the Party programme, even understand it, and even consciously and fanatically will it. It is difficult to read the mind and spirit of so many. Clearly, dictatorial Party leaders are far from complacent. Experience shows that it is very difficult to maintain the flame of conviction, the permanence of devotion, and the fierceness of the party warrior simply by reasoning alone. The maintenance of cohesion and force in the Party membership is promoted by two devices. One is the continuous emotional, ceremonial, and ritual procedures and evolutions designed to enhance the self-importance of Party membership, arouse the feelings and appeal to the aesthetic element, agitate the sentiment of belonging to a great collective body, and this is accompanied by argumentative appeal. The second element promoting cohesion, though not exactly belief, is the vast 'patronage' and 'spoils' in the hands of the dictatorial parties, immeasurably greater than any democratic party has ever had. All the jobs, all the professions, all the occupations, all the symbols of social prestige are in the gift of the dictatorial Party, and Party members come first and necessarily hold the key positions in that society—so in the civil administration, so in the conduct of the national economy, so in the control and conduct of education, so also in the armed forces, though as to the latter there has been considerable resistance by the professional officers of the German army.   With less spoils there would be less loyalty ; take away the jobs and there would be smaller Party membership and a less intense prosecution of its duties.   It need not be laboured that Party and State are intimately linked.   The leaders at the various levels of the Party machinery either have, as in Germany and Italy, by law an *ex officio* right to certain positions in the State, *de facto*, as in Russia, Germany, and Italy, hold the key offices in the State, regional and municipal government, and so, all through the apparatus of society and economy.

In spite of all that has been said regarding the appeals for personal loyalty, the acceptance and understanding of the ideology of the Party, the privileges of leadership and the penalties of expulsion, the leaders in all dictatorial States frequently reproach their following with lukewarm faith.   After the victory of the British Navy at Taranto in 1940, Fascist leaders publicly bewailed the survival or return of a slack ' bourgeois ' spirit ; and years before, indeed, during the Abyssinian war, Fascist critics cried out that the Party membership had become over-intellectualized, over-critical, slack in its political duties, and that a war was needed to recover the intense ardour of the original movement.   Within the Nazi Party a reign of terror has to operate, and incessant fervent pleading is necessary to maintain the degree of conviction and driving power the leaders deem indispensable to the remoulding of the nation.   In Russia, the facts which have been reviewed have already indicated a certain falling away from the standard which the leaders regard as the minimum for success.

It has been necessary to dwell at some length on the characteristics of parties in dictatorships, for there the party replaces the sovereign legislative and executive element that is the normal apparatus of the democratic State.   All the rest is a shell, while the party is the motor force and sits at the wheel.

The contrast between modern non-responsible or dictatorial government and responsible or democratic government is now more clearly seen.   The former rests upon a pretension that a monopolistic and imposed party possesses the ultimate truth about the political destiny of humanity.   That conviction was definite, sharp and fanatical, and therefore brooks no opposition.   But democracies admit the pragmatic nature of their search for such perfection, and recognize that of perfection there is no single exclusive principle.   Yet they surmise that if there should be, it is one yet to be discovered in a process of evolution, and that if the unfolding is to arrive at soundness, it must depend upon the unfettered expression and interplay of all opinion.   Hence, in the democratic states, the acknowledgement of rights of dissent and opposition, of rights of freedom of opinion and expression, of free association, of free elections, of easy entry and exit from political parties and the scrutiny of and contest for leadership. Even the known deficiencies in the practical working of democracies with existent economic inequalities, do not substantially offset these values. In the dictatorial State the pattern of man's perfect character is one man's vision; the teaching of ' character ' means the imposition of that mould, while good citizenship consists of submission to its confinement. In the democratic State, since perfection is yet to be discovered and is contingent on a continuing quest, the nature of the preferred character is the one that accepts plasticity and the principle of live and let live, of adventure and of self-expression leading to that end. While the dictatorial State thrusts the main emphasis upon obedience, the democratic places the accent upon the conditional terms of consent and the expression of disagreement. The dictatorial State removes responsibility from the conscience of the individual Party member and tries to chloroform or hypnotize the mind; in the democratic the conscience of the individual is fully responsible, refreshed by the beating waves of dynamic opinion, and troubled. Therefore, where dictators rule, the peculiar duty of a party member seems to be harder than that of the democratic citizen, but, in truth, the implied responsibilities of democracy are much more exacting. For self-government means, first, the government of one's self. That is why the democratic States vibrate, sometimes violently, and seem and are unstable. It explains why, therefore, the democratic States are not yet as fully democratic as the tasks implied in their own principle require; for the burden is heavy on citizens and party members who take their responsibilities seriously, and so too few of them do. Political parties, well-organized, conscious, competitive and honourable, can make the tasks easier to fulfil. The dictatorships show that there is a clear alternative to the burdens of democratic citizenship; but is it nice? At the end of these chapters, we shall show that this is the crucial problem in the future of the democratic State, for here all have the burden of leadership.

We argued that non-responsible differ from responsible governments not only in principle but in consequent institutional arrangements, one cardinal feature being the monopolistic party. The second is the practice of propaganda. After some two decades of propaganda as a deliberate arm of government in Italy, and the practices of Dr. Joseph Goebbels in Germany and the world at large, some conclusions can be drawn regarding its nature and effectiveness.

Propaganda is not mere education or instruction, though some instruction and education is propaganda. It has been said that ' propaganda is violence done to the mind ', and the meaning of the epigram is that the purpose of the propagandist is not to instruct in order that the latitude and initiative of the person instructed may be increased, but, the exact contrary, to affix blinkers and blind the subject to all courses except that imposed. Education is to open all doors of the mind ; propaganda to thrust you through one door of somebody else's will. It deliberately destroys part of the subject's mind and distorts the free operation of his senses to achieve a result desired by the propagandist and not, originally at any rate, required by the propagandee.

Now facts are a necessary basis of belief and action ; yet belief and action are affected by a citizen's proneness to believe some things and not others, and his disposition to act in certain ways. This proneness is dependent on two factors : the biological constitution of each person, and his social and economic situation which includes his education and experience. To affect belief and action, the propagandist must reach both of these factors, an extremely difficult task. It is easier to affect social status than biological disposition ; but since our biological heritage determines, to a very large extent, our outlook, which is otherwise formed by our social and economic situation and related influences, even if the latter can be affected by direct action and by persuasion, biological disposition is still a formidable obstruction of the propagandist's aim. It is indeed a very stubborn obstacle. He may turn the twig against its natural bent, but—and this is the first rule of the propagandist if he wishes to be successful—he must continue to bend it in his direction if it is to remain bent. This gives rise to the propagandist's principle of reiteration ; but it brings decreasing returns.

Since a Goebbels must find a strong instrument with which to combat a person's natural proneness to go his own way, he looks to the various implements in the theory of suggestion.[17] First, he finds an attachment or a fixation, that is to say, the particular love or hate to which a person is prone and the idea of destiny and self-importance entertained by his subject, and thus by flattering the latter, by pretending that what Goebbels wants will further the particular love or hate of his subject, he may gain a control over mind and action. It is his job to represent that what he wants is for the sake of the individual. Secondly, since most human beings are desperately subject to perplexity regarding the meaning of the world they see, and are avid for a confident and simple explanation, or even if they are merely curious, then a Hitler, a Lenin or a Stalin can achieve enormous success, especially in the short run, by giving a confident answer, particularly if this takes the form of a world historical or messianic doctrine which seems to harmonize and illuminate all the welter of every-day happenings which overtake and affect the ordinary citizen and to which he must make a response. Thus, if his every-day job is made to seem a part of a ' national ' movement ; if the national movement is represented to seem part of the future extension and glory of his particular national culture; if that, again, is made to seem a contribution to the evolution and sovereignty of a master race, a race of heroes, this may be the answer to his perplexity about why he should accept certain restrictions, longer hours, lower wages, high taxes, be subject to the unfettered control of his employer, applaud martial preparations and adventures, and, as the dictatorial oath requires, 'if necessary, die'. If one single explanation is inadequate to impress all, the propagandist's skill has lain in a clever variation of themes to suit the different strains and outlooks among the population, combined with a tricky keeping apart of the various publics to avoid any comparison of notes. The democratic countries have failed to invigorate, as they justifiably and rightly can, the stability and understanding of the democratic principle : they have not woven its significance into the stuff of the multifarious and apparently unrelated facts of life by which the man on the bus, and the newspaper reader, are slapped every day.

Thirdly, the propagandist, then, functions incessantly : this lends importance to his gospel, for reiteration in all the different organs of opinion, at all the gathering places, and in all the homes, operates as the herd operates upon the individual: it reduces the average individual to self-distrust : 'Who am I to contradict so many ? ' Incessant operation excludes from the mind other influences, and inhibits the asking of questions. Fourthly, the propagandist proceeds by devices to make conspicuous and vivid his suggestions by lending mystery and importance, and by arousing curiosity. So he penetrates through apathy and preoccupation and so attracts and commands attention as a preliminary to practising his other arts. As has so often been said, he appeals less to the intellect and more to feeling—a factor which, as a later work will show, has not been given adequate attention by political scientists, I mean, the effect of varying intensities of feeling. He pretends to show his own belief in what he says and so encourages others; it is influenced by the force of (pretended) example : if it is good enough for him . . . He operates by using existing vogues. Men and women are receptive to fashionable phrases and ideas, even the most schooled and intellectual of men and women. Thus, for example, ' self-determination '; ' race '; ' *lebensraum* '; ' justice '; ' reason '; ' the Bible ' (because the Bible tells me so). This burglarious entry into the spirit was practised by Mark Anthony : ' I tell you that which you *yourselves* do know.' Authority has an influence in matters of opinion to which it is not always entitled.

Another device is the reduction of mental defences by reason, when reason happens to be on the side of the propagandist. So he obtains a lever on other areas of the propagandee's mind by ridiculing and stigmatizing his demonstrably mistaken opponents and so demonstrates his superiority to them.   Specimens are the German appeal for colonies, and equality of armaments.   There is the censorship of ideas and information, that is, the hiding, the destruction, the cancellation, of ideas which might dissipate his spells by their own independent appeal and their competition with those which the propagandist is anxious to implant.

At the foundation of propaganda is the implement used with such effect by the Nazi Party, the instrument dedicated to it by the supreme inventive genius of their own Leader, that is, the Lie Enormous—so enormous in its shock to morality that the average citizen cannot believe that any one, that is, the propagandist, could be so dishonest and wicked as to use it, and therefore goes to the other extreme of believing that it is true.

All these devices have been used against the proclivity of the individual to pursue his own course as set by his biological character and his social and economic situation.   The experience of the last two decades has shown the measure of the toughness and resistance of these factors.   The greatest success is among the young, for they have no settled store of tested values, and being generous, trust what they are told.   But more generally, except for short periods, from day to day almost, there is a limit to propaganda in the native common sense and experience of the citizen.   The longer the time span over which the propaganda functions, the longer the experience, by direct individual observation, and hearsay, of the citizen.   Sooner or later, it is impossible for him to withstand the effect of practically demonstrated errors and inconsistencies on the part of the propagandist, the clear and inescapable perception that propaganda and what he directly senses for himself are poles apart.   The story is not true !   Moreover, since human beings are different, their social outlook and interpretations are different.   If there is any discussion at all, it is impossible to maintain complete identity of world outlook ; and the dictatorial parties, as we have described them, highly integrated and crushing as they are, are still insufficient, by a wide margin, to wipe out all discussion, for there is still that which occurs even only as an exchange of glances.   In democratic States there is much propaganda also, but free discussion soon dissipates untruth.

Therefore, no dictatorship relies upon propaganda alone or even upon propaganda mainly, excepting where there is a highly primitive population who, by reason of illiteracy, lack of education, and, perhaps, religious credulity in the past, are unable to exercise independent criticism and so are ready to accept anything.   Propaganda seems to be successful only if assisted by a heavy supplement of force.   Propaganda has never been used in our time without the accompaniment of drastic force—force to expel and annihilate the opposition, the questioners, the animators, the agitators of other interests and views.

What we see, then, is the success of propaganda when upheld by favourable conditions, and then, for the rest, the attainment of civil obedience, but not of social belief, by the threat or the exercise of force, whether in its direct brutality and nakedness, or the taking of family hostages or the withdrawal of opportunities of earning a living. The crassest mistake of the propagandist is to believe in the pure and durable transferability of fanaticism—Hitler's favourite belief. Hitler's decisive self-deception lay in believing that echoes and reflections of himself represented will, and that men remained of the same mind when they stepped, as most do, away from the peculiar environment of a meeting or radio address back into their every-day atmosphere.

CHAPTER III

THE NAZI STATE [1]

MORE grimly than any other the Nazi State recalls St. Augustine's classic question: 'Without justice what are States but bands of robbers?'

The Weimar Republic fell chiefly, but not only, because enough Germans felt the shame of defeat in the First World War sufficiently to follow Adolf Hitler in a movement to wipe out the shame, and so also to entrust him with the total government of the nation. For Germany, World War I could not and did not end in 1918. Of this Hitler directly persuaded only a small minority; but the intense fervour and propaganda of Hitler's followers irresistibly attracted a congeries of other groups for other purposes. These had ambitions which could be satisfied or fears which would be soothed if the Nazis attained power. Thus, some groups nursed designs of European and even world supremacy. Some in the upper and middle classes were obsessed by fears of the rise of the urban working classes and of the Communism of Soviet Russia. Others were filled with hatred and bigotry, either against the Jews or the British or Americans. A craving for power and high social status possessed vast numbers of misfit adventurers and millions of unemployed youth, who had never found a place in civil life after the war. Worries arising out of economic insecurity were endemic and wide-spread, especially among shop-keepers, clerical and administrative workers and the peasantry. Again, workers of all kinds were afflicted by mass unemployment growing more severe from 1929 and rising in 1932 to 6 million, that is to say, one out of every five of the gainfully occupied. Hence, eventually, there was gathered together, not a permanent coalition with common convictions, but an expedient combination of sectional and heterogeneous votes, headed by the hereditary aristocracy, the military profession, the agrarian Junkers, and big business. The women voters were especially enthusiastic for Hitler.

In troubled times, the misfit may find a chance: Hitler's was a mission for the greater glory of the German Reich. He had thanked God when the war of 1914 broke out. When the armistice, sealing the defeat of Germany, was announced, he had a nervous collapse (he said) and vowed national resurrection. It was certain when he entered German politics—and that is why he was allowed and paid to enter—that he would strive to re-fight the world war, and this time win. So much was written clearly in his own confessions, *Mein Kampf*.[2]

N.B.—The Notes to this Chapter begin on p. 173.

It is unnecessary here delicately to distinguish the ultimate separate interests of Hitler and the social groups which combined with him. To a point their interests were identical ; beyond it, there was a divergence, which ultimately would have produced their suppression by Hitler, or civil war. By the time they realized the gulf between them, they were gagged and bound in the crushing machinery of Hitler's total and unrelaxing terror. They agreed on the reawakening of Germany, the development of a mighty German people (*Volk*, or race), a war of conquest bloody or bloodless, the domination of Europe, the conquest of ' living space ' (*Lebensraum*) in the East, the weaving of Europe into a single economy subservient to the end of German politics. These aims implied certain instrumental organization : non-responsible, dictatorial régimes ; the abolition of parliamentarism ; the abrogation of civil rights ; complete control of the nation, adults and schools ; a sense of national unity produced by indoctrination and coercion ; the abolition of all voluntary associations ; a system of police and terror to eradicate the mental and spiritual onset of dissent. No further risk of differences of outlook could be tolerated, for as in 1918, a future enemy might, by psychological appeals, develop them into social divisions. Long and careful meditation on 1918 had taught the lesson of a solid home front and never again a ' stab in the back '. A totalitarian state was needed for total war.[3] Beyond this, Hitler contributed additional political aims, partly as factors in militarist efficiency and partly as social reforms for themselves. He advocated the expansion of social welfare services ; the national organization of labour to realize the ' high social significance ' of work, and therefore to combine classless discipline and ' honour ' accorded by the employer to the employee ; the harnessing of all employers into a totalitarian planned military economy ; the erasure of traditional social distinctions and groupings like the *Studentenkorps*, and the formation of a new hierarchy of virtues, promulgated by Hitler, going far beyond what was necessary merely to establish the amour-propre of the defeated military caste on the one hand, or the economic interests of big business on the other.[4]

Various earlier literary and Pan-German and nationalist party sources,[5] furnished a chauvinist and romantic policy. From social frustration, an inferiority complex and innate confusion of his own mind and megalomania, Hitler had concocted a social outlook well-known to those whose mentality was formed in the *fin de siècle* and the first decade of the twentieth century. This included belief in the survival of the fittest (' social Darwinism ') eugenics, the breeding of a higher race by social controls and laws ; the artist and the creative genius above morality ; contempt for the stupidity of existing middle-class conventions of responsibility ; scorn for middle-class timid and tepid notions of truth, justice and tolerance ; rejection of its easy-

going good nature, small lies, unheroic muddling along ; bitter repudiation of existing social distinctions inimical to the rise of capable
young men to the top, where they had the right to be and to marry
the brilliant and wonderful females and breed a finer race to direct
the destiny of nations ; scoffing at religion, especially the prevailing
ideas of God and Christian tenets ! For the son of a minor civil servant
who began his testament with a sour sneer at his father's profession,
and who had conducted his self-education by steadily discarding all
history that failed to support his ignoble juvenile day-dreams of
romantic success, this, in his day, was a not unnatural state of mind,
and many café-politicians shared it. It was not unknown in the Café
Royal in London at the end of the nineteenth century.[6]

But Hitler's habitat was Germany and Central Europe, the lands
of many races, each insecure and hating or holding others in contempt
according as it was a dominant majority or a minority being ground
into obedience. Hence, the super-race became the Nordics, the
Germans ; the superman *pro-tem*, Hitler. As he says in *Mein Kampf* :

Everything we admire to-day on this earth, science and art, technique and
inventions, is the creative product of but a few peoples and perhaps originally
of one race. On these, therefore, depend the existence of the whole of this
culture. If they perish, the better part of this world sinks with them into the
grave. . . . All we can see to-day in the way of human culture, the achievement
of art, science, and technique, is almost exclusively the creative product of the
Aryan.

It is not possible in the present text to depict the Nazi creed in
any detail.[7] But its principal features at least need indication :

(1) It is misanthropic : it disrespects, even hates, the common
man. When the dictator's lot was as lowly as that of other men, he
detested them, for in them he saw his own social mis-esteem ; but
when he rises high, he despises them because they are still to him
nonentities, and yet they live and dare to claim their rights. In Nazi
language : Once he was *Dreck* and they were *Dreck* ; now they are
still *Dreck* while he is Chancellor, and they protest they never were
and are not *Dreck* now ! The trouble about the superman is not so
much that he regards himself as a superman, but that to him other
men are not men but submen. ' The majority of people are simple
and gullible. In every nation there is only one real statesman once
in a blue-moon, not a hundred or more at a time, and secondly the
masses have an instinctive prejudice against every outstanding genius.'
(2) The Nazi creed is, therefore, physically and spiritually unscrupulous
and cruel and vicious without limitation. For it admits no restraint
in a law common to all. A constitution may be defined as a pattern
of applied scruples. But the Nazi system accepts no constitution,
except the mental and physical constitution of the leader which is
synonymous with his caprice. It accepts no notion of rights or the

keeping of promises, but lives by regular treachery. It rules by mass
extermination of body and mind. Its natural fruit is the Lie.

The German has not the faintest idea of how a nation must be swindled, if
one wants to have masses of supporters . . . the size of the lie is a definite factor
in causing it to be believed, for the vast masses of a nation are in the depth of
their hearts more easily deceived than they are consciously and intentionally
bad. The primitive simplicity of their minds renders them an easier prey to a
big lie than a small one, for they themselves often tell little ones, but would be
ashamed to tell big ones. Such a form of lies would never enter their head.
They would never credit to others so important a possibility as the complete
reversal of facts. Even explanations would for a long time leave them in doubt
and hesitation, and any trifling reason would dispose them to accept a thing
as true. *Therefore something of the most impudent lies always remains and sticks,*
a fact which all bodies and individuals occupied with the art of lying in this
world know only too well, and hence they stop at nothing to achieve this end.

Contrast this with the democratic attitude to the people. Even
when the democratic is half-hearted, it postulates the nobility and
dignity of man, his perfectibility and faith in illumination to raise
himself. It predicates the duty of those who claim his leadership not
to obscure the truth ; indeed, it announces that the truth shall make
man free ! Moreover, the institution of free and competitive associations of citizens in quest of political power is a safeguard against
electoral demoralization, and an assurance of the triumph of at least
relative integrity and decency above the baseness avowed by Hitler,
such baseness, in fact, as to be maintainable only by the forcible
suppression of protest.

(3) The Nazi doctrine and movement are fanatically nationalist,
because the grouping of the people at home, the *Volk*, despised as they
are, are still the leader's instrument and the base of his personal
pyramid. Despicable as they are, they must at any rate be better
than any other race, for their leader has emerged from their blood
and soil. This nationalism is unappeasably fanatical and reposes on
unbridled brutality. Two quotations clarify this :

In my Ordensburgen a youth will grow up before which the world will shrink
back. A violently active, dominating, intrepid, brutal youth—that is what I
am after. Youth must be all these things. It must be indifferent to pain.
There must be no weakness or tenderness in it. I want to see once more in its
eyes the gleam of pride and independence of the beast as eradicated in thousands
of years of human domestication.[8]

These words of Hitler's are copied closely from phrases of Oswald
Spengler's *Man and Technics* (1932, New York), a few phrases of which
may be cited to show the spiritual foundations :

Man is a beast of prey (p. 19) . . . The animal of prey is the highest form
of mobile life (p. 22) . . . The tactics of his (man's) living are those of a splendid
beast of prey, brave, crafty and cruel, he lives by attacking and killing and
destroying. . . . The character of the beast of prey passes over in its essential

character from the individual to the organized people, the animal with one soul and many hands. . . . There are peoples whose strong breed has the character of the beast of prey, seizing, conquering and lording people (p. 67).

(4) Hitler's is a doctrine of non-responsible government. The leader is answerable to no party, parliament or people, and responsibility connotes only a dependence on the conscience, ability, and historical discernment of the leader. We have already illustrated this. Responsibility upward is responsibility to the great void.

(5) The Nazi doctrine is ' creative ', or, as the German goes, *schöpferisch*. The leader plays the part of the potter in classic philosophy (how eternally fallacious !) and moulds the masses to fit his concept of the highest good. This view, to a degree far greater than with other peoples, who maintain a tolerant scepticism of genius and a tolerable respect for themselves, suits the Germans. For they are in general romantic, mystical and exuberant, tend to arrogance and the excessive use of power, and are credulous of the most grandiose generalities.[9] They lack irony. Being idolators of genius, they are prone to be cheated by quacks.

(6) The movement is total : it is all-pervading, denies the independence of any individual or fraction of the whole community, and founds itself on a mystical doctrine of the natural biological one-ness of the whole *Volk*, or race.

(7) The system is, therefore, completely corrupt, and recognizes no limits to the degeneration to which it may reduce the masses. This limitlessness is itself a technique of government, for it excludes any sense of reciprocity with other groups or leaders in the nation who, some day, might be in power. It grants the right completely to destroy those hostile to it, if it cannot insure their submission by guile or coercion. The leaders for themselves, and the small minority of the nation which forms the party, are brought into a tightly woven conspiracy which is committed to acts at home and abroad so terrible that the conviction that they will never be forgiven, that they are outlaws, becomes its basis of cohesion, loyalty and further evil-doing. As Himmler, the genius of the Gestapo, has often declared : ' There is no way back.' This murderous harshness may be compared with the democratic tenets like ' live and let live ', ' fair play ', ' rules of procedure ', and the rest.

This organization of hatred, enmity and corruption has, so far as required, a theoretical basis in works like those of Spengler, Junger, and Alfred Rosenberg. To this, Professor Carl Schmitt, who began as a Catholic theorist with a strong authoritarian bent, and later found his spiritual home among the Nazis, has made a neat academic contribution.[10] According to Schmitt, ' the specifically political distinction, to which political actions and motives may be referred, is the distinction between Friend and Foe '. Even if it is thought that such a relationship between man and man is an atavistic relic of barbaric times, the contrast is still existent, and is a reality. When Schmitt says Foe, Schmitt means Foe, and not merely a competitor, rival or opponent. He envisages battle, and especially the real possibility of physical killing. However, in fairness to him (which some of his recent German critics now abroad have not rendered) he does say that this extreme of the Friend-Foe relationship is not necessarily normal or everyday, nor must it be considered as an ideal. But it is in view of such possibility that men group themselves into unities of Friend and Foe, each seeking sovereignty. It is not possible here to proceed to further exposition and critique of this argument. Only four things need be said briefly. The first is that, though with qualifications, it smells like a doctrine of uninhibited force. The second is that it views with contempt the setting of moral purposes for the State for the benefit of the individual. Thirdly, the doctrine was a useful slogan for the Nazi illiterati. Finally, any one may define politics in any way he pleases ; but how he defines it reveals his own state of mind. Politics may be defined as the pursuit of the good life in society, and its means are many ; or it may be defined, as Schmitt does, as a process which separates men and nations.

The definition tells a story of the mind of the man who made it, the aspirations of his society, and the bitterness and turmoil of his time.

* * * * * * *

Only the salient facts regarding the fall of the Weimar Republic may be indicated. The democratic forces of Germany, that is to say the Social Democratic Party and the Trade Unions, the Liberals and the Catholic Centre, neglected to destroy the political power of the traditional groups when this might have been possible between 1918 and 1920. This was due to a division among themselves or within their parties. We consider the Social Democrats only. These were still in a state of mental and spiritual deference to the traditional governing classes. They had minority minds. Terrified by the Soviet Revolution and by German left-wing movements, they longed for order. Ebert, the first President of the German Republic, declared : ' I hate revolution like sin ', but he sought assistance from militarists who loved reaction like god. His followers subscribed to what a great English socialist a little later called : ' the inevitability of gradualness '. At any rate, they lacked revolutionary feeling, a secular deficiency it is suggested, of the German people. The Germans have never been regicides like the British or the French, nor forcibly expelled a king or his system like the Americans. Executions in Germany have been executions of humble workers and their leaders carried out by a small governing class, traditional or Nazi. Where, it may be asked, are the Pyms, the Hampdens, the Cromwells, the Tom Paines, and the John Wilkes ? Where are the Dantons and Robespierres ? Where the Patrick Henrys, the Jeffersons, the Washingtons, the Adams, and the rest ? The so-called revolution of 1918 was hardly more than a short flash of discontent, war-weariness, and resentment against the governing classes of the Empire. What is the cause of this lack of democratic self-respect and temper it is difficult to divine. Perhaps in the Thirty Years' War the hardier natures were destroyed. Or, the long serfdom, lasting well into the nineteenth century, may have enabled the ruling class to tide over the French Revolution,[11] and thereafter to canalize the feeling for independence, if it existed, into that of *national* independence. It may be that the existence of many petty principalities, in preventing political unity, also prevented that mutual encouragement in nation-wide opposition which comes from feeling that all are linked in a mighty organization. Again, the small wars of 1866 and 1870 were large enough to offer the middle classes sufficient political excitement and gratification of power for their lifetime. Too much fancifulness and intellectual subtlety—the search for what is metaphysically ' real '—may have caused the pallid cast of conceptual thought to freeze the energy of action and cloud the recognition of opportunity, as in the Frankfort Parliament of 1848, where the Liberals continued to debate the fundamental rights of Germans until the reactionary forces recovered and chased them away still absorbed in debating the concepts of liberty. Many socialist leaders left Germany during Bismarck's savage campaign against them —' the enemies of the State '—in 1878-1890. Nor is there any record of a substantial return from exile to resume the battle. Neither in 1919, nor in 1933, were the workers ably led ; and even if they had been, we still have no assurance that they would have responded and forcefully cast out the ruling class. There was ardour enough in the Nazi Party ; but its revolution was anti-popular and militaristic.[12]

Another suggestion is that the Republic lacked defensive morale due to the destruction of the coherence and drive of the workers' movement, through the increase of unskilled and semi-skilled workers and of supervisors, managers and salaried employees.

This complaisance or constitutional respectability left the grim core of force, as Dr. Fried [13] has conclusively demonstrated, in the hands of the Reichswehr and its friends in the Free Corps ; executive authority to the unpurged Civil Service, though many openly expressed contempt for Parliamentary democracy ; and justice in a judiciary composed chiefly of men hostile to social democracy. Nearly 50 per cent. of the Nazi political leaders in 1933 had participated in the World War and the cruel years after the armistice. Leading non-nationalistic figures were murdered : Liebknecht, Luxemburg, and Haase of the Left-wing Socialists, Walther Rathenau, a Democrat, and

Erzberger of the Catholic Centre. From 1918 to 1922 political groups of the Right killed 354 opponents : those on the Left killed 22. In the year 1930, political murders rose to 20, whereas for 1924 they had not been above 6. Political murders by the Right and attempts at *coups d'état* went practically unpunished, while violence by Republicans or Socialists was met with prompt conviction and sharp punishment.[14] There was a State behind and within the State ready to emerge when the time was ripe ; and Hitler had, after various internal struggles,[15] been confirmed as its leader, for he was the most forceful, unscrupulous, and fanatical of all. Deficient in political experience, the Germans were not sceptical towards his possessed oratory, or the uniforms, the swastika, the military, ecclesiastical and ceremonial enticements. No technique is adequate to ascertain the number of believers or the intensity of their convictions. In all the post-war discontents of Germany, especially economic discontents (shared by many countries), a promise was found by the Nazi movement for each particular complainant group, however impossible the total effect.[16] Yet, always certain notes were struck : the ignominy and treachery of the so-called ' November criminals ', that is, the Social Democrats and others who took over the Government in 1918 after the defeat and signed the Treaty of Versailles ; Parliamentary incapacity and corruption ; the misery of Germany under high finance and capitalism, and international finance ; the humiliation of Germany by the dictated peace ; the inherent superiority of Germany—' a master race '—to all other nations, and the right of Germany to equal international treatment and self-determination ; the bestiality of Communism (and it must be remembered that Russia is much nearer to Germany than to Great Britain or U.S.A.) ; and the spiritual and political disintegration of Germany by her Jews. The Germans had been accustomed to a stable executive power, even if it were non-responsible ; they were themselves unready for the burden of sovereign power, and were disconcerted by the instability of coalition governments.

After the failure of the uprising in Munich the claim was made, however, that power must be won legally, through the constitutional form of the Republic—a tactic especially designed for the bourgeoisie at home and abroad, though the murders and the street riots continued. As Dr. Goebbels declared on 30 April 1928,[17] ' We enter Parliament in order to supply ourselves, in the arsenal of democracy, with its own weapons. We become members of the Reichstag in order to paralyse the Weimar sentiment with its own assistance. If democracy is so stupid as to give us free tickets and salaries for this bears' work, that is its affair . . . we do not come as friends nor even as neutrals. We come as enemies. As the wolf bursts into the flock so we come.'

Now, a careful analysis of German election statistics from 1919 to

1933 shows an unmistakable correlation between economically troubled times and support of first, the nationalistic parties, and later the Nazi Party which outbid the latter and finally became heir to practically all their votes.[18]   In 1919 the non-nationalistic vote was about 96 per cent. of the total.   Then came a reaction (monetary inflation, disgust at the Treaty, occupation of the Ruhr) and the non-nationalistic vote sank to 59 per cent.   By May 1928, after some recovery of foreign prestige, employment, and the Dawes reparations settlement, the non-nationalistic vote recovered to 68·5 per cent. of the total.   The Social Democrats were the largest single party and had the leading position in the Cabinet.   Between the election of May 1924 and that of May 1928, Hitler's Party lost more than half its votes : it sank from 1,918,000 to 810,000.   It may be noticed, also, that Communist votes in May 1924 were nearly 3,700,000.   Then, towards the end of 1928, the Great Depression set in in Germany.   In the election of September 1930, the Nazi vote rose to 6,410,000 (taking away millions, perhaps, from the other nationalistic parties) ;   in July 1932 it rose to 13,746,000 ;   and sank a little (through internal Party difficulties) in November 1932.   It is most important to notice two other things : that the Catholic Centre gained ;   that the Social Democrats and Communists together kept their substantial vote intact, nearly 30 per cent. of the total, but that Communist votes were nearly 5·3 million, while the Social Democratic vote was just under 8 million—that is, the working class vote was seriously split.   It is believed that the great addition to the Nazi vote in July 1932 came from new voters, especially young people (brought up in an atmosphere of insecurity, unemployment, ' the shame of Versailles ', and all sorts of violent alarms) and from the Nationalist Party, the People's Party, and many of the Democrats who were of very mixed interests and very amenable to the Nazi anti-bolshevik appeal.

Two other things may be remarked of the Hitler following : its relative weakness among the urban workers, yet its general strength throughout the country and all the different social groupings.   Thus, the critical elections of 1932 and 1933 show [19] that all the big cities and the industrial districts (Berlin, Hamburg, Leipzig, Cologne, Dresden, the Rhineland and Baden, but *not* Silesia) were strongly against Hitler ;   while the East and North, especially the more rural areas (East Prussia, Schleswig, East Hanover, Pomerania, and Silesia) were strongly for him ;   in the centre of Germany (between Rhine and Elbe) there was quite substantial support.   It is exceedingly important, however, that the easy argument from the figures of 1930 and 1932 that the economic depression converted Germans into Nazis be tempered by the realization that the Nationalists or/and Hitler had millions of followers before these years, a constant following apart from economic depression, which, added to those who voted the party ticket out of desperation, subscribed a big enough percentage of the total vote at elections for the Nazi Party to claim office. Many of these were militarists—either aggressive, or revengeful, or revisionist. An analysis [20] of Nazi Party membership in 1933 and 1935 shows that manual industrial workers were very considerably under-represented in the Nazi Party compared with their proportion to the total gain-fully occupied in Germany ; that ' white-collar ' employees (in English, ' black-coated ' workers) were extremely strongly over-represented, and even more so were the independent groups, like skilled artisans, merchants, shopkeepers, professional workers (to the extent of double their proportion to the percentage of the total gainfully occupied) ; that officials were substantially over-represented, especially *after* Hitler's advent to power, and that the peasantry were considerably under-represented.

The votes for Hitler's Party were never a majority, not even in the election of March 1933 after he had been three months in full unconstitutional control. The decisive change occurred when the Party benefited from the heavy unemployment of 1932 and was able to win the confidence of the unemployed. It may be taken as certain that Hitler was never given all his votes, or even the majority of them, as active support for all that his Party afterwards did or anything approaching it, still less to prepare for war, still less to make one. There were undoubtedly some, millions, indeed, for all these things (there are $2\frac{1}{2}$ million Party members) and there were some, too, who did not vote for him in the free days, who wanted war. But reflection on the voting figures and the timing of the increase in his votes suggests that, like the Italian people with Fascism, not all of the German people knew to what they were committing themselves and the world. They believed in the ' legal State ', and believed that under Hitler it would continue much as before.[21] Nor did important observers outside Germany believe otherwise. The German voters were principally culpable of political ignorance, lack of civic prescience, insensitivity to anti-democratic forces, and democratic responsibilities, and indi-vidually selfish regard for their own immediate short-run convenience. The menace grew too slowly to be noticed ; or the Nazis disguised it. The threat to the Republic was always either too feeble to be worth challenging or too strong for assault. Hitler was either too consti-tutional for force or too forceful for any constitutional resistance ! Yet, from March 1933, it was certain what must happen sooner or later. All voting after that date proves only the efficiency of the terror, of gratitude for jobs in industry and in the Party ; for we can never truly distinguish the part played by obedience due to conviction, as compared with obedience due to terror. One other thing is certain —that Heinrich Himmler acknowledged in 1939 that the first country that would have to be conquered if war came would be Germany itself.

In all this the Communist Party played an unfortunate part. They were anti-parliamentary; entertained a creed of anti-bourgeois morality analogous to that of the Nazis; they were anti-capitalist. They drew away considerable support from the democratic socialist movement, but not enough to overcome the non-Communist electorate; they made parliamentary government impossible by their tactics; they derided and discredited the Social Democrats and trade union leaders and destroyed the faith of many workers in these organizations.[22]

In January 1933, the Nazi leader was, partly accidentally, appointed Chancellor as a result of a series of doddering moves by the aged President Hindenburg [who had governed from 1930 through minority cabinets] persuaded thereto by Baron von Papen acting for the Junkers on the belief that Hitler would be merely their agent.[23]   The acceptance, by Hindenburg, of a Chancellor whose Party had vowed to destroy the Constitution he had sworn an oath to defend, was in itself manifestly unconstitutional in spirit.   More deadly for the German people and the Republic was the Decree of 28 February 1933, signed by the President.   Ostensibly an answer to the Reichstag fire (evidence convicts the Nazis as incendiaries), the Decree was issued in pursuance of the Constitution, Article 48, Section 2 (see Vol. II, p. 1152) permitting the suspension of certain constitutional guarantees in a state of high emergency.   These guarantees are the buttress of democracy; their abridgement the foundation of dictatorship.   Personal freedom, free expression of opinion, the press, association and meetings, the secrecy of letters, post, telegraph and telephone, judicial control of search-warrants, and protection of property were abolished.   From that moment Germany was totally in the hands of the government of Hitler.

On 24 March 1933 the new Reichstag passed the ' Enabling Act for the Relief of the Distress of the Nation and the Reich '.   Involving constitutional amendment, this Act required a two-thirds majority of both Houses.   The Nazi Party had only 228 seats and adding 52 seats of the Nationalist Party, 340 out of 647.   Two-thirds majority of those present at the session was required.   It was as simple as could be. The Communists with 81 seats and 26 Socialists were kept out by exile, imprisonment, or threat of murder.   The 94 Socialists present courageously voted against the bill.   All depended on the votes of the Catholic Centre.   That Party was persuaded : all present voted in favour; none abstained.   The Party believed still that this authority would lead to the triumph of a legal Hitler over his homicidal followers. The Enabling Act (twice thereafter extended) provided first, that all laws, including financial, might be enacted by the Government outside the procedure of the Constitution.   This, then, virtually abolished the legislative assemblies, the Reichstag and the Reichsrat as more than ornamental furniture. It is true that the Reichstag continued to exist and still exists, that in 1936 there was a Reichstag election (the candidates chosen by the Party, the electorate voting for the Führer's list and not for individual names), and that it still retained power to make laws should the Führer ever ask it to. Secondly, the laws thus made by the Government were permitted to deviate from the Constitution, excepting as far as the status Reichstag and the Federal Council were concerned. But these had already been gutted when the plenary law-making power passed to the Government, and when, simultaneously, the governments of the States represented on the Federal Council had been forcibly co-ordinated, that is, taken over by the Nazis by main force. The law kept the prerogatives of the President ' untouched ', but the ' Old Man ' (Hindenburg) was manageable ; and then, soon, on his death, the Chancellor (Hitler) absorbed his office also. Thirdly, all constitutional procedural guarantees regarding legislation were abolished.

On the death of Hindenburg, 2 August 1934, Hitler by decree-law merged the Chancellorship and the Presidency, and so became Führer and Reichskanzler ; thus, the Führer absorbed all the President's prerogatives (Cf. Vol. II, pp. 1144 ff.) ; and on 19 August 1934 a plebiscite ratified this change, needless to say with an overwhelming majority (and yet about 16 per cent. of the voters voted ' No ' or spoiled their ballot papers). A plebiscite was strictly not necessary but the Führer so loved his people : ' the people themselves shall give their decision ', he said in the Reichstag. In July 1935 the title was changed simply to ' Der Führer ' : it was announced that ' Chancellor ' sounded like a functionary, whereas ' Führer ' indicated the beloved leader of his people !

Two more steps were necessary for the fundamental transfer of sovereign authority from the constitutional organs of legislature and executive to one man. First, to cast out all other parties and then submerge the State in the Party. On 14 July 1933 the ' Law Prohibiting the Formation of New Political Parties ', provided that the Nazi Party was the only political party in Germany and prescribed severe terms of imprisonment for any one undertaking to maintain any other party organization or form a new one. Of course, as the Act indicated, there might be other much severer punishments under other legal provisions, for example, acting as an ' enemy of the State '.

The ' Law on the Unification of Party and State ' of 1 December 1933 provided that : ' Since the victory of the National Socialist Revolution, the National Socialist German Workers' Party has become the embodiment of the idea of the State and irrevocably integrated with the State.' As Nazi constitutional lawyers and politicians (and they are the same thing) say, the Nazi Party is the ' bearer of the State idea of authority '. The Act assigned to the Party the status of a public corporation which, in effect, gave it certain guarantees of its funds and property, before the courts (as though that were necessary) exempted it from taxation and assigned to it ' the directing power of the National Socialist State '.   All public authorities were enjoined to render assistance to the Party in its functions.   The law made representatives of Hitler, as Party Leader and Chief of Staff of the Storm Troopers, members of the Government.   Powers are given to secure discipline within the Party and over the Storm Troopers to be implemented by the Reichchancellor as Leader.   In the Law of 20 December 1934, protection was given the Party against ' insidious attacks against State and Party ' and those who ' undermine the confidence of the people in the political leadership '.   All suits against illegal actions committed in connexion with the national revolution go not to the ordinary courts, but to the Ministry of the Interior which deals with them ' in equity '.   (!)

Thus, the Party is supreme and unique ; its leader is leader in the State ; its leader forms the Government of the State ; the Government, which is dismissible by the leader, is endowed with the power to make laws and change the constitution ; it parallels and interpenetrates the whole hierarchy of State authorities.   There is no authority below the leader except what he devolves ; there is no power parallel with that of the leader ; there is no power above him.   The Führer is the absorptive unity in a triple chancellorship, the chancellorship of the Reich, the chancellorship of the former Presidency, and the chancellorship of the Nazi Party ; and he is, again, a unity of the triple powers of government—the executive, the legislative and the judicial.

To complete the picture of the unreserved dictatorship, a few more touches may be added.   On 7 April 1933, notwithstanding the articles previously mentioned, safeguarding the position of the Federal Council, the Reich Government passed the ' Law on the Unification of the German States ', empowering the Federal Government to appoint Governors of the States, who, in their turn, would appoint and remove the governments of the States, dissolve the legislatures, order new elections, make and publish State laws, and appoint and dismiss the higher officials and the judges.   By designating the government of the States, the Führer made a mockery of their representation in the Reichsrat.   But a subsequent law of 30 January 1934 (' for the Reconstruction of the Reich ') passed by both Chambers unanimously, was decisive for unification.   Authority for this was taken from a plebiscite of November 1933 on Germany's withdrawal from Geneva, which was alleged to prove that ' the German nation has attained an indestructible unity superior to all internal subdivisions of a political character '.

The law decreed : no more popular representation in the States ; all State rights transferred to the Reich ; all State governments

placed under the Reich; the governors of the States to come under
the supervision of the Reich Ministry of the Interior. In January
1935 any remaining individuality of the States was removed by an
'Act Relating to the Reich Governors', which subjected them to
supervision, no longer by the Ministry of the Interior, but by the
various ministers of the Reich Government. The Reich Governor is
a Reich official appointed and dismissed by the Führer. All dualism
between Reich and States is supposed to have disappeared, but war-
time experience shows very considerable restiveness by the Reich
authorities at the survival of the particularist spirit.

A high centralization of local government and its subjection to
the Nazi Party was introduced in the German Municipal Code of
30 January 1935.[24] All municipalities are subject to the supervision
of the Reich Ministry of the Interior; their budgets require advance
approval by the Reich; the Ministry of the Interior appoints the
mayors and councillors of cities with a population of over 100,000,
while in smaller cities appointments are made by the Reich Governors
or other Reich officials. The Burgomaster is chosen by the Ministry
of the Interior or the Reich Governor from among three candidates
proposed by the local Nazi Party Delegate. Thus appointed, the
Burgomaster has full and exclusive responsibility for the government
of the municipality. The councillors are a mere body of advisers,
chosen by the Nazi Party Delegate (himself appointed by the Führer's
deputy, usually the local Nazi leader) for their 'political reliability,
capability and character'. The Burgomaster must consult the
Council but need not be guided by the result. The councillors are
supposed to maintain contact with the people and secure from them
'a sympathetic understanding for the measures taken by the mayor'.
This function might be a useful check on the mayor for the higher
authority, but it is difficult to fulfil in a despotic system; so the law
goes so far as to *command* the councillors to give expression to dis-
agreeable criticism. The 'leader' of the German League of Municipalities admits the failure of the councillors; they have neither time
nor will for their job.[25]

Prussia is thoroughly incorporated in the Reich. The Führer is
the governor of Prussia; but the Minister-President of Prussia,
Goering, exercises the region's power devolved to him. He is responsible, therefore, only to Hitler. All members of the Reich Cabinet are
ex officio members of the Prussian Cabinet, except the Minister of
Finance. All Prussian administrative departments are absorbed by
the corresponding departments of the Reich. This situation is the
reverse of that established in the Bismarck Constitution (Vol. II,
Chap. X). Prussia is intermerged with the Reich, but the Reich
dominates. The Nazis talked much in their early years of plans for
the establishment of economic-physiographic regions in place of the

historic dynastic State boundaries. The Nazis had this in mind, together with some return to ancient tribal regions (Gaue) as parts of the Reich. The matter was lost to view against occult resistance : it probably never meant anything but romantic talk as compared with present military-economic tasks.[26]

Since it is not intended to cover all the details of the dictatorship, reference need be made only to three other matters : the Plebiscites, the Constitution, and Education for Political Leadership.

Claiming to be a ' real ' democracy ; ambitious to unify the *Volk* as a solid, excited, palpitating, unthinking but responsive fanatical following ; anxious to intimidate foreign countries by a show of unity and will ; and with an urgent appetite for approval and acclamation, the Nazi Government established the referendum of 14 July 1933. But this referendum was to be at the instance of the Government, and was in no wise at the initiative of the people, as permitted by the Weimar Constitution.   There have been three plebiscites : 12 November 1933, already mentioned ; 19 August 1934 on the fusion of Chancellor and Presidency ; 10 April 1938 on the German-Austrian Anschluss *post facto*.   There was no referendum after Munich, and there was none before the war against Poland.   Nazi apologists are always anxious to observe that the Führer needs no sign of popular assent. The whole Nazi system postulates a mystical solidarity among the people and with the Führer, and no distinction between their authority can be admitted.   The plebiscite is merely the ceremonial of solidarity, not its establishment.   Four months before the referendum was enacted, a Ministry of Public Enlightenment and Propaganda was established : ' for purposes of enlightenment and propaganda among the people concerning the policy of the Government and the national reconstruction of the German Fatherland.'

The general constitutional system merits a few reflections.[27] Whatever formal obstacle stands in the way of the Führer's will may be removed by him by a simple decree, which, if it should happen to be challenged before the law courts, will prevail in the sense the Führer declares to be his wish.   This is the doctrine of ' the legal last word of the Führer binding all judges '.   It was fully expressed in a German law journal in relation to the case, won in the first instance but finally lost, brought by Jehovah's Witnesses to save their property from confiscation.[28]   They claimed the religious tolerance of the Weimar Constitution (Article 135, unrepealed) while the Nazi prosecutor claimed they were not acting religiously when (on the ground that only God could give ' salvation ' (' Heil ! ') their members refused to give the salute ' Heil Hitler ! '   This is the Nazi doctrine : The judges, still afflicted with a Weimar mentality, were looking for a formal document by which to determine what parts of the Weimar Constitution had been cancelled or amended, and what parts stood.   In part, this

was perfectly clear, since some laws had been passed on the basis of
the power clearly given by the Reichstag to the Party and Hitler.
Elsewhere a rule of interpretation was required. A constitution is
necessary : ' National life needs a container in order to be able to
utilize the forces active within it . . . this foundation of national
being is the constitution.' It is ' the fundamental order in which a
political people forms itself in a State '.—' A constitution is not a
number (or assemblage) of individual constitutional laws but an
enclosed whole made up of all the principles, the spirit, and the nature
of the national being. . . .' The justification of a constitution, that
is, the Weimar Constitution, is lost as soon as it ceases to be appropriate
to the idea and existence of a new political order. ' In the programme
of the Movement, we possess a catechism of political world outlook
which provides a criterion and principle in the decision of questions of
constitutional law.' The principles have triumphed ; they are actually
might, might founded on a spiritual, moral element, and that might
prevails. Therefore, the latest addition to Party principle by the
Führer supplements the factual order, and this is supreme over written
law. To this the judges must submit, for the judge is below the
legislative. The judge must interpret according to ' the unambiguously
expressed will of the Leader '.

Two conclusions may be drawn from this : one regarding constitutional amendment, the other regarding the separation of powers.
When commenting on the political problems of a very rigid amending
process, the hypothetical question was asked (Vol. I, p. 126) what
would happen to a single dissenter in a country where constitutional
amendment required a unanimous vote ? It was suggested that the
dissenter would be put away by violent means. In dictatorial countries the constitution of the country is the physico-psychic constitution of one man. To amend the constitution is impossible without
amending the constitution of that man. In a democracy, the constitution is a promise to the people, in a dictatorship a weapon of the
rulers ; in a democracy the constitution makes flexibility available to
the governed, but therewith makes guarantees ; in a dictatorship the
constitution is fully rigid for the governed but totally flexible for the
rulers ; in a democracy the constitution is made in order to enable
people to live securely and in reasonable tranquillity ; where dictators
rule, the constitution, on the other hand, is adopted to enable the
dictator to live dangerously, and to exact the price in the abject
obedience of the people. How did the Poles get over the difficulties
of the *liberum veto* ? Those who agreed met at a snap meeting in a
locked room, keeping the dissentient out. One such dissentient came
through the chimney in time to vote, but missed the roll call because
one of the nobles cut off his head before he could cry ' No ! '

Furthermore, in the observations on the Separation of Powers

5

(Vol. I, Chap. VI), it was clearly shown that only where society intends to restrict the use of political power are checks and balances and the separation of powers applied ; that this occurs in the degree required by the particular policy of moderating the use of power, and where the answerability of all the organs of government to a fundamental formal law is desired, separation of powers is a product of the principles, the material aims, and the general temper of governed and government. It is a question of degree. In revolutions it disappears altogether, at least for a time, while the principles of the revolutionary movement are being positively applied in substitution for the old.[29] The fanatical temper of the Nazi movement implies vehemence, even violence, of concentration and unity. The separation of powers is incompatible with this and therefore set aside. So Führer and Party deny the separability of the agencies of Government—they make the laws, they execute them, they appoint, dismiss and correct the administration, while the judges are regarded simply as executive instruments fully incorporated within the will of the Leader. Again and again, the Ministers of Justice and the Führer have returned to the purification of the mind of the judge, the dismissal of the untrustworthy and the appointment of accomplices. And yet, so strongly does any study of the law impress upon the mind the spiritual and practical social values of consistency from case to case, equality between man and man, and reverence for the words by which alone the spirit may be apprehended and caprice excluded, that to secure their ends the Nazis have to this day been obliged to continue to threaten, to wheedle, and to plan a reformed law education—and still many judges resist.[30]

All occupations, employers and employees, and independent workers, are harnessed in the German Labour Front, an authoritarian organization to permeate the economy with Nazi functionaries and ideas.[31] All professions are sucked into the vortex of the Party by their compulsory affiliation to it, and the dependence of the right to practise on a licence from the State, for which membership or good standing in the Party is a condition. Among such professions is the Civil Service, which in Germany includes judges and teachers as well as administrators. Of one and a half million members of the Nazi Civil Service Association, nearly 30 per cent. are Party members, and, considering the violence of behaviour and plainly declared intentions of the Nazi Movement, this is a damning proportion. All officials swear personal fealty to the Leader in these terms :

I swear that I shall be faithful and obedient to Adolf Hitler, the Leader of the German Reich and the people, that I shall obey the laws and fulfil my official duties conscientiously, so help me God. (Law Regarding Public Officials, 26 January 1937. Translation by Pollock and Heinemann, *The German Civil Service Act.*)

The Civil Service and the Judiciary were purged of 'unreliable elements' (Law, 7 April 1933), though apart from Jews not many needed to be dismissed since most, if not zealous Nazis, had never been warm friends of the Republic.[32] The Judges are ordered to administer justice on two principles, namely, on the general Nazi idea that 'law is that which serves the German nation', and the particular injunction of the Reich Minister of Justice at the Reich Conference of Judges in 1936. 'How would the Leader decide in my place . . . is this decision compatible with the National Socialist conscience of the German *Volk* ?' How far from the position of the judge in the British system in which Lord Justice Atkin could utter so potent and majestic a protest against the Executive and his own assenting brethren ! [33]

Now, it has somewhere been suggested that wholesale dismissal of public officials by the Nazis would have endangered the régime. Indeed, such action would have paralysed the State and therefore the Movement. Equally, then, a wholesale resignation would have stopped the Nazis, so strategical is the position of the Civil Service in the modern State. It is clear that a substantial number stayed because they were Nazi-minded (*vide* the numbers who were members of the Party). It can also be accepted that many others were temporizers, waiting for the situation to clarify itself, as the Nazis made their onslaught, and approached power. Vast numbers, permanently lukewarm to politics, no doubt thought first of their jobs, salaries, and pensions. The continuance of some in service, was perhaps, and 'perhaps' must be emphasized, morally supported by the principle and tradition that the civil service is a neutral servant of the State, and therefore carries out the duties required of it by *any* political party that enters office. The action of the very few who may be deemed to have been animated by this motive, in scrupulously sustained purity, and by this motive alone, has already raised in the minds of some political scientist the problem, if not the doubt, how far such a principle of impartial service ought to be commended. The answer cannot here be given in full systematic form, but some thoughts may be offered.

It has always been held that if the public official's conscience is revolted by what he is required to do and for whom he is required to do it, he should resign, and, then, as a citizen fight all evil things. That is the most honest and practically satisfactory injunction from a long run point of view. Only in what may be called law-abiding and responsible politics, the main principles of which are held in common by the vast majority, can the principle of neutrality and impartiality be expected to operate, and only there ought it to operate. The pertinent question arises always : Why should the public official be expected to boycott a party (by resignation) when all other industrial workers and shopkeepers and professional workers, and so forth,

continue to render normal service and supply goods, to the members
and followers of a guilt-laden political party ? Some might rejoin
that there is a special duty on the public official because his work is
so strategic and his resignation therefore so much the more damaging
than the work of ordinary industry. This argument can no longer
be sustained in an era or region of highly developed economies, where
the interdependence of industries on each other, and of the total
economy on each industry, is vital. Why, then, saddle public officials
with a social burden that other citizens show no drastic anxiety to
bear ? If public officials are expected to, exceptionally, they may be
made hyper-sensitive to politics, which would not be good for normal
duties.

When, then, there arises a state of society where all should withdraw service and sustenance from evil followers of destructive movements, the civil service should act likewise. Any action on the part
of public officials earlier and braver than that of other citizens who
could frustrate an undesirable political movement, is something that
cannot be demanded, though it can be praised. The issue is to be
decided in the light of John Locke's conclusion, that when the Prince
violates the principles of the constitution, there is then no way of
advance except that all enter the conflict under Heaven, that is that
each man shall fight for the right as he himself sees it. The claim that
by remaining in office in the service of that which in the civil servant's
opinion is infamous in principle and leadership, the official may perhaps thereby salvage something of permanent value to all, or to the
majority of his fellow-citizens, or to a minority which he believes to
be right and oppressed, is either a rejection of the principle of neutrality
(heroic, it may be, in the circumstances) or cowardly self-deception
of a more or less gross kind.

Supreme in the hierarchy of terror and repression is the People's
Court, the *Volksgerichtshof* (established on 24 April 1934), composed
of two trained judges and three laymen from the Elite Guard, appointed
by Hitler on the proposal of the Minister of Justice, ' on the basis of
expertness in defence against subversive activities or because most
intimately connected with the political trends of the nation '. This
Court is especially seized with ' political crimes ' which are of the
widest scope, and its victims are punished by the Secret Police. It
is secret ; and retains a squad of executioners. In order that no
formal limits should stand in its way in dealing with persons ' inimical
to the State ', the rule of interpretation, ' to judge in accordance with
sound popular sentiment ', is applied. This is based upon the laws
of 26 February 1933 and 29 March 1933, amended on 28 June 1935,
thus :

Whoever commits an act which the law decrees punishable or which is deserv-
ing of punishment according to the fundamental idea of a criminal law and

according to sound popular sentiment, shall be punished. Where no definite criminal law specifically applies to the act, it shall be punished according to law, the basic idea of which is simply applicable.

The Secret Police, the Gestapo, was founded in April 1933 by Goering in Prussia. A year later all the police forces of the Reich were centralized under Heinrich Himmler, directly subordinate to Hitler. The Gestapo is an independent branch of public adminis-tration, and is authorized to demand information from and to give orders to all State agencies whatsoever. Its acts cannot be challenged in any court or department. Only Himmler and his deputies can consider complaints made against its members. There is a close connexion between the S.S. (Schutzstaffel), *alias* the Elite Guard, *alias* the Black Guards, and the Gestapo, but these organizations are independent of each other, except for special purposes. All higher officials of the Gestapo are officers of the S.S. and many of the Gestapo are recruited from it. The Gestapo was empowered by the law of 10 February 1936 ' to uncover and combat all tendencies and develop-ments dangerous to the State and for this purpose to take all measures deemed necessary and expedient '. It is thus the final control in the totalitarian terror organization, and even holds the Nazi Party by the throat.

In a democratic State, the nature of the ultimate political good is regarded as properly and naturally the very essence of political contest : it is regarded rather as an adventure in the unknown than an organized march to a specific destination. A special education for political leadership is not regarded as imperative. A dictatorial State, however, is founded on an ardent revelation, consequent bigotry, and on a temper implying unconditional obedience. It is, therefore, faced with the problem of discovering future leaders through special mechan-isms of selection and education. The first step in this is, of course, the recruitment and training of children in the Youth Organizations, their subsequent selection as full-fledged Party members, and then a further process of selection for Party offices occurs. This, however, the supreme leadership of the Party deems insufficient, believing that a process of tuition must provide for the succession of dynamic leader-ship. It is obviously faced with a problem much more important and difficult than that of selecting mere functionaries in the intermediate level of the organization. It must provide for what may be called creative leadership. To do this, there have been established a number of schools for leadership ; they are the Adolf Hitler Schools, the National Political Institutes of Education and the ' Order Castles ' (Ordensburgen). The Adolf Hitler Schools open to boys at the age of 12 for a 6-year course. The entrants are chosen by the Nazi Party from the Hitler Youth for character, physique, and ability to lead. Only physique is really definable. School studies need be no more than 'satisfactory'. What is looked for is outstanding leadership ability. But there is no definition of character or of ability to lead. Schooling is free; the unpromising are promptly weeded out. At 18, the pupils have a choice of the university to prepare for a profession, or the army, or State or Party administration. Some 300 boys a year have been admitted into the schools. All the teachers are Party members and the essential basis of education is biology, German racial studies and orientation in history and contemporary affairs. The National Political Institutes of Education replaced the Prussian Cadet Schools. They are for the training of Stormtroopers and the Elite Guard leaders or the Compulsory Labour Service. The S.A. is in charge. There are three girl schools among the 31. The Order Castles are far more ambitious. They lead back to the castles which in the thirteenth to the fifteenth century were built for the subjugation of the Slavs in the East. They are reserved for select members of the élite of the Party, for example 1 out of 4 of the graduates from the National Political Institutes of Education are admitted. Before entering, the recruits must do one year of Compulsory Labour Service and 2 years of Compulsory Military Service. And then, before they are accepted, there is a candidature from 1 to 3 years. The course lasts 6 years. The first year is spent in the studies of racial biology and ideology; the second year in athletics, the handling of arms and parachute jumping; the next year-and-one-half in political education and intensive physical training; the next year-and-one-half in politics, especially the politics of Eastern Europe.

What is expected of this training for political leadership? The emphasis may be on obedience or domination, but what is crucial is that no candidate is permitted to entertain or utter views in opposition to Hitler or leading to a movement for the destruction of the Party. If the education does not foster those who, by brilliance of mind and individuality of character can confute the Party ideology, it is not for leadership, but only for the administration of Hitler's ideas and will, and for visiting them on others.[34] It has nothing in common with leadership as we know it in the democratic countries, for this is the discovery and pursuit of new values, while the other serves the cause of human bondage.

CHAPTER IV

FRANCE: THE THIRD REPUBLIC [1]

THE Third Republic was struck down by the German Armies in forty-five days, the culmination of seven years of military threats and of the systematic moral subornation of French leadership and patriotism itself. On 10 July 1940 the French National Assembly adopted a new constitution in the involuntary absence of one-third of the elected representatives, and on false representations by their new leaders.[2] It is not intended to examine in any detail the causes of the temporary collapse, but rather briefly to reflect on the mortal deficiencies of the fallen régime, for the future of France depends on their recognition and repair. The argument that France fell apart merely as a consequence of the class-struggle is far too simple to fit the facts.

On 18 June 1940 M. Paul Reynaud, who had just resigned the premiership to Marshal Pétain, expressed the desperate need of the disastrous hour in a single word : fidelity. It was, indeed, the want of public fidelity in the inter-war years that inexorably lead to downfall. Montesquieu, perhaps the first and easily the second in the galaxy of French political minds which have so richly endowed Western culture, affirmed that every régime is animated by a characteristic and saving spirit. A monarchy (not a despotism) lived by the citizens' ambition and their love of honours, glory and applause. An aristocracy throve by virtue, that is, probity, and moderation among the aristocrats. But the soul of the Republic was ' *virtue* ' : ' Love of the laws and of their country . . . require a consistent preference of public to private interest.' ' Now,' says Montesquieu, ' a government is like everything else : to preserve it we must love it.' [3] And even Machiavelli (who may have inspired this part of Montesquieu's doctrine) holds that no people can be free without *virtú*,[4] that is, vigour, force of character, determination. Montesquieu's virtue is a standard of social behaviour ; Machiavelli's, the virility, energy, and fortitude which would make the former effective.

The only justifiable question is not whether France could have won the War standing alone ; but whether she had prepared the moral and material power necessary to a better effort. How far, we must ask, was this duty within the power of French government to fulfil ? The answer, we shall see, was very much ; but the Government failed. France needed the ability, that is the organization, and the resolution under onslaught, to hold out until Britain in the first place, and the United States in the second, could throw into the balance their men

N.B.—The Notes to this Chapter begin on page 175.

and industrial resources.[5]   Comprehension is first a matter of appreciation of her strength in manpower and manufactures.   For in respect of these two sovereign factors in modern warfare, France was in 1939 far surpassed by Germany.

The deficiency in manpower was partly capable of correction and, therefore, partly a failure of government practice and public spirit, which inspires government, and is in turn cultivable by government. There were also, however, population factors beyond political correction, at least, in time to be effective.   The disparity between Germany and France was very considerable : the total German population was nearly 75 million, the French 41·3 million ; Germany had 25 million men between the ages of 15 and 65, France had barely 13 million ; while, if women were included in the war potential, Germany had 40·4 million between the ages of 15 and 49 and France only one-half as many.   This gap was much greater than in 1914. It developed in the inter-war years, and became a source of political pessimism in France and engendered a foreign policy of concessions. Yet governments can apply remedial population policies : Fascist Italy and Nazi Germany found ways and means.[6]

Another controllable factor in manpower is the length of service and the training period of conscripts.   But French governments adopted a mistaken policy.   The three years' military service had first been reduced to 18 months, and in 1928 to 12.   The Socialist Party steadily opposed long service for social reasons, because, until too late its doctrine was blindly pacifist ; in May 1935, when the Chamber voted for 2 years of service by 350 to 196 votes, Socialists and Communists voted against.   But other parliamentary groups also opposed the longer period of service, since it meant increased public expenditure and took men away from industry and the farms.   The powerful Radical Socialist Party was, by general doctrine and political composition, a staunch friend of short service, while the reduction had indeed been made by a Conservative (Tardieu) Government.

In the harsh light of sheer self-preservation (and this should have been immediately seized as the closely approaching ordeal) a similar political error was committed in the mal-distribution of manpower between industry and the armed forces.   A proper allocation to the manufacture of arms can go far to reduce disparities in the gross populations of enemies.   Since 1919, a remarkable increase of industrialization had occurred in France (the iron-ore deposits of Lorraine were now fully hers), particularly in industries like automobiles and aluminium.[7]   But industrial manpower was not adequately organized to meet war commitments, because there was faulty judgment whether there would be a war at all, the kind of war to be fought, and, therefore, the kind of equipment which would be needed ; and because few would face the sacrifice of the standard of living this implies : short-run commodity was preferred to long-run good. Also in 1936, the Popular Front Government under Léon Blum introduced various social and industrial measures, in themselves very desirable and long overdue, but unfortunately out of time with the prodigious re-arming of Germany.[8] For the 40-hour week and the paid holiday meant an average week of 38 hours and 20 minutes ; and, as somebody said, France was the only country with two Sundays per week. (In England, at this very time, there was obstinate refusal to create Ministries of Supply and Defence.)

So far, it has been intended only to suggest that the spirit of French Government and her political institutions were in large degree at fault, and that the failure was no accident. The rest of this discussion pursues in turn the weakness of the men and the inadequacy of the machinery. There was too little public fidelity.

Now there are many orders in which it is possible to explain a political catastrophe. One could begin with social and economic popular divisions and ascend to political leadership at the summit. Or one can begin with the leaders at the top of the political pyramid, exhibit their qualities, survey the system of institutions in which they operate and which exert a reciprocal effect on their functioning, and thence probe forward to the part played by the people and their divisive groupings. The former method puts the emphasis on the deterministic inevitability of disruption, the latter at least suggests alternatives in the free resolution of men to be masters of their social cleavages, for national union and democratic order which is their more fundamental and long-run good. Were there no social divisions there would be no need for leadership, for leadership undertakes the task of adjustment. We regard events in France from the top of the pyramid where the leaders stand ; supporting or undermining them, or splitting the pyramid on which they might stand and advance into unbridgable and unmergeable parts, are the people. This latter approach involves some repetition, but it is the more instructive. Therefore, the order of discussion is as follows :

   I.   The deficiencies of the Statesmen.
  II.   Faults in the manners and organs of government.
 III.   Social and economic divisions of the people.

I. *Deficiencies of the Statesmen*

It has been urged that France failed from too little public fidelity. Now fidelity is incarnate above all in political leaders. But after the death of Clemenceau and Poincaré, the Third Republic lacked leadership adequate to survival in a Europe menaced by Fascism, and more especially by the grandiose and deadly ambitions and ruthless technical efficiency of the Nazis. Until a people of forty million are able spontaneously to think for themselves, in a world perspective embracing the very complicated present and the dim but exigent future, to organize themselves and act in undirected yet appropriate collaboration, their happiness, peace and survival must depend on the assistance of their leaders. The peculiar circumstances of the European situation required that such leaders should be personally capable of summoning forth the painful sacrifice and protracted effort equal to the impending ordeal, that is, they required attributes which could persuade Frenchmen to conquer their personal and group egoisms, steadily to pay heavy taxation, accept lower standards of living, and, in the end, if the show of armed resolution failed to thwart the menace, offer life itself. Above all, the leaders must be capable of overcoming in themselves their personal dislikes, their differences of doctrine, and their social and economic antipathies, at least to the degree and for the time necessary to meet the crisis of domestic disruption and external attack—assuming that for them their nation means more than their like-minded social groups in foreign lands, perhaps their *national* enemies.

Within the whole body of a democratic polity, containing its diverse individuals, its political sub-leaders, and what may be called *clots of interest*, the vital organs can respond and function only if there are leaders (not dominators) who inspire faith, for faith generates movement. They, too, in this era of acute social division, must be moved to surmount their differences at the minimum for defensive unity. The masses will move, and in moving, fortify and accompany the leaders along the necessary road, if they can be convinced that it is necessary, and so by willing collaboration, contribute to their own leadership. But in a time of trouble, exceptional degrees of the attributes of leadership are demanded. At the fatal moments, the Third Republic was bankrupt of eminence. No one replaced the dead Clemenceau's combination of insight and comprehension, his cynicism, roughness, his Jacobin energy, his absolute patriotism, his quaint manners, with equal or better. No one else could have saved France in World War I, and he only just succeeded. His able lieutenant, George Mandel, might, if given time, have accomplished a second miracle ; but he was placed in minor office for he was a Jew. Almost alone on the Right, in March 1936, he urged action against Hitler's march into the Rhineland. André Tardieu also might have preserved France, but in 1936 he retired from politics, disgusted by the negligence which was leading to destruction. Nor could either of these men have had a popular following in party or parliament : distinctly, they were not men of easy political virtue.

Estimable men in some respects, none of the French parliamentary leaders possessed the whole range of qualities indispensable to the situation. Unlike England, France was unable to advance from a Chamberlain to a Churchill. That such leaders had not been born was a natural misfortune, just as it was a natural affliction that some, like Pétain, had lived too long for the nation's well-being. The fact must be faced that it can happen that the indispensable leader is not at hand, in spite of a widely held theory that at a crisis forces and events are sure to bring the destined hero on to the stage. Yet a nation's institutions, that is, the various groupings of men endowed with authority and responsibility, are also conditions of the timely emergence of leaders, and determine whether they shall be supported or smothered. General de Gaulle was such a possible leader; no one can say whether, had he been Minister of War, he could have averted disaster. Long before the last desperate moments when he received a minor appointment, Daladier as Prime Minister bitterly opposed his recommendation. All the leaders prominent enough to deserve consideration, if strong in some aspects, failed in others; while the governmental system itself and the colleagues of the chiefs did not, by the working of collective leadership, repair their inadequacies.

It is not possible to present these personal failings in full detail, but to offer a foundation for an understanding of the respective effects of personal and institutional deficiencies, some indications at least are due at this point.[9]

M. Edouard Herriot, for many years the principal leader of the Radical Socialists, possessed all the democratic virtues. His integrity was altogether above the mud-line of scandal. But when, in 1937, he became President of the Chamber of Deputies, en route, he hoped, to the Presidency of the Republic itself, he defaulted in his duty to remain fully in politics and form a strong government of the Left at the crucial moment when it came. Perhaps he hoped to be in reserve for the mortal crisis. But he neither rose to the Presidency, from which Poincaré, in the First World War, had been able to assist the cause of victory (for Daladier, who detested Herriot, his former professor of history and rival for the leadership of the Party, manoeuvred the re-election of the dullard Lebrun), nor did he re-enter the arena until too late. He disapproved of Munich, but led no crusade against it. Offered the Ministry of Foreign Affairs by Prime Minister Daladier at the outbreak of War, he distrusted the offer, and was finally vetoed by Marshal Pétain, who had also been suggested for appointment, on the ground of Herriot's former pro-Soviet policy. Herriot fought the capitulationists desperately as the hands moved to twelve, but July 10 he abstained. Having everything that France needed, he still lacked the fighter's fury, and a champion's intrepidity.

Leader of the same Party as Herriot, Edouard Daladier's relationship with his own and other parties exposes above all a wavering, hesitant will. He moved from the extreme Left of his own Party, to the Centre and the Right, in his friendships. After the riots of 6 February 1934, wilting under the uproar from the Right, in reality

a definite Fascist challenge, he resigned. The great strike demonstration that shortly followed showed that he had cast away the most
dependable of popular forces and support. He preferred to move to
the Centre rather than rely on the Left ; and in late January 1934
had created a cabinet of the Left only after he failed to secure a cabinet
of the Centre. He participated in the Popular Front Government
under Blum in 1936, but though supporting the social reforms and
the Spanish non-interventionist policy, his loyalty was under suspicion. In April 1938 he leaned heavily on the Right ; and concluded
that year with Munich, and with measures of force against the trade
unionists and strikers (the future armies) who detested his foreign
policy.

After the occupation of Austria his foreign policy was robustly
patriotic. But he committed two fatal mistakes : a bitter campaign
against the Communists that began when the Russo-German Pact was
signed and culminated with police persecution, the dissolution of the
Party and total expulsion by unanimous vote from the Chamber of
Deputies (not that the Communist Party was without fault !). His
second mistake was the steady uncritical tolerance of the defensive-war
theory of the Generals Gamelin, Weygand, and Pétain. Especially
did he turn a deaf ear to the views of de Gaulle and Paul Reynaud.
Daladier's error in this respect is a fault not fully his, but goes back
to military administration in France which held its doors closed to
vitality and genius.[10] But increasing international danger gave
Daladier almost unlimited authority ; and still he lacked the character
to put the General Staff on its mettle. Though Chairman of the
Superior Council of National Defence, a meeting of that body or its
reformed successor was never called.[11]

Yet Daladier was also unfortunate, for when he attempted to form
a Government of National Defence in September 1939, the men he
called on would not collaborate in the same Cabinet. In the eleventh
hour, also, France was unfortunate, for Daladier and Reynaud were
so antagonistic to each other, in mind and character, that though
Reynaud was a member of Daladier's Cabinet, and then later Daladier
of Reynaud's, the two men could hardly speak to each other.

Typical of a number of men in the second rank, yet decisive of the
strength of the first among the leaders, was Camille Chautemps. A
member of a well-known republican political family, he was among the
leaders of the Radical Socialist Party. He was Vice-premier in the
Blum Cabinet of 1936, Prime Minister after Blum in June 1937, and
retained the Vice-premiership until the fall of France. Political
power—or, rather, office—was to him an objective in itself. No
important statement of social policy, or decided assertion of political
principle ever came from him. A successful lobby intriguer, with a
coalition government as his supreme object, he found his way to

Pierre Laval and the Right. He was a friend of Franco, Munich, and Hitler. He was derelict in his official responsibility to unearth and convict the Cagoulards : in 1944, Joseph Darnand, a Cagoulard, was the Himmler of France. Misfortune giving him the deciding vote when capitulation was in issue, he took a foremost and fatal part in the proceedings leading to it. He served in Pétain's Government.

Paul Reynaud was the last legitimate Prime Minister of the Third Republic, when by his resignation power passed to Marshal Pétain. Reynaud was a conservative, a man of the moderate Right, and a member of the Democratic Alliance Group, until antipathy to Pierre Etienne Flandin, the President of that purely log-rolling Group, the tall, hollow man and appeaser of Hitler, caused him to quit the Group. Reynaud was a far-sighted patriot ; his mind was modern and fresh ; his policy was anti-Fascist, anti-Laval, anti-Hitler, and anti-Munich. To energy he joined considerable intellectual strength, and his moral courage was clearly manifested when, during 1936, he opposed his own Group which was villifying Roger Salengro. However, a wealthy man, and under the influence of a mistress who was a capitulationist, his own will disintegrated in the hour of crisis.

Leading to the capitulation was Reynaud's choice of men in his three Cabinets of March, May, and 6 June 1940. He omitted Léon Blum. He included reliable and able men like Louis Marin, Mandel (Minister of the Interior, to control the civil organization of the whole country), de Gaulle (Under-Secretary of State), and Daladier (later expelled). But he also included Munichites ; a friend of the leader of the *Croix de Feu* ; Pétain and Weygand, the former as Deputy Prime Minister ; and most sinister, Paul Baudouin. In other words, he invited into his Cabinet the cancer of defeat. A word on Paul Baudouin confirms the weakness of the French system to expel its destructive elements. Baudouin was an official in the Finance and other Ministries ; then a manager and Director of the Bank of Indo-China ; in 1937 a financial expert to advise Léon Blum's government ; a confidant of the suspected Georges Bonnet ; and well-known as a Fascist ready to make concessions to France's enemies. No one has yet discovered why Reynaud confided in him, except that he hoped to use the brilliant intellect but ignore the political views of his man. Baudouin's mind, flamboyant romanticism,[12] and personal fascination won Reynaud and Reynaud's mistress ; and Reynaud's will was destroyed. Even after the British offer of union with France was rejected by 13 to 11, he might by force of character have still defied the influences which prevailed on him to resign on 16 June. He failed to stand the strain. No force remained around which resistance could rally.

It was not until the year 1932 that the power of the French Socialist Party became a major factor in French politics. Thenceforward, Léon Blum, its leader, was an important force. With remarkable intellectual gifts, sincere, democratic, socialist, he nevertheless could not resist the moral and political pressure which aligned him with the ' non-interventionists ' in the Spanish Civil War, to the encouragement of the reactionary forces and the disheartenment of the working classes. He had not the strength to oust men from the Party like Paul Faure and his pacifist followers who voted in favour of the Munich pact. His social reforms were untimely. His dissolution of the French Fascist and military leagues was a patriotic act. But he could not galvanize the nation, or heal its divisions.

Finally, there was Pierre Laval. He commenced politics on the extreme Left, and moved with quiet dexterity to the Centre and Right.[13] When the socialist voters of Aubervilliers abandoned him on piercing his disguise, he was elected to the Senate. Its constituencies are small enough to be wheedled and suborned ; and Senators (perhaps the most senile assembly in the world), in a time of social conservatism and hostility to Russia, could be persuaded one by one out of their immediate aversion to him. With friends in every quarter he had especially firm ones in the *Croix de Feu*, and exercised a specially strong influence over Chautemps.

Employing his principal quality, a genius for surreptitious manœuvre, the butcher's son made fast political progress, acquired a large fortune, a radio station, and two newspapers (of rather different politics), and married his daughter into the family of the aristocratic diplomat, de Chambrun. It became difficult to find people who would swear that political and common honesty must have resulted so quickly in such rewards.[14] Laval was involved in the Stavisky scandal, but avoided open implication. No one could recount his political principles. The facts, however, lead to the opinion that political power was more important to him than its national objects. It appears as though he became anti-British and a friend of Mussolini out of personal ambition. For the sake of an understanding with Hitler, and to gather friends on the Right to compensate for his permanent rejection by the Left, he manœuvred the non-ratification of the Franco-Soviet Pact of 1934 (the most probable salvation of France, if it had been ratified *and implemented*), long enough to be disastrous to his country, chiefly to obtain or retain power.[15] Yet he was not ostracized, in spite of his persistent intrigues in the parliamentary lobbies and the Senate's Foreign Affairs Committee. With Chautemps, Bonnet, Baudouin, and too many others he laboured discreetly for a premature peace. Earlier than anybody else he suggested the inclusion of Pétain in the Cabinet. That his longing, finally avowed, for a German victory was not discerned and condignly punished in proper time under the Republic, is a fault of the rest of the leaders.

II. *Faults in the Manners and Organs of Government*

Thus, even the best of French statesmen fell far short of the dreadful needs of the day. But the governmental system contained no virtues reparative of the personal shortcomings of the abler leaders, nor could it vomit forth the incapable and corrupt.[16] On the contrary, it sapped the vigour and confidence of the more stalwart, and sheltered those who misunderstood their country's need, or, understanding, betrayed it. Leadership was emasculated by (1) slander and scurrility ; (2) by the permanent lack of a parliamentary majority for any one leader ; (3) by the want of a united following behind each of the contending leaders ; and (4) therefore by the debility of French Cabinets all of which were coalitions.

(1) French politics were notoriously scurrilous and blemished by defamation and personal malice. It is true that some polemics and cartoons are diverting. But parliamentary government is only another name for temperance, sobriety, and magnanimity of political conduct. This is not a doctrine to kill journalistic gaiety, or reduce debating tactics to dinginess, or blunt incisive exposure or restrain the pungent demonstrations of opposition in the public interest. But manners maketh parliaments. Without moderation, there is no preservation of a common foundation of mutual respect and confidence. (Cf. Vol. II, Chap. XIX). What follows must be, as it became in France, a spectacle of bickering futility, or what it threatened to become, a dictatorship or civil war. It is excessively simple to weaken trust in democratic leaders, by reducing them and the system to ridicule ; the electorate is merely invited to enjoy a jolly snigger, or to indulge in fits of hatred and spite, and for the moment it costs them nothing. In France, attempts made to regulate the most scandalous behaviour of the Press were necessary but failed.[17] Certain political scandals, too many indeed, if the period since 1871 is scrutinized, lent substance to the denunciations, and opponents of the parliamentary system made the most of them.[18]

Four events among others in the decade before the outbreak of World War II, gave special occasion for an outpour of personal poison, since politicians, lawyers, the Banks, even the Bank of France, the police and the administration of justice were in various measures involved. The first was the Oustric financial scandal (1930) ; the second, the suicide of Roger Salengro, Socialist Minister of the Interior (1936), so inhumanly and falsely baited for cowardice in World War I ; the third, the momentous Stavisky affair, an enormous and filthy financial and police scandal ; and fourth, the riotous aftermath of this affair in the early months of 1934.

On 6 February 1934 the rising hatred and arrogance of the Royalist Camellot du Roi, various other Fascist groups supported by moneyed men like the perfumier Coty, the Fascist *Croix de Feu*, certain ex-soldier organizations whose innocent exasperation had been perverted by Fascist slander, burst into riots before the Chamber of Deputies. They might have set fire to it and even to France, if the police and special guards, under extreme provocation, had not dispersed the rioters by shooting. There were 20 dead and 1,500 wounded, of which one-third were police and mobile guards. A mighty scream arose from the guilty Right, and its journals. The parliamentary inquiries into the Stavisky Affair and 6 February were stigmatized as the Thieves' Committee and the Murderers' Committee respectively. Daladier was dubbed 'the gunman', and the press of the Right cried out for his lynching. Daladier resigned the premiership. This most unfortunate overthrow of a government by other than constitutional means dealt a hard blow to the Left and all anti-Fascist elements, and, moreover, set an example of successful disorder to the workers, bearing fruit later in the sit-down strikes. The events paved the way for a marshalling of the forces of the Left, leading in 1936 to the Popular Front electoral victory and Blum's government.

Four journals were especially responsible for a continual campaign of excitement. They were the *Action Française*, whose editor Charles Maurras was in 1936 sentenced to imprisonment for his campaign of hatred against Blum which led to an almost fatal assault upon the latter by Royalists. *Gringoire*, a weekly, with a circulation of half a million, especially among the young people and the middle-class, was virtually an organ of Italian Fascism and violently anti-British. Its most notorious article among many, bore the heading: 'Is it necessary that England should be enslaved?' The director was a son-in-law of M. Jean Chiappe, Police Prefect of Paris, a Bloc National appointee, implicated in the *Croix de Feu*, negligent in the Stavisky Affair, and at least a passive conniver at regular Fascist-fomented street-affrays before his dismissal in February 1934. (*Je suis partout*, edited by Jean Prouvost, later Vichy Minister of Information, was another weekly organ of Fascism, its financial support unknown. In July 1939, it set itself against the coming war—'the war "for justice and right" to re-establish a Republic in Germany (but without dismembering her), to assure the prosperity of the Jews, to construct a mythologic Czechoslovakia, to leave the miserable old men of the French democracy in their sinecures? We might just as well capitulate right now and save two or three million young corpses.') Finally, *l'Humanité*, the organ of the Communist Party, was in tactics and language well to the fore in the vilification of the day.

One certain way to kill the Sovereign is to pour poison into his ear. No political leader escaped aspersion. The practices of the French press were a queer invitation to the toiling peasants and workers to sacrifice and endurance for the national cause.

(2) No one of these leaders, capable or inept, spotless or mud-spattered, ever had a majority in the Chamber in the right of his own Party. That is, of course, a commonplace in the Third Republic, amply discussed in Vol. II, Chap. XXIV. In the elections of 1932 and 1936, the distribution of parliamentary strength was as follows : [19]

1932		Votes (Million)	1936		Votes (Million)
Right		2·26	*Right*		2·25
Independents	14		Republican Independents	13	
Independents, economic, social, and peasant	7		Republican Federation	59	
Republican Federation	41		Popular Independents	16	
Republican and Social Group	18		Independent and Agricultural Republicans	40	
Centre		2·23	*Centre*		1·94
Popular Democrats	16		Popular Democrats	13	
Republicans of the Centre	6		Left Republicans and Independent Radicals	44	
The Republican Centre	34		Democratic Left and Independent Radicals	38	
Republicans of the Left	29				
Radical Left	48				
Left Independents	23				
Left			*Left*		
Radicals and Radical Socialists	160	1·81	Radicals and Radical Socialists	111	1·46
Socialists, Republicans, and French Socialists	28⎱		Socialists and Republican	29⎱	0·52
Independent Left	15⎰	0·51	Independent Left	28⎰	
Socialists	131	1·93	Socialists	149	1·92
Group of Labour Unity	9		Communists	72	1·50
Communists	10	0·50			
Non-Party	26		*Non-Party*	6	
	615			618	

The largest representation ever attained by any single party was in 1932, when the Radical Socialists had 160 seats out of some 615 ; a close second to this was the 149 of the Socialist Party in 1936.

(3) These parties could hardly be called strong ; but what was the strength of their leaders (and there were always several rivals) in view of the internal weakness of their own parties ? As earlier suggested, the Radical Socialist Party had its wings, indeed it was hardly anything but wings : because it represented the better-off peasants, the shop-keepers, the petty doctors and lawyers, the middle and lower civil servants, the small urban bourgeoisie. It was largely a party of negation. Its chief purpose was to be left alone by the government, and to reduce taxes, no matter how low they were. But it solicited political favours and material advantages. This largest single party in France was a party of small forgotten men whose chief desire was to forget the State, excepting occasionally to touch it. If it were jostled by the parties on its Right or Left, if it were threatened by events, then one of its wings would shift from a Herriot, a Daladier, a Chautemps

and throw its weight to another. The Socialist Party [20] was divided between followers of Léon Blum and the pacifist followers of Paul Faure ; and further, there was always a cleft between the international, democratic and reformation wing of the party, and men like Marcel Deat, Marquet and Montagnon, concretely shown in the secession of the 'neo-socialists' in 1933. The latter were activists, anti-democratic, anti-Marxist, and with their slogan : 'Order, Authority, Nation,' almost identical with the National Socialists of Germany. Of course, they became collaborationists on the capitulation of France. During the War, the Socialist Party was in a difficult situation, for the pacifists were unreliable, and the Right Parties were so incensed with Blum that Daladier had not the courage to include him in the Cabinet.

These were the ministrable parties. There was another party which had sharply increased its parliamentary representation and its votes in the country : the Communist Party. In 1932, it had 10 seats ; in 1936, 72. But at a turning point in French history, the Blum Popular Front Government, the Communist tactic was not to participate in the Government, though supporting it, even as, until 1936, the Socialist Party itself had held aloof from office when offered inclusion. The Communist policy was to discredit all other parties, above all the Socialists, then the Radical Socialists. Against these the Communists made common cause with the Right. The survival of France was not the Communist Party's first concern. Was it in this representative of its voters ? When, however, it became the policy of the U.S.S.R. to have strong friends against Germany, the French Communists became the most ardent patriotic force working for military strength. Too late : for the party had undermined popular confidence in the Republic, helped to alienate the masses from the national course, and had organized and aggravated strikes in war factories among others. They were a force of disunion. The signature of the German-Soviet Pact made them enemies of the French war effort, even if not all Communist Deputies were serious, and even if many of their followers were doing what electors have no right to do, playing make-believe.

(4) So, in the critical years there were shortlived coalition Cabinets. From the Laval Cabinet of 27 January 1931, which lasted a year, to the Daladier Cabinet (the so-called Government of National Defence) of 13 April 1938, there were not less than 17 governments, their average duration being some 5 months. Only two, Laval's, and Blum's first Popular Front Government, lasted a year ; the rest lasted from 8 or 9 days up to 9 months. On the day that Hitler marched into the Rhineland, there was only the caretakers' Ministry of Albert Sarraut ; on the day of the corruptor's march into Austria, France was without a cabinet altogether. And thus, as throughout its

history, the Third Republic was in the years of decision a prey to the natural results of shaky and evanescent executive authority. These were feebleness in domestic and foreign policy; a fumbling touch in the Executive, and haziness of vision in the daily march of administration (for example, whether the military credits were being promptly converted into the appropriate war weapons). The number of public officials grew excessively, but was unaccompanied by a firm gearing of their efforts to the policy and tempo required by domestic and foreign convulsions. Consequently, since France is a highly centralized country, only a palsied grip held the provinces to their role as the indispensable second line of civil defence against the State-cracking tactics of modern *blitzkrieg*. Most immediately disastrous was the lack of a steady, comprehending, and resolute scrutiny of the General Staff, for that was permanent, while the Prime Minister and the Cabinet were ever-changing. With so short a span, so many enemies, and such doubtful and provisional colleagues, Ministers never had the time, the insight, the energy, or the self-confidence to challenge the prevailing doctrine of war and its consequential provision of training and equipment. France descended into governmental indolence : all energy was exhausted in polemics. Fresh vigour could not expel that choking French practice of *papier timbré*, the octopus regulations of nightmarish complexity, designed to frustrate purposeful activity. The Third Republic died of a surfeit of *papier timbré*.[21] Furthermore, the Senate, composed too largely of men well on their way beyond senility, and by age, temperament, and electoral remoteness from the people, hostile to action, especially in a socialist form, forced the resignation of four cabinets in six years : Tardieu in 1931, Laval in February 1932 and Blum, refusing the latter ' full powers ', in 1937 and again early in 1938.

It has been said in fallacious defence of the French party and coalition cabinet system, that, after all, the Chamber, divided into Left and Right, is comparable to the two-party divisions in other countries, where within the two-party system each party contains wings. The argument misses the crucial point, for elsewhere each of the two parties has a discernible common doctrine and certainly a common electoral organization and popular contacts ; they are truly articulated, though less so in U.S.A. than Great Britain. The second-ballot system established in France to secure the democratic equity of avoiding minority victories in three-cornered election contests required agreements among parties. (Cf. Vol. II, pp. 912 ff.) Such agreements, however, were made not between positively like-minded parties but only less hostile to each other than they were to others, and even that was doubtful. The obligation was not to a single fellowship in ideas, with the public good in mind, but to vanquish the other side. Each politician thus elected, was himself a coalition, so to speak, but not an emulsion; [22] a focus, but not a resolution, of conflicting loyalties; beholden to other men and groups as to principles and interests and jobs. It is true that some continuity of and specialization in policy was secured in the Parliamentary system by the membership of former Ministers on the Commissions of the Chambers.[23] But these again merely disrupted the unity and authority of the Government, and impaired and confused the responsibility of individual ministers, while their own policies rarely reached executive or legislative fruition. Nor can the reservice of former Ministers in ' re-plastered ' Cabinets be regarded as any adequate mitigation of their weaknesses; such practices rather added to ministerial cynicism.

Two bids were made in 1933 and 1934 to reform the system, one by André Tardieu and the second by the aged Gaston Doumergue. They were altogether unsuccessful.[24] For the problem was to give the Executive a means of discipline over the factiousness of the Chamber of Deputies; the proposals, almost identical, were to furnish the Prime Minister with the right to dissolve the Chamber of Deputies without consulting the Senate (Vol. II, Chap. XXIV). The Chamber did not collectively intend to cast away its dominating position in the balance of governmental powers; nor did any individual deputy intend to make a sacrifice of his personal political power. The Radical Socialists and the Socialists were agreed on this.

It was said above that not only were the abler leaders of France obstructed, but that the incompetent and guilty were not expelled. In 1914, Robert de Jouvenel in his *La Republique des Camarades* (' The Republic of Pals ') condemned the laxity with which Deputies tolerated each others' deficiencies and misdemeanours. Yet in the most dangerous period for France since 1912, men like Laval, Henri Bérgery, Phillipe Henriot, and pro-Fascist and Cagoulard leaders were permitted to remain in or around the offices of State and gnaw away at public morale, especially the resistance to Italy and Germany. It was well enough known what was being said in the lobbies, in the *salons* of the wealthy, that funds were coming through Ribbentrop's emissary Abetz, and Fernand de Brinon, the leader of the *France-Allemagne* Committee, a link dear to the leaders of the *Comité des Forges*, the political consortium of heavy industry. The Italian subsidies to certain newspapers were known accurately enough. The activities of Georges Bonnet and Pierre Etienne Flandin before and after Munich were suspect and public. Yet no will or power existed to sweep these men from their positions where their intrigues could cast away the interests of their country. Only a few months before the War, two journalists were convicted of receiving money from Germany, one the head of the news-service of *Le Temps*, the organ of the big French employers. The Cagoulards actually had arms-dumps provided by Germany and Italy, yet they were not brought to book.

Could the public have faith in a governmental system where such political morals were a matter of course ?   Disgust and cynicism and impotent desperation must be the public result.   From their Government's actions the people learn even that which Governments are unconscious they are teaching.   It is, of course, a fair question whether the public wanted honesty and firmness.   When we consider the condign judgment passed between 1919 and 1939 on at least two British civil servants and one politician whose private interests and public duties got mixed up,[25] what a laxity seems to have smitten the Government and people of France !

In addition to these deadly weaknesses in the political system, there was no Clemenceau or Lloyd George or Churchill to say as they had all proved, and as the first-named said : ' War is too grave a business to be left to the direction of the soldiers.' [26]   In military preparation and in action in the field the General Staff failed,[27] and its failure threw all the weight of disaster on a feeble State structure.   And one of the most serious aspects of the defensive war theory was the inertia produced in soldiers and citizens alike.   We have only to compare this with the Nazi policy of making beasts of prey out of their youth.

Yet is not democratic leadership a product of the whole people ? Did not the French masses have the open opportunity to perceive the fatal errors, and had they not the wholesale strength by their clamour to repair them ?   All bear a heavy responsibility, but only a few fulfilled it.   But a more fearful responsibility lies on the one or two thousand leaders at the top of the political pyramid and in its secondary strata.   For just as a *levée en masse* is useless in modern wars, so ineffective also is a *levée en masse* of political opinion.   For modern States are founded not upon one great united public, but primarily on many little publics and individuals ; and as the polls of public opinion constantly reveal everywhere, very large proportions of the population have ' no opinion '.   Only leaders can create the national (and international) public : the State is still very young and growing. The people alone cannot achieve a resistant conscious national unity, even after the most chastening lessons of defeat and distress.

III.   *Social and Economic Divisions of the People*

France was divided by prime differences of interest and outlook, both of occupation and of psychological disposition, and these and other (e.g. traditional political) differences were sharpened by groups hostile to each other, sometimes for foreign purposes and sometimes by foreign agents.

There were divergencies of interest arising out of the different occupations as, for example, agriculture (where one-half of the population still finds a living), industry, finance, and small traders and bureaucracy.   There was another type of divergency arising out of class groupings, such as the employed industrial and clerical workers, employers, government employees. (The peasants were taught by some propaganda that in the event of war they would fight in the trenches, while the skilled workers would live comfortably in the factories.) This clash of interests, normal in any democratic State, was aggravated in the inter-war years in two ways. France, like other countries, was, even if unperceived by her citizens, one link in a world economy. That economy was first subjected to the catastrophic strain of transition from war to peace, and later to the cyclical depression (coming rather later in France than elsewhere) which smote the whole world, and variously and in different degrees struck at the workers in their many occupations, at investors, and holders of savings (including millions of workers, peasants and lower middle class) and property. Each individual, socially and in economic groups, did his best to protect himself, and this meant throwing the strain on some-one else ; and for this purpose each spurred on or established some political party. For a time even a violent Peasant Front was organized by one Dorgères, with a slogan : ' Up With the Pitchforks.' But, secondly, beyond this, came the pressure of the general challenge of our time, which may be briefly called the socialistic demand on the State, that is the demand of all groups without exception, but especially of the poorer and the propertyless, that the organization and authority of the State be employed to protect, maintain or augment their eco-nomic welfare. Once the State assumes such responsibilities, then, instead of the free conflict and eventual adjustment of the diverse claimants, the State is faced with the problem and duty of establishing what, for want of a better word, is usually called a ' reasonable ' settlement. The general nature of such an accommodation is essen-tially arbitrary, even though it be attended with care, responsibility and good will towards even the weakest of the parties concerned. It is not easy for any group long to remain content with the proportionate claim on the national production thus allotted to it, through all the changes of outlook in a spiritually restless age and in a world economy subject to constant and often exceedingly sharp fluctuations. Thus, the political institutions of France became subject to an intolerable strain ; the strain was aggravated to a destructive degree by the exigency and recklessness with which all groups pressed their claims and opinions.

Concerned too strictly with their own comfort and notions, all sections forgot Adam Smith's maxim that ' defence comes before opulence '. It appears also that French social habits and outlook were grossly influenced by the less fortunate aspect of American wealth and materialism.[28] The preference for comfort overshadowed recognition of the need for sacrifices to strengthen the nation ; a pre-occupation with money and pleasures blinded people to danger from

Germany and Italy, and, indeed, induced them to admire the authoritarian systems which, full of colour, preserved power and status for
the wealthy, and offered bread, parades, pleasure trips and cheap
motor-cars for the rest.

From 1919 to 1939, France's politico-economic history was marked
by large State budgets, by continual demands for increases of expenditure from almost all sections of the population, and by the simultaneous
unwillingness to pay taxes. Among those in the higher tax groups
there was considerable evasion, furthered by a taxes administration
that was at once too complicated and too feeble. Faced with the
stubborn taxophobia of the electorate, Prime Minister after Prime
Minister sought *pleins pouvoirs* from the Chamber so as to make
drastic economies or raise loans or deflate the currency, and in particular
to cut the salaries of the public employees and the expenses of the
social services (not so highly developed as in Britain or in Germany).
Budgets were voted many months in arrear. The French Treasury
was frequently in deficit,[29] and had to apply to the Bank of France for
advances. Since the loans which the Government might raise were
prescribed by statute, the Bank management could always throw an
embarrassed Government upon the mercies of a hostile Assembly,
rather than find an indirect way to accommodate it. The Bank,
nominally a private organization, had been established in 1806 with
statutes designed by Napoleon to secure State control over it. But it
was the property of its shareholders, and in particular of those two
hundred families who, holding the largest number of shares, formed
the General Assembly and exercised all the power of the shareholders,
in particular the election of the Council of the Bank. In one way or
another in all the major State financial transactions (loans, the valuation
of the currency, credit policy) it had or assumed a strong and even
decisive power, and thereby attained a power over Governments.[30]
Indeed, in several Cabinet crises or during the formation of Cabinets,
the policy of the Bank had to be ascertained by the parties in negotia-
tion in order that the possible adherents might be able to gauge the
feasibility of the policy proposed as the basis of coalition. Its influence
on the policies of inflation and deflation affected the economic tug-of-
war of the many diverse groups within the country, and the place of
France as a whole in the system of world prices. It could retard the
progress of social legislation. By their shareholdings, the big industrialists and financiers had a controlling influence on the Board of
Regents (some of which, by the statute, had to be elected from among
banking firms). From time to time, especially when Governments of
the Left were in office, capital fled abroad. Government deficits and
the flights of capital and the general public opprobrium (for the
majority of French citizens have public savings) dashed freezing water
on the warm social intentions of these Governments, and, assisted by

the Senate, cut short their lives. The Popular Front Government under Blum reformed the Bank. Its governing body was widened to admit government representatives, trade unionists, representatives of co-operative societies, business and shareholders and employees of the Bank, while its Governor, always appointed by the Government, was no longer required to satisfy the original rule that he must be an owner of Bank shares, for this stipulation had made the nominee beholden to the rich bankers for the loans needed to acquire such shareholdings.

There were, then, in France many sides, not merely two. There were the liberal republican groups and interests which followed or revolved in the vicinity of the Radical Socialists. There was the very large following of the Socialist Party with its democratic, mildly collectivist and international programme. From 1932 the Communists were strong in the Chamber of Deputies with $1\frac{1}{2}$ million votes out of a total of some 10 million. It need not be pretended that the extreme views held by any section of the parties mentioned were meant to be applied wholly and at once. But that they represented the views of millions of Frenchmen for the establishment of a State radically different from the existing one—of this there can be no doubt ; though here, again, it is fair to make a strong reservation regarding the drive and pace which the constituents would have tolerated in their leaders, had the latter hurried towards fulfilment.

Another segmentation of opinion was caused by the cleavage among the Socialist, the Communist and the Catholic Trade Unions. Big business, many of whose members were solid with the fascist militant groups, and indeed their subsidizers constituted another egoism which damned the consequences more than most.[31]

Political opinion was further disturbed by royalist circles. Though (in the main) profoundly anti-German, these were excited by the flashy style of Mussolini ; their press fomented discord, and the activities of the *Camelots du Roi* were more socially disturbing than the mere royalist prejudice which caused their formation. Royalist authoritarian antipathy to the Republic was shared (of course, with organizational differences and an immeasurable gulf in social and economic purpose) by Marcel Thorez and his Communist followers. The royalists themselves were further divided between those who, like Alphonse Daudet and Charles Maurras, applauded Mussolini, and those who, like the pure-minded Jacques Maritain, detected and repudiated the malignant corruption in the dictatorial régimes.[32]

There were sections of the nation which had developed in all good faith a pacifism paralleled in England by the 'peace balloteers' and in the United States by certain Isolationists. They have a horror of power and force, due sometimes to sheer hypersensitivity, but more often their disavowal of power is the result of mental confusion regarding the place of power and force in all government, democratic, national

and international. There were conscientious objectors. There were
also people who believed that international affairs could be conducted
on the basis of patient and reasonable discussion and good will, mutual
understanding, of disarmament, that reconciliation with Hitler and
Mussolini was possible, perhaps at little cost to the French Empire.
There was division, cutting across other divisions, between those who
genuinely believed it possible to maintain the French leadership of
Europe, and those who resignedly thought that France must ineluct-
ably submit to being second to Germany. The first believed that in
alliance with Great Britain, and with the benevolent interest of the
United States, with the organization of the smaller countries in Europe,
especially the Little Entente, and with a long-term pact with Russia,
and, furthermore, with unremitting insistence upon the sanctity of
treaty obligations, collective security and sanctions (without which a
policy of disarmament would leave France vulnerable), France could
maintain her primacy amidst the growing might of Germany and the
importunities of Mussolini. This view was held firmly by some members of the Right, for example Tardieu, Marin and Reynaud, and also
on the Left by most of the leaders and rank and file. Yet it must
not be ignored that there were many on the Left who recognized the
weakness of France, for example M. Jouhaux, the Socialist Trade Union
leader ; and others again who had rather confused ideas on the merg-
ing of France in a European system. On the other hand, there was
a strong current of thought widely affecting the Centre and on the
Right, and groups between the Centre and the Left, pessimistic and
defeatist : that Germany in Europe was to be preferred to Soviet
Russia, that England would or could give only too little and too late,
that the United States was not to be relied on ; and that nothing
could prevent Germany's superiority of industry and population from
putting France in the second place. There were other good things
in life, besides international status, they said ; and if France were
obliged to seek for special dignity and power she could find it in a
Latin *bloc* along with Italy and Spain.[33]

It is impossible to attempt to unravel in each man and each group
what was of personal economic interest and what was genuine ideological belief : in part there was a coincidence of economic interests
and national and foreign policy, but to a very important extent, as
we have seen, motivations which were not economic in origin. This
complex disintegration of ideals and interests and social purposes
produced the disruption or enfeeblement of a united French governmental organization in face of her resolved destroyers. Individuals
and associations indulged their resentments against their hostile
fellow-citizens so savagely that they were blind to the fact that
every insult and blow was always a stab at the State. These differences, as has already been indicated, were much emphasized by

the world-wide propaganda battle of States claiming to be new civilizations, and by wars in which France was not directly involved, but in which she permitted her strategic assets to be filched from her. From Germany's exit from the League of Nations in October 1933, a sub-revolutionary period set in for France. Both the Italo-Abyssinian War and the Spanish Civil War tore the tissue of France's national opinion to shreds, set all antagonisms ablaze and produced the well-known historical phenomenon of some Conservatives' preference for a foreign invader to the victory of the progressive social forces in his own country and some workers' and intellectuals' repudiation of loyalty to their own lands.

Hence the will to prepare to fight and endure was sapped. Always in the French mind there was the grievous memory of the losses in the last war (1·4 million dead, and 4·3 million wounded). The third French Republic was defeated in 1940 by Germany at the Battle of Verdun in 1917. For though that city never fell, the German Army's purpose in that campaign to bleed France to death was achieved. That cost in blood caused all nations to seek for a bloodless war, but each in its own way. Either not to have a war at all, or to get someone else to fight it ; or, if fighting were unavoidable, to fight it defensively on the Maginot model or on the British, by a blockade ; or, in the case of the Nazis, to divide the enemy internally, so that while mutually hostile sections of the country killed each other, their armies would be scattered by a swift, brusque war of movement, and sympathizers with the victims would be kept neutral by well-publicised terror.

Thus, besides a true humanist pacifism, there developed a great trepidation and indolence, of which Paris, ' an open city ', was the fruit. To overcome the creeping inertia, to cultivate its opposite, to encourage a spiritual resistance, to coax the people as a good officer coaxes his soldiers, required official candour to the people regarding their world position, comprehension of Hitler and his intentions, and public admission of the cruelty and corruption of his régime. These things were especially required of the Right and the Centre parties in France, but their narrow interests and stupidity combined to defeat democracy, though it must be emphasized that a part of these groups was loyal to the best interests of France. On the other hand, leaders like Tardieu or Mandel who were of the Right could find no support among the parties, and their voices fell silent. The Blum government, choosing non-intervention in the Spanish Civil War, also felt obliged to evade clear explanations to the public who, in the final resort, would be commanded to make sacrifices, and so once again the pro-French and anti-Fascist forces were weakened. No one with a solid enough following could raise the cry as in the last war : ' *Debout les morts !* '

To the last minute, then, there was hesitation to enter the war ;

and when it became inevitable, most people were content that it should
be a war of waiting, except those we have mentioned who looked to an
early negotiated peace.   Under the first charge there was collapse ;
and among most leaders no moral recovery.[1]   Among those who saw
in their hearts that they were to blame, some experienced only an
instinct to grovel, and called it repentance.   But there were also
those in whom there surged the resolution to build anew.

[1] The proceedings at the Pétain trial seem to me to have re-demonstrated
the incompetence of the returned political leaders who testified against him.
Defence counsel seems to me to have diagnosed their situation unerringly : ' They
have made of the trial an attempt to recover their political virginity.'   Léon
Blum alone had the sensitiveness to weep.

In the General Election of 21 October 1945 (women voting for the first time),
for a National Assembly, and for a definition of its powers to write a new constitution, the results were (New York Times, 23 October 1945) : Communist Party,
152 seats ; Socialists, 142 ; Mouvement Republicain Populaire, 142 ; Radical
Socialists, 25 ; Moderate and Right Parties, 67 ; Independents, 18.   The first
three parties obtained respectively : 4·6 million votes ; 4·5 million ; and
4·0 million.

What is notable about this result is the reduction of the traditional party
of negation : the Radical Socialists ; and the failure of the Communists at a
propitious time to gain more than one vote out of every four.   The M.R.P. is
a new party with a conservative Catholic basis, perhaps an inclination to social
action, and a supporter of Charles de Gaulle, President of the provisional régime.
The Assembly has seven months in which to write the new constitution.   Some
92 per cent. of the voters favoured a new constitution to replace the Third
Republic ; only 72 per cent. for keeping the Assembly weak in relation to the
President and his Cabinet.

There is nothing in the situation to indicate any change from the pre-war
régime of unstable coalition cabinets.   There is everything to indicate that the
Assembly intends to remain the firm master of the Executive.   A Communist
minority wants no strong Executive ; the Socialists under Blum have never
desired it.   The Fourth Republic will bear the essential features of the Third,
whatever it may be baptized.

CHAPTER V

GREAT BRITAIN

BETWEEN 1932 and 1939 there was much strain and an acute sense of crisis in Great Britain, yet whether owing to temperament, experience, or institutions, the course of events was milder than in France, Germany, or the U.S.A. More excitement might have served the nation better, for the comparatively subdued reaction to world economic slump and the creeping 'white' war caused insufficient preparation for defence and the fulfilment of moral obligations to the balance of Europe, obligations of direct survival utility to Great Britain herself.

The principal centres of disturbance were mass unemployment; the manœuvres of the political extremes, Fascists and Communists; [1] the unsuccessful agitations for a Popular Front [2] composed of the Labour, Communist and Liberal Parties to fight against the 'National' Government; the relationship of Great Britain to Italian aggression in Abyssinia, and to the Civil War in Spain; [3] the rising tide of Hitlerism and the diverse reactions thereto of the various political parties and especially of the Conservative Party; two elections (1931 and 1935), and their aftermath; the rapid road to war; the frantically excited and bitter tension in the House of Commons. These urgent forces strained the conventions of the Constitution almost to breaking-point.

So unfluttered, comparatively speaking, was the nation that another level of political action developed in an atmosphere hardly less nonchalant than the most normal dog-days. We refer to such peaceful evolutions as the abdication of King Edward VIII, the Ministers of the Crown Act of 1937, and the status of the Speaker. The more convulsive forces of the political earth must be discussed first, however.

*　　*　　*　　*　　*　　*　　*

The high and special quality of the unwritten British Constitution is founded on the conventions, especially those concerning the relationship between the Cabinet and the House of Commons and the electorate. In turn, the democratic serviceability of these conventions depends to a very large degree on the quality of the constitution and practices of the political parties. Consequently, the fate of the nation in an era when the State has so extensively been assigned responsibility for domestic and foreign welfare, depends on certain vital elements in the functioning of the political parties. These are: whether the parties assist the public to a full, all-round, clear and honest com-

N.B.—The Notes to this Chapter begin on page 177.

prehension of policy at elections and between them; whether or not
they confuse the electorate, purposely or through ineptitude; whether
the parties select candidates for Parliament possessing vigour, ability,
and independence of mind, or whether they seek or by their practices
produce the docile; whether the Cabinet is or is not sensitive to
Opposition opinion, or exploits its majority status down to the last
vote and obstinately rides roughshod over the Opposition or the
minority in its own following; whether the Cabinet is courageous
enough to take the people into its confidence about grave events
calling for sacrifices; whether the parties act, allowing for their many
unpleasant tasks, so as to elevate rather than depress and demean
the political process and engender and reap disgust.

Therefore, since the parties are the springs of the conventions of
the Cabinet system, which is the heart of the system of government,
their quality in the midst of moving events must be the principal
theme of what follows.

Chronic tremors arose out of mass unemployment. This produced
bitter dissension between the two parties. The Labour Party representing many millions of workers, and knowing their lives at first hand,
pressed for unemployment relief, for relief on a subsistence level, for
relief without the indignity of a test of needs or means, and especially
for relief without those conditions which burdened other members of
the family.[4] Furthermore, not being in principle a friend of private
enterprise, the Labour Party was unconcerned that its demands for
reducing unemployment might lead to State intervention in industry
and therefore away from capitalism to socialism. It pressed strongly
for measures to rehabilitate the distressed areas even if this meant
the establishment of industries based on State subsidies or a command
to private industry to settle in those areas.

The Conservative Party were more concerned for the fate of foreign
trade, the increase of industrial production and the maintenance of
free enterprise than about the distress of the unemployed. Both
parties were sensitive to the great dependence of British prosperity on
exports. Yet there was a clear cleavage between the two on the effect
of the cost of the public social services on the cost of production of goods
competing in foreign markets. On the Conservative side there was
no special impulse to remove the pain and deterrency from the existing
system of industry. In the long run, they argued, the system would
arrive at equilibrium, a necessary economic law. Prices and wages
would decrease; the unemployed in the long run would find new work.
Substantial relief payments would obstruct the search for and acceptance of available jobs. Every effort was made to prevent solutions
which involved the competition of nationalized production with private
industry or compulsion upon industries to remain where they were
or to set up in areas directed by the Government. The Conservatives

thought rather in terms of the transfer of men to industry (but not at Government expense) while Labour thought more in terms of transferring industry to where the men already lived. Conservative Englishmen consigned solutions to 'the long-run', the modern Greek kalends : Englishmen in misery stubbornly refused to be the victims of postponement.[5]

This divergency of opinion and interest affected fiscal policy. The Conservative Party urged a balanced budget by means of a reduction of public expenditure and of taxes. The Labour Party claimed that for a period an unbalanced budget was justifiable,[6] that subsequent prosperity would wipe out the deficit, that such prosperity could be attained by increased incomes which would increase consumption and therefore the demand for more production. Moreover, any increase in taxation, they thought, could well come from the high income groups, and certainly should not be imposed on the lower. Out of this contention arose another, namely, whether Britain could improve her world commercial situation and therefore her home manufacturing position by tariffs. That she could and should was the traditional claim of the Conservatives, who at this juncture preferred this course to increased taxes. The Liberal Party was directly hostile to this view. But Labour was uncertain since the Party was largely founded on the Trade Unions,[7] and some trade unionists, at any rate, were allies of their employers regarding protective duties so far as their industries were concerned.[8] Since the respective attitudes of the disputing parties implied a vastly different view of the relationship between the economic system, its social utilization, and the tasks and rights of political government, and since, in the background, the question of the regulation or entire control of private enterprise loomed large, and since also the streets were full of unemployed and the homes of misery, hunger and squalor,[9] an intense feeling of crisis and impending disaster persisted through many Parliamentary sessions.

The most spectacular and critical effect of the tension was the fall of the Labour Government in August 1931, and its replacement by a 'National' Government headed by the defecting Labour Prime Minister, Mr. Ramsay MacDonald. Some attention to this phase is essential. The Labour Government of 1929 was a minority government.[10] It could not handle unemployment without the generous and sensible co-operation of the Liberals and Conservatives who together could outvote it. By 1931 the burden on the Budget of social service expenditure and unemployment allowances posed the questions : More taxation ; tariffs for revenue and for the protection of British trade and employment ; reduction of unemployment allowances ? A budget deficit, not of large proportions, but sure to increase unless instant action was taken, injected the temper of desperation into the political struggle. The British Treasury warned

Mr. Philip Snowden, the Labour Chancellor of the Exchequer, and the May Committee [11] reinforced the warning, making drastic proposals to meet the deficit. At the request of Mr. MacDonald and Mr. Snowden a majority of the Labour Cabinet were ready to meet the 50 per cent. of the deficit by reduction of social expenditure and the rest by increases in taxation, but refused to reduce unemployment allowances. The Conservative and Liberal leaders, largely the voice of the industrialists and the bankers, were consulted by Mr. MacDonald, and required more considerable reductions of expenditure than the majority of the Cabinet were prepared to make, for 75 per cent. of the deficit was to be met by reductions and only 25 per cent. by more taxes. Mr. MacDonald could make no headway with a large majority of his Ministers. As a next step the Cabinet expected him to resign and so report to it; and that Mr. Baldwin would be called on to form a Government, when the next step would probably be dissolution and new elections. But, abandoning his Labour colleagues of more than a quarter of a century's partnership, and with several friends of the moment, principal among them his Chancellor of the Exchequer, and with some exiguous Labour support in the country, Mr. MacDonald formed a Ministry under his own premiership composed of a Labour contingent, Conservatives under Mr. Baldwin, and some Liberals headed by Sir Herbert Samuel (without Mr. Lloyd George's consent [12]). This solution of the immediate crisis raised the issue [13] of the King's political neutrality. It was alleged that King George V had personally appealed to the outgoing Prime Minister, Mr. Ramsay MacDonald, in terms strong enough to induce him to form a coalition government with members of the Conservative and Liberal opposition parties, though the consequences must be his abandonment of the Labour Party. A critic observed that *if* this were so, the King had violated the convention of his neutrality, which, in the practice of forming a cabinet, required that he should entrust the Government to the leader of the majority party, that should this party be defeated, he should then accept the resignation of the leader, and call either for a dissolution of Parliament, or entrust the government to the leader of the next largest party, i.e. in this case the Conservative Party. In spite of the difficulty of arguing from tangled precedents, the propriety of the Royal action on this occasion depends upon whether the allegations referred to were true, but far more on whether, there being three parties, none of which has a clear majority over the others, the King may not properly seek a coalition promising a stable government rather than a dissolution, probably inconclusive, so shortly after the last general election. In Volume II, Chapter XXII we suggested that the existence of three parties in the House of Commons might make the experience of the formation of cabinets in continental countries a necessary instruction, rather than a subject of horror. These recoiled from prescribing a diet of dissolutions. But it seems unlikely that three parties will persist of such strength as to deny any one a majority over the others.

This coalition was a spectacle for at least two things : that such heterogeneous elements could be marshalled in a single government, and Mr. MacDonald's defection, so at variance with his public professions of loyalty to the Labour Party, and so dismaying and confusing to the Labour following. Mr. MacDonald's mental confusion and strange character need not occupy us. But something more must be said of the coalition experiment itself.

' The Agreement to Differ '

In spite of the Government's severe economies, the drain on the Bank of England compelled the abandonment of the gold standard by 2 September 1931, one of the remedies earlier proposed in MacDonald's Cabinet but rejected as blasphemy. The National Government had by now carried out its purpose, that is to say, re-establishment of the national financial balance. (The abandonment of gold was virtually a subsidy to exports.) However, it found new reason for continued indispensability : the uncertain situation produced by the abandonment of gold, and even more, the need for a clarification of national issues by a new electoral mandate. In October occurred a general election on the Government's slogan of securing ' a doctor's mandate ', a general licence to take all measures necessary for the patient's good. The parties to the coalition were much embarrassed by their principles, especially regarding free trade or protection. It was, therefore, decided that at the election all parties should go forward as National Government candidates but that they should not stress their disagreements. They would emphasize the exceptional nature of the situation, its special urgency, and therefore the need of abnormal measures. The Conservatives, however, could not avoid giving prominence to tariffs in their election appeals, nor could the Liberals avoid extolling free trade, and so incurring the wrath of their coalition partners. The country was certainly in a panic, and it was made more acute by Mr. Snowden's broadcast appeal that the Labour Party's policy was ' bolshevism run mad ' and would result in the loss of the people's Post Office savings. This was a blow beneath the belt with a glove loaded with the iron that Mr. Snowden knew from long years of confidential relationship with the lowly would be felt by most workers and lower middle-class voters. For in 1931 there were nearly 10 million members of the Post Office Savings Banks with an average of £29 per account. The National Government won an overwhelming victory, with 554 seats to the Government, against 52 for the Labour Party, and 4 for the Free Liberals. Of the Government majority, 471 were Conservatives,

13 were National Labour, 35 were Liberal National, and 33 Liberals. The Labour Party had polled over 6½ million votes (for 46 contested seats) and the Government 14½ million (for 493 contested seats), of which 11 million were Conservative. It was urged by students of electoral statistics that the loss of Labour support was due to confusion caused by Mr. MacDonald's transfer of loyalty, and the financial panic of the ' white collar ' voters, a class of increasing importance as compared with the rich and with the manual industrial workers.[14] The Conservative Party's victory was so overwhelming that henceforward responsibility for domestic and foreign policy must perforce be exclusively ascribed to that Party. The shock of defeat, and of the steps leading to it, were so sharp to Labour, that many members looking back on the ignominious record of two years vowed that they would never again accept office as a minority,[15] for it was believed that as a minority government the Party had been obliged to act so feebly that the country came to despise them. It is difficult to see how such a vow could be fulfilled under the British Constitution, yet one precedent at least lends it some respectability.[16]

The Government was soon smitten by internal troubles, for the difference which it had sought to avoid—protection—burst out. Nor can it be left out of account that many people believed, rightly or wrongly, the recent ' crisis ' had been engineered, at least highly exaggerated, partly by the Conservatives and Liberals for policy and office, and partly by Mr. MacDonald for personal ambition. It was also claimed that the election was fraudulent, being run on false issues and asseverations regarding the Labour Party's policy. Such charges of bad faith, especially if they were justified, were noxious to national morale in relation to the sincerity of democratic processes, and the results came home to roost later. For if Mr. Baldwin and his advisers were clever enough to outwit the Labour Party and the electorate it was a different matter when they later came to ask for its moral support against Hitler. The Party was throwing away democratic credit. The Conservatives in the Government moved fast, and a public dispute regarding the adverse balance of trade was precipitated. On 21 January 1932 a majority of the Cabinet Committee recommended a general tariff of 10 per cent., with three Liberals and Mr. Snowden dissenting. Normally the dissentients should have resigned ; but resignation would have meant damage to the ' national ' façade of the Government. A formula was hatched : ' the agreement to differ '. It ran :

The Cabinet, however, is deeply impressed with the paramount importance of maintaining national unity in presence of the grave problems that now confront this country and the whole world. It has accordingly determined that some modification of usual ministerial practice is required, and has decided that ministers who find themselves unable to support the conclusions arrived at by

7

the majority of their colleagues on the subject of import duties and cognate matters are to be at liberty to express their view by speech and vote. The Cabinet being essentially united on all other matters of policy believes that by this special provision it is best interpreting the will of the nation and the needs of the time.[17]

Thus, the principle of Collective Responsibility was jettisoned. Compelled to defend the Government against such a charge made by the Opposition, Mr. Baldwin first pretended to show that what was ' constitutional ' in British practice had always been uncertain, but he concluded on an entirely different note : the expediency and the practical wisdom of the tactic. Thus, ' Is our action constitutional ? Who can say what is constitutional in the conduct of a National Government ? It is a precedent, an experiment, a new practice, to meet a new emergency, a new condition of things, and we have collective responsibility for the departure from collective action . . . it is approved by the broad common sense of the man in the street.'[18]

It was not long before the vessel foundered, though not with all hands. For Sir Herbert Samuel's criticism of the tariff proposals was sharp. He aroused Conservative resentment in the House and in the country. He counter-claimed for the right to liberty of opinion. Lord Snowden, now in the Lords, diverted his vitriol from the Labour Party to the tariff.[19] In April 1933 at the Liberal Federation's Annual Conference the Party denounced the connexion : for Liberals in the country were bewildered : they thought the proposals mischievous, and found it a strain not to be able to follow their leaders. Late in July came the Ottawa Agreements ; by the end of September the Cabinet was resolved upon their acceptance, and Samuel and Snowden resigned. The Liberal Ministers declared ' It is plain that the difference is so fundamental upon matters of such high importance that it is impossible for us to remain members of a Government which is bent upon giving to those agreements the force of law '.[20]

Facing Aggression

Another struggle even more exciting and fearsome was proceeding : over the security of Great Britain and her relationship to the aggressive dictatorships in Europe. Now, it cannot be said that upon this subject the Labour Party was always completely united and consistent. In the main, it stood sincerely for collective security and the effective use of the League of Nations, with all the consequential obligations. Yet some reservations must be made, especially on the latter part of this sentence ; and there were other uncertainties implied in the confusion of Labour, whether war was the result of capitalism, or whether capitalist governments could make peace at Geneva.[21] The Labour Press was easy with Germany's re-introduction of conscription and the re-occupation of the Rhineland ; it was certainly not war-like firmly and unitedly. Such qualifications produced a confusion of public opinion and to some extent gave the MacDonald, Baldwin and Chamberlain Cabinets some assurance that their policy of appeasement would not be squarely challenged. The Labour Party's voice was largely pacifist—it voted against the Army Estimates—until 1937, when disillusioned after nearly a year's support of the Government's policy of non-intervention in the Spanish Civil War, it began to take the European situation far more seriously than the Government did. Thenceforward, it supported re-armament, and was far ahead of the Government in demanding resistance to aggression and in its insistence upon the sanction clauses of the League, and immediate and massive preparations for defence including the establishment of a single Ministry of Defence and a Ministry of Supply for production. But, between 1933 and 1937 there was parlous disunity in the Party regarding war as an instrument of foreign policy. The Labour Party is in the main composed of average British working-class men and women of the Trade Union and consumers' co-operative society type. It includes, also, various minority groups and individuals of manifest and even of startling sincerity, often sectarian, often extreme purists, and sometimes visionary.[22] Such were some pacifist groups symbolized most conspicuously by Mr. George Lansbury who from 1931 to late in 1935 was Parliamentary leader of the Labour Party.[23] They disavowed power and confided in Christian meekness. But the world, including the vast majority of the Labour Party, still continued its wicked ways ; and Mr. Lansbury's missions to those lions, Hitler and Mussolini, though magnificent, were not peace. Furthermore, at critical times, as during the Abyssinian War, some men of influence like Sir Stafford Cripps, instead of calling unambiguously for sanctions, fled from them alleging that sanctions would put arms into the hands of the government of the day which was ' capitalist ' like any other government with whom Britain had relations.[24] There was even a suggestion (rejected) at the Labour Party Conference of 1934 that in the event of war, the trade unions should call a General Strike.[25] The electorate could not but be puzzled by such splits in the mind of the Party. Nor was this all. Had the Government taken the proper measures for the support of France in the event of war, it would have involved conscription in Great Britain. Conscription was not feasible for two reasons : (a) because the Government did not want it, as it would then have admitted that appeasement was either insincere or impossible, and (b) because the Labour Party would not tolerate military conscription except in extremes, fearing that if the principle were admitted then industrial conscription must be implied, putting the workers at the mercy of a capitalist government. In the circumstances, neither side could trust the other. And even in 1939, the

Government did not introduce the Bill till in desperate straits ; Labour opposed it as unnecessary and because it feared its powers over the workers. Not till the war had started was the National Service Act passed.

The Government's appeasement policy sprang from several sources. In one sense it may be credited, as Labour may be, with not wishing war ; for no democratic government can or wishes deliberately to pursue a policy which is likely to bring war and its modern horrors upon their fellow citizens ; or, if one cares for cynicism, to the voters. Moreover, it was conscious, as all governments in Britain of whatever colour must be, that Britain is a Great Power only on certain delicate conditions : far-flung tenuous maritime connexions ; friends along the sea routes to distant overseas supplies ; and friends to contribute their industrial capacity should a preponderance of Continental power threaten Britain's own considerable but not unlimited manufacturing ability. And in so deep an economic depression, the Cabinet studied all ways of stabilizing peace and increasing commerce. Yet in this respect, its commercial outlook, its ' city ' horizon, especially under Mr. Chamberlain, was so inordinate as to act like a blinding bandage on its international vision. It came to speak, and even to think, as though the increase of commerce would please Hitler and Mussolini as much as it would please Mincing Lane, and forgot there were broader interests still, the interests of the millions, their lives, indeed, to be saved only by timely preparation for defence or unlimited respect of the League. That is, the risk of war had steadfastly to be assumed.

But there were more dubious elements in Great Britain's policy of appeasement. It almost appeared as though the Government believed that an Empire can be enjoyed without the full payment for its defence, that songs were enough. Such payment is usually exacted in one or all of three forms. In peace, empire requires the payment of taxes and firm controls over industry to strengthen armament.[26] In war, under modern conditions, one must face the loss of property by air bombardment,[27] the loss of ships, and also a loss of population (and Britain's population is declining).[28] And as regards the governing class itself, there would be a fearful addition to those grave casualties suffered by its sons in the war of 1914 to 1918. Nevertheless, if enemies arise, the heavy price is indispensable if it is desired to uphold the power and standard of living of a small country with one of the densest populations in the world, a small island growing only one-third of its food (not of full dietetic range), a small island, which geographically is nothing but a minute pimple on the shoulder of the vast land-mass of Europe and Eurasia.

In the critical years, faced by an inevitable aggressor, Hitler, and a practically certain accomplice, Mussolini, the Conservative Party showed itself unready to foot this bill. Instead, its leaders seemed to believe that it was possible to overcome by reason, blandishments, and loans, the plain and oft-recited designs of the dictators, bound inevitably for an offensive war on Britain, or such a domination of the Continent and the seizure of Soviet territory and wealth, that Britain would be in virtual servitude. The failure to resist Italian aggression in Abyssinia, the toleration, and finally the support of Franco's Government in the Spanish Civil War, the lack of encouragement to France in resistance to German demands, the hostility towards Soviet Russia, that Eastern arm of the permanent two-front nut-cracker, seemed to be total blindness even to the patriotic values involved. Surely, the saddest moment in many decades was experienced at about half-past three on 14 July 1937 when the Government spokesman [29] evoked Conservative hilarity by announcing that a British merchant ship had actually been captured by the forces of Franco—hilarity all the shriller, because it shouted down conscience, and because the announcement was a turn of a red-hot poker in the flesh of the writhing Labour Opposition. It was overlooked that that red heat scorched the flesh of Britain more. And indeed, it must be confessed, that two catastrophic mistakes were made. First, the complete misunderstanding of the aggressiveness of the dictators and their systems ; and this was a fault partly of the diplomatic representatives abroad, but principally of Ministers who appointed and instructed them and utilized their reports.[30] Secondly, the authoritarian régimes were not altogether uncongenial to Conservative leaders faced by economic and social troubles and a vehement Opposition which advocated equal opportunity, fuller and better education, a juster distribution of national wealth as well as serious changes in the organization of industry.[31] For these demands seemed to drive towards a policy like Soviet Russia's, regarded as black sin by Conservatives, and advertised to them by Hitler, the champion of civilization, as the devil, to be fought by himself and the British in jocund company, he firmly guaranteeing the British Empire, while they gave him a free hand in Eastern Europe.

How was it possible that a Party, solidly entrenched in power as few governments have been since 1832, and itself so frequently claiming the monopoly of patriotism, could bring the whole nation including itself to the brink of defeat and even slavery ? What were the causes of this singular and prolonged aberration, almost patricidal in its result ? A century and a half before Edmund Burke had admonished their predecessors, saying ' a great empire and little minds go ill together '.

The answer is secreted in the social and economic composition of the Conservative Party in Parliament. The organization is a party of really rich men, rich by occupation, inheritance or marriage, connected among themselves by family relationship into a great modern

' cousinhood ', holding numerous directorships and multiple directorships in British industry and commerce at home, abroad, in the
Dominions and Colonies, in an age when there is an extremely high
degree of industrial and financial concentration, and these men dominate the House of Commons by election, the House of Lords by heredity
or recent peerages, while by family or economic connexions a tight
web connects Commons, Cabinet and Lords. Thus, it has been com-
puted that a man who in pre-war years was not a surtax payer with
an income of two thousand pounds a year or over, had hardly any
chance at all of becoming a Conservative member of Parliament.
This economic basis of the Party is, of course, accompanied by a
common outlook acquired by education at the same or similar public
schools and Oxford and Cambridge. For example, in the Parliament
of 1936, 30 per cent. of Conservative members came from Eton and
Harrow, while more than another 35 per cent. were educated at other
public schools on grounds of expense and family tradition, and sometimes religion. Besides this, others were educated by private tuition.[32]

The descendants of this same class (admittedly with renewals)
have ruled for many centuries, since British Government has at no
time admitted, even in the revolution of the seventeenth century, the
sudden and total incursion of the lower classes, but has handed down
liberties and rights in limited doses at the last moment before a mass
movement might overturn the whole edifice or incur permanent
rancour. In particular, the opportunity of education—the gateway
to self-development and public power and service—was until very
recently dependent upon the wealthier class's concession of education
supported by public funds.[33] These opportunities are still very small,
especially compared with the price the wealthy pay for their own
education, estimated at about a thousand pounds for the university
and about the same sum and perhaps more for the public school.
The result in part is a continuance to a substantial degree (even if
annoyed and less complaisant) of that social deference which 80 years
ago Walter Bagehot declared to be the principal characteristic of
English political relations.

Attention has already been drawn to the advantages accruing to
this Party by its control over the Press and various factors in the
electoral process (Vol. I, Chaps. XIII and XIV). All in all, then,
the Party is marked by a very high degree of social solidarity and
pride, as well as the attitude that political power is its unchallengeable
heritage and mission, and that all other contenders, notwithstanding
their unadulterated and ancient British lineage, are upstarts, unpatri-
otic parvenus and unfit to govern. It must be admitted that the
querulousness of some members of the Labour Party encouraged this
conceit, and its leaders have from time to time needed to urge a change
in demeanour.[34]

The constitutional structure of the Conservative Party follows from its social homogeneity. One of its most notable features is the regular recruitment of young men, possible because they are masters of their own time. Their youth contrasts markedly with that of Labour Party recruits to Parliament. Thus, taking a percentage of all the members elected for the first time between 1918 to 1936 the Conservative age-group 26–36 is 25 per cent. of the total, but of Labour a little less than 10 per cent.[35] The middle age-groups are also more heavily represented in the Conservative Party than in the Labour Party as compared with the older men. It is paradoxical, but true and significant, that the larger number of young men entering the Conservative Party results not, as one might expect of youth, in the independent virility of the Conservative younger generation, but (in contrast to the Labour Party) in a domination of youth by their distinguished elders. The political induction of Conservative youth is part of the normal deliberate and firm social grooming in ' good form ' operative in all phases of the life of the governing class. When they enter Parliament the Leaders receive the same deference as did prefects and headmaster at school. Membership of a small social class, possession of a fortune frequently unearned, are not likely to cause an individual to be stubbornly independent of his social and political leaders. Like the selection of candidates by other British parties, the local and central organization are not subject to any statutory prescription. The practice of ' endorsement ' of Parliamentary candidates by Conservative Party headquarters, and still more the attitude of local Conservative associations, give the decisive preference to the rich aspirants, the elders an almost absolute control over the political career of the young recruits. They are fastened on when they are young enough to be grateful for a start, before they are sufficiently mature to practise an experienced and resolute independence. There have been many complaints regarding the selection of Conservative candidates not for mind or independence or character, but for the financial ability to contribute their election expenditures (nearly £800 on the average per member in the election of 1935, that is, more than double that spent by Labour members), and make substantial contributions to local charities, sports and other objects, and no doubt to give thereby a guarantee of their political conformity and reliability.[36] It has been disclosed [37] that there are roughly three categories of Conservative candidates : those with an excellent chance of adoption, that is, willing to pay all their election expenses from four hundred to twelve hundred pounds, and in addition to subscribe from five hundred to one thousand pounds a year to the local association ; those with a reasonable chance of adoption, that is, willing to pay half of the election expenses and from two hundred and fifty to four hundred pounds a year ; and those with hardly any chance at all, that is, those unable to pay any election expenses and able to give only a hundred pounds a year or less to the association.[38] The best constituencies therefore go to very wealthy men.   Nor do the figures mentioned take account of the contributions to Conservative Party headquarters and entertainment. Those must come from the gifts of wealthy men. This serves as a partial explanation of the Nazi belief that they could find negotiators of peace in the House of Lords.

The objective observer must confess that the history of Britain's decline in foreign relations to the grim brink of ruin between 1933 and May 1940 could thus be written in terms of the constitution and taming methods of the Conservative Party. As Mr. Churchill ruefully observed after Munich, ' Had there been one healthy growl ' from the benches behind His Majesty's Ministers, there could not have been the descent to Munich ; ' But honourable gentlemen above the gang-way, pledged, loyal, faithful supporters on all occasions of His Majesty's Government, must not imagine that they can throw their burden wholly on Ministers of the Crown. Much power has rested with them.' [39] But, there was hardly a whisper even until Holland and Belgium were struck down ; and even then, the new Prime Minister, the truth of whose warnings were now so dreadfully demonstrated, for long continued to be greeted with coldness by many who had followed Mr. Baldwin and Mr. Chamberlain.

The strain on British political conventions of supporting the leadership of Mr. MacDonald and Mr. Baldwin in company up to June 1935, of the latter alone after that time, and of Mr. Chamberlain from 1938, was enormous. The majority of the nation was anxious for peace, yet many leaders, the Trade Unions above all, in conjunction with numbers of Liberals [40] and a score or so of Conservatives following Mr. Churchill, saw that peace could not be enjoyed unless the country were organized for an early stand against aggression. The Fulham election of October 1933 had shown a strong peace sentiment and confidence and support for the League.   In November 1934 an organization of men and women of all parties began to take a kind of referendum on the subject of peace and war : The Peace Ballot. The results of the long campaign, headed by Lord Robert Cecil, but supported by politicians of all parties, were made public on 27 June 1935. The questions and the votes were these. 1. Should Great Britain remain a Member of the League of Nations ? Yes : 11,090,387 ; No : 355,883 ; the rest doubtful and abstentions. 2. Are you in favour of an all-round reduction of armaments by international agreement ? Yes : 10,470,489 ; No : 862,775 ; abstentions, 213,839 ; a few doubtful. 3. Are you in favour of the all-round abolition of national military and naval aircraft by international agreement ? Yes : 9,533,558 ; No : 1,689,786 ; abstentions, 318,845 ; a few doubtful. 4. Should the manufacture and sale of armaments for private profit be prohibited by international agreement? Yes: 10,417,329; No: 775,415; abstentions, 351,345; a few doubtful. 5. Do you consider that, if a nation insists on attacking another, the other nations should combine to compel it to stop by: (a) economic and non-military measures? Yes: 10,027,608; No: 635,074; abstentions, 855,107; a few doubtful, and Christian Pacifist. (b) If necessary, military measures? Yes: 6,784,368; No: 2,351,981; abstentions, 2,364,441; a few doubtful, and Christian Pacifists. But this ' referendum' confused the situation with its ambiguities.[41]

As early as November 1934 Mr. Churchill had warned the Government of growing German strength. From time to time the Government declared its preference for action through the League of Nations —the popular mood. But within its own ranks the Government was urged to appease Hitler, even to return the German colonies. In March 1935 Hitler reintroduced conscription. With certainty, there was from that moment no ground for anything but the swiftest preparation. This was an excellent occasion for a Government appeal to the people. Instead, it persisted in trying to overcome the threat by moral suasion, and quarter measures, if any. In May 1935 the Government declared its intention to create an air force equal to any within striking distance of Britain. But in June 1935 it made a Naval Agreement with Germany, alleging that it was democratically bowing to pacifist sentiment at home, as demonstrated by the peace ballot campaign.

Now, it is not valid to argue that at this juncture Ministers were acting properly because their policy, as they claimed, was consonant with majority opinion in the country, even if they might have proven the claim by the kind of surveys subsequently made by *Mass Observation*. For popular political judgment is not spontaneous, but is largely formed by instruction from Government sources about everyday political events, inferences regarding the meaning of the facts, official prognosis of future developments, and therefore an indication of the character of the public's duty. This observation holds for the course of action, of Ministers and their Parliamentary supporters also down to Munich; and even down to and beyond 3 September 1939; and even to May 1940.

The Italian attack on Abyssinia offered the Government an opportunity of an appeal to the League and to its British supporters. It took it in a masterly intervention at Geneva in September 1935, but apparently soon concluded that if it proceeded to serious sanctions it would do so practically alone. Laval then ruled French foreign policy. Its display may have been made chiefly to demonstrate that international support for military sanctions was unreliable. It would not face the Italian threat, ' Oil or war!' It goaded the Opposition as ' warmongers'. Then, with high prestige for this peace-ensuing policy, it decided on a General Election. It appealed to the country on its peace-seeking record and its further hopes of peace and of the League; it pledged 'no great armaments' to the Peace Society. (But its reference to League action in the official election address is equivocal.) [42]

The electoral vote suffered a serious decline to 11,789,575 against a total opposition vote of just over 10,000,000. The decline is usually put down to the movement of middle-class, especially clerical and professional suburbanites, who believed that Labour would save them from a war, and voters who realized that the scare of 1931 had been exaggerated for electoral purposes. The Conservative Party obtained 385 seats; the Labour Party 154 ($8\frac{1}{2}$ million votes); the National Liberals 32; National Labour 8; and Liberals 21. (The unproportional representation in Parliament, especially between the Conservative and Labour Parties, may well be noticed.)[43] Whatever the voting meant the Government alone might guess, for it had forced the issue in the election. One thing was certain—it had overwhelming Parliamentary power. It could very possibly have obtained power otherwise, and it may be even more, if Mr. Baldwin had chosen to be entirely frank about the menace of the international situation and consequently regarding the grave measures and decisions it imposed. The Prime Minister, according to a subsequent Parliamentary confession, decided not to be frank, but instead to exploit the prevailing mood of good pacific feeling and aversion to war as a ladder to his Party's power.

I put before the whole House my views with appalling frankness. My position as the leader of a great Party was not altogether a comfortable one. I ask myself what chance was there—when that feeling that was given expression to in Fulham was common throughout the country—what chance was there within the next year or two of that feeling being so changed that the country would give a mandate for rearmament ? . . . Supposing I had gone to the country and said that Germany was rearming and that we must rearm ? . . . I cannot think of anything that would have made the loss of the election, from my point of view, more certain.[44]

Thus, the power was in the hands of the Cabinet, and almost with cold hatred it turned its back on the League. There was still an alternative : to arm. To achieve this successfully, it was a supreme duty to tell the public *all the facts* about Germany, including the atrocities which were infallible evidences of character and intention. Instead, it misinformed the public about Germany's rapid progress in re-arming, pooh-poohed the information offered by others, for example, the Churchill group and various newspaper correspondents, played down the cruelties, and sometimes praised the Italian and German governments. Then, later, it confessed that its own preparations were outstripped by Hitler's, in a manner which implied that confession was adequate repair of the military weakness. It followed by consistently refusing to take the measures appropriate to the kind of war that the coming one would be, that is to say, total, stern, and swift. It spurned the establishment of a Ministry of Supply (preferring a Cabinet Committee of Defence Requirements) on a variety of grounds, chiefly economic, arguing that while there was no ' cogent proof of danger ' it would be wrong to convert a peace into a wartime economy. It rejected the setting up of a Ministry of Defence to fuse the three fighting services on the grounds that the Prime Minister could not admit a Minister of Defence who, to do the proposed job, would need to be a man towering above himself and that such a Ministry would be an admission of the inevitability of war. It relied on the shaky co-ordination of the Committee of Imperial Defence with the Cabinet, without giving adequate drive to the former's loose organization of committees and sub-committees.[45] In short, it did not produce the arms.

Above all, by far the most damaging mistake, governmentally, among the many serious ones made by the Government, was its want of frankness with the public. Is it to be argued that the total duty of a government ends with respect for the electorate's mood, even if in dangerous error ; or that the voters must not be informed of the harshness of political facts ? What is democratic education but the direct, open enlightenment of contemporary experience ? May the desire for power of a Party be set above the good of the Commonwealth, as seems to have been done in the light of the Baldwin confession ? It is surely the basic and indispensable condition of democracy that the people be truthfully informed by its Government. For, if it is informed, and things fall out well, democracy is fortified ; while if things fall out badly, the people may learn by responsible experience, and may collaborate the more earnestly in redeeming the error, because they realize that they have participated in its making. But if a misinformed people becomes cynical about untruth in high places, and the bonds of their sincere loyalty to their State are weakened, they become, as after Munich, sick at heart. The political manipulator may, then, underestimate his own people, and order or connive at actions they still have the backbone to repudiate. Thus, there was a revulsion of feeling at a critical moment when the Hoare-Laval proposals were made public in December 1935. ' Something has happened ', the appalled Mr. Baldwin declared, ' that has appealed to the deepest feelings of our countrymen, . . . some note has been struck that brings back from them a response from the depths.' [46] Indeed, popular instinct on ' the ground of conscience and honour ', as Mr. Baldwin called it, was sounder than the comprehension of the leaders, and also regarding the nature of the dictatorial States.

A demonstrative test came in the Spanish Civil War. The Government played the policy of 'non-intervention'. But its pro-Franco attitude became ever more plain and it more jubilantly popular with its followers. The Opposition was almost entirely for the Spanish Republic, although at first allowing itself to be compromised by the Government's policy when it believed the Government was sincere. The Government steadily, day after day, stubbornly, and even jeeringly, denied what everybody had the right to consider abundant and sound evidence of Italian and German intervention. Secure in its majority, and inveterately iron-handed in policy, the Government took exceptional joy in taunting, even tormenting the impotent Opposition.

The issues of the time, being war and starvation, both of which arouse primitive passions, threw an intolerable strain on representative institutions, for though the country survived, it was touch and go whether it would. Democracy was retained, but its operation was debased. For one thing, the election tactics of 1931 exploited financial panic ; in those of 1935, as openly confessed later, a considered deception was practised on the electorate. Again, the harsh and arrogant use of the Government's overwhelming majority on the issues of war and unemployment, troubled consciences with the question of how far a democratically responsible government may go in jeopardizing the nation irredeemably, except by perhaps the sacrifice of millions of lives, regardless and even disdainful of reasonable and loyal opposition. There is a point at which it becomes an abuse of responsible government, to act so that a reasonable Opposition cannot influence the course of events by the constitutional means open to it. Indeed, dangerous doctrines were being talked, such as, that it was unnecessary to call Parliament together or to keep it in session during the grave international crises ; or again, the opinion of *The Times*' leading article of 17 October 1938, that Mr. Chamberlain ' has been able to give peculiar encouragement to believers in the democratic system by showing the vaunted *Führerprinzip* can exist and operate within the framework of Parliamentary institutions '. Such methods threaten to demoralize public morale by inducing popular disgust at the mis-information, cynicism and callousness of its Government.

In the high moral tension, the dreadful atrocities committed by the Nazi Government against its own people were ignored or minimized, though they were important demonstrations of the spirit which that Government was applying to its relationship with other countries, and illustrations of what democratic peoples were spared. So was there for too long an ignoring of the brutalities and incitements of the British Union of Fascists whose unprecedented exhibition of violence at a meeting in Olympia was actually condoned by some Right-wing politicians, even in the House of Commons, as being justifiable owing to previous Communist rowdyism.[47] An uncomfortable suspicion arose that politicians who were hostile to sanctions against Italy, hostile to the Spanish Republican Government, friendly to Hitler's cunning advances, haters of Russia, were not unwilling to see in the British Fascist movement an executioner of Communists and, indeed, the Left in general. It was not until 1937 that this movement was disciplined by the law prohibiting political uniforms.[48] The tension led to the passing of an act dealing drastically with Incitement to Disaffection among the armed forces.[49] The Official Secrets Act was severely applied to prevent journalistic transmission of information from official sources to the public which might use it in criticism of the Government's policy.[50] This enforced pacification of the country was spectacularly illuminated in the case of Mr. Duncan Sandys, member of Parliament for Norwood (son-in-law of Mr. Churchill) who, having secured information about the shocking state of anti-aircraft defences, and being about to raise a question in the House of Commons on the matter, was practically threatened by the Attorney-General with prosecution—a matter so serious in its interference with the privilege of the House of Commons that the House revolted against the Government and virtually censured it through the House and a special committee.[51]

The policy of the elders of the ruling party could only be carried through by the strictest control of their followers, for there could not but be severe crises of conscience among them as one asset after another in Britain's international position was cast away, and as this decline was agitated by a group of Conservatives led by Mr. Churchill. This control was symbolized and engineered in Parliament through the Government Whips and particularly by the Chief Whip. But the Chief Whip can only exert the power put at his disposal by the Government. The leaders wanted unconditional obedience and all signs of independence were swiftly crushed. It is not a good recommendation for those who submitted. Just before World War II when the fruit of repression within the Party came to be seen in manifest and proximate dangers to their own land, strong protests were uttered against the power of the Whip's Office. And even in the ' phony ' phase of the War this iron hand persisted. In a protest of unprecedented severity, Captain Vyvyan Adams, Conservative Member for West Leeds, attacked the Chief Whip and his tactics. He complained that the Chief Whip had succeeded on many occasions in muzzling Parliamentary freedom, complained that he had successfully worked to exclude Mr. Churchill from the Government until the War came. ' The Right Honourable and gallant gentleman has tried to convert this first assembly of the world to which our constituents elect us to use our own judgment, into a school with himself as the chief usher . . . never has the country or a great Party suffered such injury from a single individual so powerful.' [52]

When such a fierce light beat upon the Government, and consciences were so deeply stirred, it was inevitable that the convention of the neutrality and anonymity of the Civil Service should be involved. Occasionally during the Italo-Abyssinian War the Opposition complained that the Foreign Office officials were hostile to British reliance on and co-operation with the League of Nations, and there was even a suggestion that the staff of the Foreign Office be required to take an oath of faithfulness to the principles of the League. Argument revolved around whether the advice of Sir (now Lord) Robert Vansittart, then Permanent Under-Secretary of State for Foreign Affairs and later Chief Diplomatic Adviser to the Government,[53] was being ignored by the Government in its policy of appeasement and what that advice was.[54] Later still, in the months preceding the Munich Agreement, the unprecedented reliance of the Prime Minister in life and death foreign negotiations upon a high Civil Servant, Sir Horace Wilson, Chief Industrial Adviser to the Government, absolutely unversed in diplomatic experience or training, and the extensive publicity of their names and photographs, caused much dissatisfaction in Parliament and the nation. The Opposition criticized the unconventional selection of advisers and the publicity, but met with the Government's disingenuous rejoinder ' deprecating any departure from the well-recognized tradition which precludes public references—whether in the House, in the Press, or elsewhere—by name to individual officers of the Crown Services. . . . It would be contrary to the public interest if the practice were to grow up of seeking to identify individual Crown servants with particular actions or particular developments of policy.' [55]

In a democracy the people look to their leaders for moral guidance or see in actual policy a moral standard. A long and steady course of promises of action which remain unfulfilled, a stream of explanations which claim to be realist but are only gross, pretensions to vision which turn out to be merely the eye-straining of the wilfully blind, and a decade of impure tergiversation masquerading as ' official ' facts, are not calculated considerably to elevate the standards of citizenship. For plain men, as well as gentlemen, may acquire a taste for cynicism, desiring to emulate their betters and suspecting that it pays. It is an error on the statesman's part to believe that the making of the laws does not influence morals, on which future laws depend, not excluding the fundamental law itself. Fortunate, indeed, the State whose people are nobler than their statesmen, for then, in their ' darkest hour ' they may still shine, alone. But they deserve statesmen who do not lead them down to dark hours bereft of economic opportunity and the company of their loved ones.

*   *   *   *   *   *   *

The abdication of King Edward VIII in 1936 was important to students of political science because it revealed the strength of the Monarchy, and secondly, distinguished and reinforced the conditions of that strength.[56] To abolish the Monarchy occurred to nobody, though in the past there had been considerable anti-monarchical movements, and public feeling. Indeed, when in 1935, Sir Stafford Cripps, in the course of a political speech in the country had referred to ' interference from Buckingham Palace ', there was a sharp outcry, not least from members of the Labour Party. The existence of the Monarchy was and is taken for granted by all classes : exceptions are negligible. This nation-wide sentiment is based upon an appreciation of the political utility and social amiability of monarchy. Provided this is not outweighed by the occasional constitutional disadvantages of the Crown in the British Constitution, and the social snobbery which nourishes itself on a symbolic figure at the apex of society,[57] the sentiment is assuredly strong and lasting.

The conditions of durable esteem became clear upon the disclosure of the relationships between the King and Mrs. Simpson and in relation to the issue whether a marriage or any other relationship between them was compatible with Edward's retention of the kingship and his coronation by the Archbishop of Canterbury. There were men in every party prepared to defend the domestic freedom of the King, and for a little time it looked as if a severe parliamentary and public conflict might arise. Some Conservative politicians, most prominent of whom was Mr. Churchill, sided with the King, and there were rumours of a ' King's Party '. On the constitutional side, the major criticism was directed against the Prime Minister, Mr. Baldwin, on the ground that he had conducted negotiations for rather too long before seeking the counsel of his whole Cabinet and of Opposition leaders, and facing Parliament with the King's wish for a law to make possible a morganatic marriage.

More important than this was the attitude of the country. Every social grouping of the nation had its own idea of what the British monarchy should be. The established Church, led by the Primate, had one view : complete conventional propriety. Working class men had another view, largely that the King should be free in his domestic affections. Working class married women were fearful that the example set would have a generally bad social influence. Working class young unmarried women were more tolerant towards the King and Mrs. Simpson. The provinces were more strait-laced than the Metropolis. The upper classes in general were strongly opposed to the King's domestic freedom ; anything else was not ' good form ' ; yet many denounced the cant that the King must sacrifice himself to duty. Some intellectuals threw scorn on middle-class respectability. A small number of socialist rationalists favoured the King's marriage ; Fascists were for the King against the Government; Catholics were for the King against Parliament. And so one could report even more minutely the results of a careful contemporary analysis made of the reactions of the various social groups.

Though the House of Commons could have rejected the solution proposed by the Prime Minister, it acceded to his policy after a few days.[58] For Parliament found that on the whole public support of propriety, puritanism and respectability predominated. Britain was a socially conservative nation, founded on widely accepted standards of public respectability, and a sense of what was properly fitting for the social and constitutional function of the Crown. As a man he might have his own ideas and pleasures. But as a King, he was made in the image of the people, that is, of the large majority. It was particularly stressed in public debate that the actions of the man were the actions of the Crown, and they must be such as to unite the greater number of citizens, and not contribute to social dissension. In other words, he must be the exemplar of Civil Service. His actions and his friends must be such as not to diminish his dignity or the purity of his political influence; his inclinations and diversions such as to contribute to the despatch of business and not waste ministerial time. Nor, finally, could any possible affront to the moral code of the Dominions be tolerated, for a diminution of loyalty to ' the golden link' of Empire meant a loss of respect for the Mother Country, and a weakening of the sentiments of imperial unity. Finally, Britain's world position required that the most majestic symbol of its dignity should not be the object of scurrilous tales.

Ministers of the Crown Act, 1937 [59]

In 1937, the Ministers of the Crown Act was passed, with the principal object of levelling upwards the salaries of members of the Cabinet and other Ministers. It also made dispositions regarding the numbers of Parliamentary Secretaries who could be appointed to assist certain Ministers, and thus touched on the serious problem presented by the fact that so large a proportion of the membership of the House has paid employment with the Government and that this reduced the independence of mind and the freedom of criticism of the Commons. (This issue was again raised in 1941 during the debates on the House of Commons Disqualification—Temporary Provisions—Act.[60] The problem gave rise to a Select Committee, whose *Report on Offices &c. Under the Crown* [61] is a very important addition to the interpretation of the constitution.) The correction of some historical anomalies in the relationship between the payment of Ministers and their respective duties entailed certain constitutional changes of some interest, in particular the statutory mention of the chief executive organ of British government, namely the Cabinet, and of the national political leader, namely the Prime Minister. As the statute made a distinction between the salaries of Cabinet Ministers and other Ministers, members of the Cabinet had to be defined, and they were henceforth so defined as those notified in the *London Gazette* as being members of the Cabinet. Their exit is similarly notified. It also became necessary to mention the office of Prime Minister : ' There shall be paid to the person who is Prime Minister and First Lord of the Treasury an annual salary of ten thousand pounds.'

Of more interest to the operation of parliamentary institutions than these arrangements was the establishment of a salary for the ' Leader of the Opposition ', again the first time that this recognized but conventional office received statutory basis. As has been amply explained in Vol. II, pp. 990 ff., the British political machine depends for its efficiency upon the existence of a steady, organized, coherent, forceful opposition (known as His Majesty's Opposition), vehement and frank in its intention to reveal, by magnifying for popular vision, the shortcomings of the Government, and stimulated in this by the possibility to supplant the Government at some future date, an alternative government with a widely contrasting political policy. Its vigorous pursuit of these aims imposes on the Government the task of explaining itself and, as a consequence, of correcting itself. That such an organized and determined Opposition can operate without being regarded as an ' enemy of the State ' must be recognized as a very high degree of political attainment. Instead, it is a friend of the State, precisely because it is a rival of the Government of the day. The small number of men, about 20, who lead the Opposition, must, if they are to fulfil the function which convention has assigned to them, be full-time and even hard-working politicians. Even more responsibility and onerous duties falls upon the Leader of the Opposition, virtually the prospective Prime Minister. In the Canadian House of Commons, for many years past, the weight of duties on the Leader and the possibility that he might be a man lacking ample means, has been met by a salary. A similar arrangement was introduced in the Ministers of the Crown Act. The Leader of the Opposition is defined in the statute as, ' that member in the House of Commons who is for the time being the Leader in that House of the party in opposition to His Majesty's government having the greatest numerical strength in that House '. It is further prescribed that, if there is any doubt as to who shall be designated Leader of the Opposition, the Speaker of the House is to decide and his decision is final for purposes of the Act. If the Leader of the Opposition happens to be a former Prime Minister, which is very possible, and so in receipt of a pension as such, he receives no salary, or if in receipt of a pension under the act of 1869, it is by that amount reduced. The amount is £2,000 a year and, in order that it shall not be the subject of annual debate, is included in the Consolidated Fund.

8

The then Prime Minister, Mr. Baldwin, strongly emphasized the need of economic independence of the Leader of the Opposition.[62]

> The Leader of the Opposition is the one man who must always be here as the one man who leads his party. It is he who consults with the Leader of the House. On him too rests the responsibility to maintain the traditions of his House. He is probably a potential Prime Minister, or he may have been Prime Minister. In that case, he cannot make much money outside of this House and I think it is right and indeed necessary that that one man . . . should be made independent. Independence in politics is worth a great deal . . . the Leader of the Opposition ought to be in that same position.

Mr. Arthur Greenwood, the spokesman of the Labour Party, observed the fact that the arrangement was in a sense a challenge to the totalitarian states, since they abhorred tolerance of minorities and opposition. It showed that the British system of government was hostile to ' the militarization of politics '.

There was some opposition to the principle. It came particularly from the Liberal Party, though some Labour members also were afraid of the effects of the stipulation. The opponents argued that the liberty and vigour of thought and criticism of the Leader of the Opposition, would be reduced by his acceptance of an official position. Anxiety was expressed that the House of Commons would degenerate into the subservience of civil servants. It was suggested that the public would regard a paid Leader of the Opposition as less their champion, than if he were unpaid. The present author's own opinion is that the fundamental forces of British politics are quite adequate to maintain the independence of mind and the critical force of the Opposition.

The Speaker of the House of Commons

In the Election of 1935, the Labour Party broke a very venerable tradition by putting up a Labour candidate to oppose the Speaker of the House of Commons in his constituency. The reason offered was that a local conservative association conducted a campaign in opposition to the Labour Party. It was a petty and ill-advised action, whether the provocation was local and the reason genuine, or whether caused by the increasingly bitter relations between the Opposition and the Government. For it is more than ever essential in the British parliamentary system to maintain the impartiality of the Speaker, since his duties of common service to the House and the parties are constantly increasing, and require the support of a publicly accepted and expressed convention of his neutrality. And if the Labour Party were anxious about the Speaker's use of his power under the Parliament Act to certify and determine what is a Money Bill, which may go to the root of social reform, then the better course is to deal firmly with the House of Lords problem. All other parties and groups rallied to the Speaker's support, who won his seat. Many suggestions were advanced in the Press to meet the alleged difficulty arising out of his political impartiality, namely that his constituents were thereby 'disfranchised' or unrepresented. A Select Committee of the House of Commons on Mr. Speaker's seat [63] was appointed, including former members of the House of all shades of opinion. It scrutinized the history of the Speaker's status, the various suggestions, and the parliamentary practice in foreign countries. It concluded that all alternative proposals to present practice suffered from serious parliamentary disadvantages. It recommended that well enough should be left alone ; it was urgent that the Speaker should be elected in an ordinary constituency like his fellow-members of Parliament ; and this meant that the Speaker's constituency would be liable to contest, if any opponent thought this fitting. This undesirable event should be met by 'fuller education of the electorate towards the recognition and increased understanding of those vital democratic safeguards which it is the duty of the Speaker to defend '.

* * * * * * *

Therefore, as could be predicted (cf. Finer, *Canadian Journal of Economics and Political Science*, Sept. 1942), in the post-war General Election (results 25 July 1945), the first in nearly ten years, Conservatives suffered a great defeat, while the Labour Party gained a decisive majority. A strong Labour Government took office. The results of the Election may be recorded :

Party	Votes	Seats
Labour	11·99 million	394
Conservative and National	9·98 ,,	216
Liberal	2·21 ,,	11
Independents	0·52 ,,	13
Communist	0·10 ,,	2
Independent Labour Party	0·0467 ,,	3
Common Wealth	0·11 ,,	1

A substantial degree of socialization will follow, with considerable development of social security and the social services. This must give rise to some important problems. The first is the recruitment of a civil service more attuned than hitherto to the positive initiating tasks of enterprise and management assumed by the State. The second is the measure in which the workers will freely and loyally discipline themselves to fulfil the obligations involved in the successful conduct of socialized industry and professional services. No one yet knows the answer to the second, indispensable to decisions in the social advance of all democratic nations in the twentieth century. A final question arises : What conceivable social policy can a Conservative Party formulate likely to attract an electoral majority ?

CHAPTER VI

THE U.S.A.: THE NEW DEAL AND BEYOND [1]

THE Great Depression revealed profound financial, agricultural, industrial, and commercial distress and weakness throughout the nation, and in every social group. On the inauguration of President Franklin D. Roosevelt, in March 1933, the index of depression showed itself starkly in the closure of two-thirds of the nation's banks. It was estimated that more than fifteen million were unemployed, most of them fully.[2] Some communities had even resorted to barter and the issue of local scrip. Neither the Federal Government nor the States, with negligible exceptions, had, at that time, anything approaching the social security services or the organization, experience and personnel, which enabled some European countries and Great Britain to alleviate, however inadequately, their own economic distress.

The disaster had begun almost half-way through the Presidential term of Mr. Herbert Hoover, at a time when the prosperity which had begun to mount shortly after the First World War, seemed certain of unhindered advance to some fantastic zenith. Financial specu-lation among all classes had, however, masked grave weaknesses in the economic system, and, indeed, enhanced them—among them were over-speculation, heavy private debts, instalment purchasing and indebtedness, foreign trade undermined by the war debts tangle and European difficulties, greater industrial and agricultural production than could be bought or consumed at the prices anticipated and asked for by the producers. The President, a distinguished engineer, cele-brated as an administrator of food relief in Europe in World War I (but also, as such, the uncompromising leader in 1918 of opposition to Inter-Allied continuance of joint governmental relief arrangements for Europe), a life-long devotee of *laissez-faire* and rugged individualism, was, by temperament, habit, faith, or political acumen, not able to conceive and apply the bold measures required to meet so dreadful a crisis.[3] Indeed, its character and extent were not even appreciated by the President and his advisers. God would provide, the President literally declared. However, visible distress and public clamour caused the President to take some action. He appealed to State and local governments to expand public works; he established (when the presidential contest was looming) the Reconstruction Finance Corpor-ation to lend funds to banks, railroads, agricultural exporters and to farmers for their crops; a law put a brake on farm foreclosures, and authorized banks to make loans to home owners similarly threatened.

N.B.—The Notes to this Chapter begin on page 182.

Furthermore, the Federal Reserve Banks were empowered to be more liberal with their discount procedure to stimulate business. In July 1932 there was forced out of the President's unwillingness an act permitting loans to State relief works and self-liquidating projects. Yet, in spite of the heavy pressure on the President, brought to bear by the House of Representatives after the Republican majority had been overturned in the Congressional elections of November 1931, he vetoed a bill providing Federal assistance to employment exchanges.

At the elections of November 1932 the ordinary swing of the electoral pendulum was reinforced by resentment at the feebleness of the Administration, which argued that prosperity was round the corner, by the negative and vague Republican programme, by the hopes reposed in the far bolder, positive promises of the Democratic candidate, and anxiety about the more deep-seated economic and social malaise. Mr. Franklin Delano Roosevelt received a popular vote of nearly 23 million and carried 42 States. Mr. Hoover received nearly 16 million votes and carried only 6 States, four in New England, and Pennsylvania and Delaware. The total vote, some three million above that of 1928, indicated a considerable popular stir.

The Roosevelt Programme was indeed comprehensive and bold. It promised unemployment relief, labour legislation, unemployment and old age insurance, the restoration of agriculture, the conservation and development of power resources, regulation of holding companies, securities exchanges, and utility rates. It promised reciprocal trade agreements, economy and a balanced budget, a sound currency, the repeal of the Eighteenth Amendment, and ' the continuous responsibility of government for human welfare '.[4]

The significance of the Democratic programme lay not merely in its width, but in the resolute spirit in which it was undertaken, its warm, generous humanity towards the ' forgotten man ', and the determination to carry the country over or through the obstacles opposed by the Constitution to positive economic and social action by government, especially by the Federal authority. It promised a ' New Deal '.[5] This spirit emerges clearly from the President's Inaugural Address, 4 March 1933.[6]

With this pledge taken (to secure the larger good) I assume unhesitatingly the leadership of this great army of our people dedicated to a disciplined attack upon our common problems. I shall not evade the clear course of duty that will then confront me. I shall ask the Congress for the one remaining instrument to meet the crisis—broad Executive power to wage a war against the emergency as great as the power that would be given me if we were in fact invaded by a foreign foe . . . we do not distrust the future of essential democracy. The people of the United States have not failed. They have asked for discipline and direction under leadership. They have made me the instrument of their wishes. In the spirit of the gift I take it.

Not merely remedial, the New Deal sought reform and reconstruction in matters upon which, it is important to remember, there had been for many decades the acutest unflagging social criticism, and which had from time to time, given rise to parties of dissent and radical reform, like the Populists, the Farmer-Labour Party, the Socialist Party, and which, moreover, had evoked from Theodore Roosevelt the promise of a Square Deal,[7] and from President Woodrow Wilson the evangel of the New Freedom.[8] In addition, then, to the distress produced by a crisis within the capitalist system, there was also a crisis of the system ; and, since the U.S.A. was the most capitalist economy in the world, the dual crisis was extremely severe and its gravity necessitated the sternest governmental measures.

Some have expressed the sum total of the New Deal as a ' revolution ' ;[9] while others,[10] appreciating the size of the achievement, deny its revolutionary quality. But, this is certain, that in the period 1933 to 1939, there was a sharp and massive rupture with the basic assumption of American society, namely, extreme economic individualism and its triplet of consequences, economic opportunity, economic insecurity and economic adventurousness. In considerable modification, if not in substitution of gallant *laissez-faire*, social provision, control, economic security and governmental planning were inaugurated. So abrupt and so extensive a change, analogous to the turning-point in British social policy under the celebrated Liberal Government of 1906 to 1914, set in train a development the path of which will not be retraced, but which is certain to be permanent and certain to be expanded. The U.S.A. had broken with the nineteenth century. The problems are henceforth permanent problems of American society and government.

In the present context, three subjects merit special interest: (1) the legislative achievements of the New Deal ; (2) the administrative consequences ; and (3) the effect on Presidential leadership, the relationships between President and Congress, the position of the Supreme Court, and the Federal system. It may be said that under the United States Constitution neither the President nor the Congress elected in November 1932, was able to take office until 4 March 1933. The gap of authority during so grim a depression was damaging, although the President-elect and the President-reject conferred during the gap. The Twentieth Amendment, proposed 2 March 1932 and ratified 6 February 1933 (a long agitated reform), closed the term of the President on 20 January, and of Congress 3 January, and this came into force, the former in 1937, the latter in 1935.

Legislative Achievements

It is possible to include only the most important measures passed in the first and second terms of the Presidency, 1933 to 1940.

In the space of a day, Congress passed the Emergency Banking

Act, 9 March 1933 : it permitted the abandonment of the gold standard and payment of gold notwithstanding the stipulation of contracts, and gave the Federal Government authority to extend and strengthen credit and support to the banks, with powers to the R.F.C. to advance considerable loans. The abandonment of gold on 20 April was ratified by Joint Resolution of Congress. Later, a supplementary statute permitted considerable issue of Treasury Notes and a reduction of the gold content of the dollar up to 50 per cent. The Truth in Securities Act, 27 May 1933 (in a later and fuller form, the Securities and Exchange Act) was passed (modelled on British legislation long in effect). This legislation arose out of the disclosure (by a famous Congressional investigation) [11] of dangerously speculative practices, dishonest bond salesmanship, scandalous breaches of trust, and shady co-operation between bankers and stockbrokers and politicians and foreign and domestic government officials. As the President declared, the law was intended to correct ' unethical and unsafe practices on the part of officers and directors of banks and other corporations '. The securities legislation required the registration of bond issues with a government Commission (soon established) of most non-governmental securities, together with the filing of full information about the securities, designed to exhibit the soundness of the venture, the integrity of the operators, and to control credit for margin and speculative loans.

The scope of the Reconstruction Finance Corporation, under Hoover restricted to assistance to banks, railways and insurance companies, was now extended to industry, commerce, and agriculture ; and out of its loins sprang a number of government credit corporations. [12] The Federal Reserve Bank system [13] was extended and its inspections made severer. The big banks were allowed to undertake branch banking to avoid excessive reliance on many petty and weak local banks, natural wrecks in the economic tempest. A Federal Deposit Insurance Corporation was established to insure bank deposits.

Laws were passed to provide work or maintenance. The States and the cities had been giving immediate relief by adapting their antiquated poor laws. An Unemployment Relief Act, of March 1933, authorized the employment of citizens in public works designed to rehabilitate and conserve forests and soil. This gave rise to the Civilian Conservation Corps, employing an average of 350,000 youths a year. The fear of wholesale demoralization (popularly and politicianly advertised as caused by the ' dole ' administered in those years in Great Britain), caused President and Congress to provide public works. Under the Emergency Relief Act of May 1933, the Federal Emergency Relief Administration was set up to administer vast sums of money by grants to the States to ' match ' their own expenditure, and to make even larger grants where the States were

abnormally poor. In June 1933 The National Recovery Act provided for a very wide system of public works, including roads, rivers,
and harbours, slum clearance, waterpower, public buildings, low cost
housing, reservoirs, sewage plants and so forth. The Public Works
Administration was set up to organize the programme, and operated
through the Civil Works Administration. Early in 1935 additional
funds and some changes in the principles of relief gave rise to the Works
Progress Administration, as the organizing agency. It is impossible,
in the present text, to state the course and results of this mighty
undertaking.[14] But this at least may be said : though there was
much waste, faulty administration, and malingering, these were small
compared with the dire needs of the situation, and the enormous
benefits accomplished. People were fed ; and that is superlative
praise. There is something permanently noble and inspiring about
the unwillingness of the U.S. Government to surrender to hopeless-
ness ; and much to be learned from the variety of socially beneficial
work-projects which can be found for government promotion when
ingenuity and determination are exerted. Many unemployed obtained
work ; private enterprise was assisted by the additional purchasing
power provided by this ' priming of the pump ' ; and throughout the
country, public works, which States and cities had long desired, but
had not been rich enough to supply, were carried through by Federal
grants or loans without interest, to the lasting benefit of those
communities.[15]

On 12 May 1933, the Agricultural Adjustment Act was passed to
raise agricultural prices and lighten the burden of loans and mortgages.
It had two general objectives : to assist the whole agricultural community to raise its share of the national income as compared with other
occupations [16] (and here it was partly encouraged and stimulated by
the historic pressure for tariffs and other measures to assist industry
and commerce), and secondly, to reduce American agricultural production to a level which would satisfy domestic requirements, but
abandoning foreign markets, which had disappointed the hopes of the
American farmer. The immediate tactics of the Government were
to make voluntary agreements with millions of farmers to reduce the
production of specified staple commodities, cotton, wheat, maize,
pigs, rice, tobacco and milk (later extended to include rye, potatoes,
sugar and peanuts). The Government raised a general tax on the
processing of these commodities, and applied the funds thus obtained,
to paying benefits to farmers who restricted their production to suit
the plan. At the same time (1935), the Resettlement Administration
began to rationalize other factors in agriculture : to improve marginal
land, to make grants to poor farm families, adjust farm mortgages,
set up camps for migrant labourers,[17] and foster rural health, housing,
recreation and education.[18] The Federal Farm Loan Act, May 1933,

instituted farm land banks and empowered them to re-finance farm loans at a great reduction on the original interest rates. In the critical years, some 10 per cent. of all farm properties had been foreclosed ; in many places farmers had rioted against mortgagees, auctions, and the law courts. In July 1937 the Farm Tenant Act provided for assistance to tenants to buy their own farms. For the President's Committee on Farm Tenancy of 1935 had shown a most remarkable increase in farm tenancy in the last forty-five years and a corresponding decrease in the number of operating owners : in 1880 some 25 per cent. of all farmers were tenants, but in 1935 this had increased to 42 per cent. Nearly half of the land, in money values, was farmed by tenants or wage labourers.[19] The Commodities Credit Corporation was established by the R.F.C. to lend money to farmers to enable them to carry stocks to a season of better prices.[20]

Soil erosion in the U.S.A. had carried away no less than one-third of the surface soil from one-fourth of the cultivated land, while one-sixth or more of the surface soil was lost from another fourth of the farm land. Other very serious damage had been done to the natural minerals of the soil which had been treated like expendable stores, not nourished by plant food.[21] The pioneers and later settlers of the U.S.A. were virile creators, but they were also fierce destroyers of the soil, the forests and the grass and mineral reserves, such as coal and oil. By 1940, the Department of Agriculture's soil erosion programme included over 270 million acres, and was being carried through by no less than one farmer out of four. All the chief natural assets were grasped and husbanded with energetic devotion by the New Deal administration. In May 1933 the Tennessee Valley Authority, a U.S. Government Corporation, was established to regulate floods, make the Tennessee River fully navigable, exploit the hydro-electric power, combat erosion, and raise the standard of living of the Valley, by the better utilization of agricultural and other economic resources and methods.[22] In the Public Utility Act of August 1935, the Federal Water Power Commission was empowered to regulate the generation, transmission, and sale of electric power and gas in interstate commerce : it could regulate the co-ordination of facilities and quash unfair charges.[23]

The Federal Housing Administration insured existing mortgages ; and in 1937 the United States Housing Authority was established to promote slum clearance and develop low cost housing by the cities and other bodies.

The National Industrial Recovery Act was passed on 16 June 1933. It had two chief objects, to regulate industry and production, and to safeguard, indeed, to grant the workers authority to organize and bargain collectively without intimidation by their employers. The first object was compassed by authority to establish Codes of business practices to be formulated by authorized representative associations of the members of each trade and industry. On receiving the subsequent approval of the President the Code would have the force of law. Where the making of a Code was delayed, the President was empowered to draft and impose such a Code. Secondly, the rights of labour were fortified in the law, by the requirement that in each Code there must be included the right to organize and bargain collectively, free from interference by employers ; while no worker could be required to join a company union or not to join any association he chose ; and further, the industry must apply the maximum hours, minimum wages, and conditions of employment, as approved and prescribed by the President. There were two corollaries to this attempt to plan production—for one of the purposes of the statute was the settlement of the quantity of production where there was excess (e.g. petroleum production). First, the Executive was given the power to restrain or forbid the importation of commodities which made ineffective or seriously jeopardized the maintenance of a Code. Secondly, the codes and other like instruments of the legislation were exempted from the force of the Federal anti-trust laws.

A gusty public campaign led by the Government, and a tempestuous upsurge of popular idealism, resulted in the establishment of some four hundred Codes in less than twelve months, and these covered no less than 90 per cent. of the American economy and the majority of the gainfully employed.

It has already been suggested that, judged by the standards of many modern democracies, America was, until the New Deal, remarkably backward in provision for the aged, the young, the sick and the unemployed. The functions involved were divided between the traditional constitutional agents of power, that is the Federal and the State governments, but were chiefly regarded as the province of the latter. However, though possessed of this rare opportunity to exhibit the value of the experimental possibilities inherent in States' rights (a subject of unremitting, stubborn and even grasping claims), only 28 of the States had by 1934 old age pensions, and these were mostly inadequate. Only Wisconsin and Ohio had unemployment insurance. The Depression sharpened existing opinion leading to a social security system, incubated also by the heat of the Share-the-Wealth agitation of Huey Long, boss of Louisiana,[24] the radio tirades of Father Coughlin of Detroit,[25] and the propaganda of Dr. Townsend's Clubs. In August 1935 the Federal Security Act was passed, providing for contributions by the Federal Government to States which should establish pension systems for the aged, the blind, for dependent workers, children, cripples, and for public health works. The Act included an old-age insurance system. Above all, it established a system of unemployed insurance, based on State administrative schemes, and financed by a payroll tax levied by the Federal Government on employees everywhere, who are given a credit of 90 per cent. for the payments they make under State unemployment compensation laws. The ten per cent. is a Federal grant to cover administrative costs.[26] Of course, the State standards of administration must be approved by the Federal Social Security Board.

It is fair to say that ' rugged individualism ' had promised explicitly or implicitly (and had survived on the promise) a fortune to anybody, if he were worth it, that is, if he could acquire it by his own lawful enterprise. Most Americans abided by and extolled the system while there was prosperity. But when prosperity vanished, they suffered ' conversion ' as the result of the revelation that there were advantages in ' security ' ; even if the economic level of ' security ' were more modest (?) than what could be gained in a régime of opportunity and insecurity.

The New Deal was immensely courageous. Without it and the relief it brought to many millions in diverse ways, there must have been nation-wide violence, rising perhaps to a revolution, with the result worse than the dreadful condition to be cured. President Hoover had sent soldiers to chase away hunger-marchers encamped near Washington. American society might well have collapsed. To keep American society and the American economy from foundering in disorder and violence, immense sums were raised by the Government, and the national debt was increased, as in most other nations at about the same time. A regular theory of ' deficit financing ', that is, of the propriety of unbalanced budgets in time of depression, of ' spending your way into prosperity ', was developed.[27] Consequently, many interests which were still relatively comfortable amidst the general ruin became disaffected. There was special hostility to the laws which controlled the operation of private enterprise, especially among the big financial and manufacturing interests, but also among the smaller business people. The Liberty League prophesied doom. Each of the New Deal reforms was of advantage to some social groups, but also vexatious to others. A storm blew up : the ' bureaucracy ' was ' swollen ' ; the constitution had been ' violated ' ; States' rights ' invaded ' ; the Presidency had become a ' dictatorship ' over nation and Congress ! Some charged the President with Communism ; while those on the Left exclaimed against his Conservatism, and even Fascism ! In the middle of 1935, American friends of the present author told him that businessmen had threatened to ' quit ' ; but how they could ' quit ', or from what, remained unexplained : the Republic was and is a going concern.

The Republican Party's presidential platform of 1936 [28] promised to preserve political liberty, individual opportunity, and the character of the free citizen. And then it promised most of the measures of the New Deal. Simultaneously it vowed to reduce expenditure, balance the budget, support the Constitution, and liberate enterprise from the bonds tied by the New Deal. However, President Roosevelt, again the Democratic nominee, by universal acclamation of the Party's Convention, confidently, and indeed, challengingly, announced his intention of prosecuting the fulfilment and expansion of the New Deal.[29] The Democratic platform declared its intention to seek such clarifying amendments of the Constitution as would ensure Congress the authority to enact the necessary laws. If the Constitution stood in the way, the Constitution must be amended. The President himself declared : ' We have had to struggle with the old enemies of the people, business and financial monopolies, speculation, reckless banking, class antagonism, sectionalism, war profiteering. They had begun to consider the Government of the United States as a mere appendage to their own affairs . . . they are unanimous in their hate for me—and I welcome this hatred. . . . For these things too (the New Deal measures) and a multitude of others like them, we have only just begun to fight.' [30]

Governor Alfred M. Landon of Kansas, a very successful but rather inarticulate independent oil producer, was Republican candidate. President Roosevelt's victory was greater than that of 1932. He obtained 27·75 million votes ; Landon, 16·68 million ; a ' Union ' Party candidate (who sought to combine the forces of Coughlin and Townsend) less than one million ; Norman Thomas, the usual Socialist candidate, one hundred and eighty thousand. The President carried all States but Maine and Vermont.

Inspiring the claim to amend the Constitution, and to strengthen the vote for the President, was the action of the Supreme Court in steadily invalidating New Deal legislation. This theme is further discussed presently. The President's determination to pursue his end was strengthened by the electoral victory which was so much greater than that of 1932, prior to the experience of the New Deal.

In the second term, further important legislation was passed, and new administrative departments set up, sometimes revised versions of invalidated legislation, sometimes fresh fields of law which now began to meet with the acceptance of the Court. Coal-mining was regulated by fresh legislation passed in 1936. The Farm Security Administration undertook to make loans, money grants, educate, train and generally rehabilitate small farmers. In February 1938 a new Agricultural Adjustment Act replaced the Soil Conservation Act of 1936, which itself was a partial substitution for the original A.A.A. invalidated by the Court in January 1936. And it re-introduced in another form (and subject to a two-third's approval of the farmers involved) [31] the fixing of acreage for certain crops, marketing control for surpluses and payments of compensation to acquiescing producers.

To secure an ' ever-normal ' granary, in order to stabilize prices the Government built vast storage space.   The benefits of the New Deal to the agricultural community were remarkable : between 1932 and 1939 cash income from wheat was multiplied more than two and a half times, from maize more than four and a half times, from cotton nearly twice, from tobacco about two and a half times, from meat animals about twice.

The Fair Labour Standards Act was enacted in June 1938.   This Act was passed to fill the gap left by the judicial invalidation of the National Industrial Recovery Act in 1935.   The immediate forces that produced it were the ' recession ' from economic recovery in 1937.   There was serious unemployment (eleven million completely unemployed and five and a half million partly unemployed).   There were many strikes, some following the French example of sitting down in the factories, and some workers were killed by the police.   The Democratic politicians from the Southern States, always more conservative than the rest, became an especially strong, steady, and irritating opposition to the liberal measures moved by the President.   The Act provided for a forty hours week, minimum pay of 40 cents per hour, and extended these regulations to all employees engaged in or producing goods for interstate commerce.   Child labour (about which there had been at least thirty years of popular agitation, and a discouraging attitude of *laissez-faire* in Supreme Court cases) was prohibited in manufactures for interstate commerce, and the labour of young persons in hazardous occupations was subjected to strict limitation.   A late-comer in the field of labour regulation, the United States by this statute had adopted, perhaps the broadest and most advanced regulation in any land.

Administrative Consequences

The New Deal was far from being founded on a socialist basis whatever the vituperation of opponents for election purposes.   For Congress and the President were far from being socialists.   Like many confronted by disaster, they were well-intentioned, but they invented their policy from day to day as claims pressed in on them ; and like all politicians in a land inhabited by struggling and virile groups in competition for prosperity, no single claim could be allowed priority over the reconciliation of all.   The New Deal, then, was founded on the system of free enterprise, but purified of the very darkest of its competitive, oppressive and speculative practices, and subject to certain modifying experiments in social security, in public works, a governmentally-managed parity between the various great producing sections of the national community, and the Government's undertaking of the conservation and development of primary natural resources.   Most of the legislation mentioned, required for its fulfilment the continuous and intensive activity of administrative agencies.

These fell into two great classes : the mainly executive and the mainly regulatory. Of the first, the work of the Reconstruction Finance Corporation, or the Housing Authority, or the Department of Agriculture is a good example ; while the second class is exemplified by the National Labour Relations Board or the Securities and Exchange Commission.[32]

Here we have space only to observe that (a) the number of public officials considerably rose, (b) the number of agencies and offices increased, and (c) among the latter, there was an increase in the number of ' independent agencies '.

The increase in the number of public officials was striking. On 10 June 1932 there were 583,196 persons employed in the entire service ; by 30 June 1936 there were 824,259 ; and by 30 June 1939 920,310. Civil Service reformers sought a reduction in ' spoils ' by the inclusion of more offices in the ' career ' service, subject to selection and appointment by the United States Civil Service Commission. Both parties promised this. President Roosevelt himself was a friend of this principle, but his campaign manager, Postmaster General Jim Farley, and many New Deal Congressmen (now that Democrats were in power with authority over patronage) as well as Republicans were not so Simon Pure.[33] In 1932, 80 per cent. of the Federal employees were in the competitive ' classified ' services. By 1939, the total number of ' civil servants ' had increased, but there was a proportional decline in merit appointments to slightly less than 70 per cent. But the President followed the recommendations of the Committee on Administrative Management and by Executive Order made very large extensions of the coverage of appointments into the classified service, ' upward, outward, and downward '. In June, 1938, full civil service status was ordered for all postmasters. In 1940, on the basis of the Ramspeck-O'Mahoney Act, the President covered into the civil service all the positions over which his authority extended, that is, practically all existing positions, with the exception of the T.V.A., the assistant district attorneys of the Department of Justice and one or two other small groups. But first, second, and third class postmasters, now put into the classified service, were to be appointable by the President with Senatorial consent. The percentage of merit appointments rose to over 90 per cent. of all appointments.

The President's Committee on Administrative Management was created by the President in March 1936 to recommend reforms in the highest levels of Federal administration. The appointment of this Committee was a specially conspicuous sign, as it was itself a towering achievement, of the remarkable progress in American administrative reform made in the decade 1929 to 1939. Some years before, the Public Administration Clearing House had been established in Chicago to bring together many organizations of public officials and public administrators under one roof, where the experience and loyalty they could draw upon from their individual and group, State and local memberships throughout the entire country, could be pooled, and transferred, developed and disseminated, their value to democratic government demonstrated, and a general rise in the prestige as well as improvements in method encouraged and assisted. This work owed much to the leadership of Professors Charles Merriam and Luther Gulick, Mr. Guy Moffett of the Spelman Fund (a subsidiary of the Rockefeller Foundation), Mr. Beardsley Ruml, then also on the Board of the Spelman Fund, and the specially gifted guidance and strategy of the director of the Clearing House, Mr. Louis Brownlow. In 1934, a masterly inquiry was conducted by the so-called Commission of Inquiry on Public Service Personnel, of which Merriam and Brownlow were members, and Professor Gulick the director. Its Report and volumes of evidence with attendant monographs focused attention on the public service, analysed its deficiencies, illuminated its opportunities, and recommended action. Now came the President's Committee: its members were Mr. Brownlow, Professor Merriam, and Professor Gulick. When its Report and results are added to the change for the better already produced, that is, taking the decade 1929 to 1939 as a piece, these men had effected an improvement in the American public service easily matching the historic and celebrated Macaulay-Trevelyan Reforms in Great Britain between 1848 and 1853. That beneficial influence was made manifest in a general rise in the prestige of public administration as a career, especially among university graduates, and in better preparation for it. It is being further developed, as was anticipated and planned, by cumulative progress among the new generation.[34] It taxes the mind to think of a more valuable gift that any three men could, in a similar space of time, contribute to their nation's permanent welfare and strength. Quiet administration hath its victories no less renowned than the barking parade of politics.

The advent of the New Deal provided opportunity for a reform, still in its experimental stage, attempting to adapt to the United States Civil Service the idea of the administrative class of the British system. American students of administration, especially Professor Leonard White, had for long appreciated the value of a group of civil servants who would not be merely technicians and special experts, but men of general education, comprehension and high intellectual ability.[35] In 1934, there was established a Junior Civil Service Examiners' Group. The minimum educational qualification of a bachelor's degree from an institution of recognized standing was prescribed. Some 15,000 applicants took the examination (itself a testimony to the enhanced interest in public service as a career) and

some 7,000 passed, of whom one thousand in due course found positions
of various types in the Federal service.   The examination was subsequently consolidated with one for Junior Professional Assistants,
and preserved the great width of its general appeal by the range of
its options in the examination. Yet, since the examination now
required special work in economics, political science and public administration, a few of the formerly eligible candidates from other fields
of study lost their opportunity of entering the civil service by this
broad route.   Ten years of experience shows that the reform is a
marked success.   Some of the ablest of the rising generation of the
Federal Service now come from this source.   Appointing officers are
most anxious to secure recruits who have specialized in social science
and public administration.[36]   (Cf. also, Public Administration Review,
II, No. 2, 1940, *The Making of Administrators*, for another view.)
The exigencies of World War II have caused the examination again
to be based on an acceptable college degree and not on special
requirements.

The increase in the number of public servants naturally aroused
vehement aversion among anti-New Dealers. It was natural that
the cry of ' bureaucracy ' should be keened by those who regarded a
capable bureaucracy,[37] even more than an inefficient one, an enemy
of ' good ' government.   Indeed, the Chamber of Commerce wisecrack,
so untrue and so pernicious to the well-being of the nation, that is,
' The best public servant is the worst one', had widespread currency.
The benefits to the public—the recipients of welfare services and
pension allowances, and national resources conserved and developed
—meant less to manufacturers, business men, bankers and some
' middle class ' groups, than the irksomeness of the controls exercised
by the government over them to safeguard the workers and the consumers, and to render long-term services of nation-wide extent to
the national economy as a whole.   The cry of ' bureaucracy ' was
levelled not merely at expanding numbers and salaries, which caused
a charge on taxes and augmented the debt, and which were alleged
to provide a band of permanent electoral supporters for the existing
administration.[38]   It was as strongly directed against administrative
and quasi-judicial procedures.   These, designed to secure prompt and
appropriate compliance with the law for the benefit of individuals or
groups, as intended by the properly enacted law, were alleged to be
violating ' due process ',[39] that is the personal liberty and property
guaranteed by the Constitution. This ' administrative justice '
aspect of the controversy resulted in sensible and liberal amendments
of procedure by the governmental agencies and commissions involved,
the trend being towards full testimony, fair hearings of the parties,
proper conduct of the examination of documents and persons, opportunity to scrutinize and rebut an order before it went into effect,

segregation of the prosecutory from the judicial function, and adequate acquaintance with the record by the official rendering the decision. The movement was, in the words of Chief Justice Hughes, towards ' the spirit of the just judge '.[40]   On the other hand, the Courts increasingly acknowledged that their role was not merely to obstruct the discretion of those entrusted with administrative fulfilment, but only to see that the administrative agencies acted within the power granted to them by the Constitution and the statutes, that Congress possessed the power to give authority in due form, and that the spirit of the just judge prevailed in the procedure and behaviour of the agencies.   Courts and agencies are means to obtain the prescribed end, and neither body should frustrate the other, but both should act in collaboration.[41]   For it was acknowledged that administrative justice was indispensable in view of the need for speed, and almost always for the technological mysteries involved, and to secure equality before the law as between powerful and concentrated interests on one side and a diversified mass of unrelated individuals (' the public ') on the other.[42]

As law followed law, the agencies of government increased in number.[43]   The agencies for the exercise of the new powers were not, as they are in normal British and European practice, fitted into as few chief departments as possible.[44]   Thus (by no means exclusively due to the New Deal), there were over one hundred separate organized establishments and agencies with the obligation of reporting to the President.   Among the one hundred, there were ten great departments ; and then came a congeries of many ' commissions ', ' agencies ', ' administrations ', ' authorities ', under the President, but not within any of these departments.   There were also some twelve agencies which were altogether independent of Presidential surveillance.   This defeated coherence of direction and co-ordination by the President. It left the President either a distant, ineffectual witness, or an impotent intruder into chaos, and gave the rein to overlapping and departmental friction and mutual frustration, of which many examples could be cited.   Indeed, the President's Committee on Administrative Management went so far as to say that ' a headless fourth branch of the government responsible to no one ' had ' planlessly grown '. The Committee proposed twelve major Executive Departments to be fitted into one all-comprehensive administrative pattern.   At the very centre of this, assisting the President, and to form a better organized White House staff, the Committee proposed six Executive Assistants to the President in addition to existing secretaries who dealt with the public, with Congress, the Press and the Radio.   Their only function and status would be : ' When any matter is presented to the President for action, affecting any part of the administrative work of the government, to assist him in obtaining quickly and with-

9

out delay all pertinent information possessed by any of the Executive Departments, so as to guide him in making his responsible decisions ; and then, when decisions have been made, to assist him in seeing to it that every administrative department and agency affected is promptly informed. . . . They should be possessed of high competence, great physical vigour, and a passion for anonymity.' The scope of the proposal is thus explained in its simplest form by one of its principal architects : [45]

The President's Committee decided to propose that the Executive Office of the President should perform only those functions, the responsibility for which could not be delegated by the President. The ' non-delegable ' functions are those by which an executive may control the policies of his departments, while leaving to the head of each department decisions which are peculiar to its activity and the work incidental thereto. . . . According to our distinction between ' delegable ' and ' non-delegable ' functions, a staff function such as purchasing may be centralized or decentralized as expediency may require, but in either case can well be delegated ; whereas the managerial functions by which an executive can control his organization, especially budgeting, planning and personnel, must be performed in the Executive Office.

Of a special importance in the reorganization proposed is the transformation of the status of the Bureau of the Budget, become a veritable centre of creative administrative management and improvement for the whole apparatus of government.[46]

The recommendations regarding departmental reorganization [47] were defeated by Congress by an altogether capricious single vote in the House of Representatives in 1938, but accepted in 1939, when some reorganization was undertaken.[48] The White House Staff was increased as recommended, though time must show whether the physical and psychological attributes proposed for the assistants have been recruited. Experience hitherto, perhaps distorted by World War II, has shown the utility of the Staff, but of a kind rather different from that which was planned and expected. A strong President, impatient of administrative apparatus in time of War, and even in time of peace, will hardly wait for his orders to sift down to the departments, or for the information to be sifted up to him. He is likely to pass beyond his administrative assistants who are go-betweens, and make direct contact with his Cabinet Officers (the heads of great departments) and the mightiest agencies. To him, his assistants will seem to clutter up the path ; and to the impatient heads of departments they must appear as obstacles to be circumvented. This is in the order of what has happened ; and the President in war-time has dealt with most agencies directly and through political confidential men and old friends.

The Committee, concentrating its attention on the President as supreme ' administrative manager ' in the national government, envisaged the assistants as administrative assistants alone. This was to under-estimate the impossibility of segregating the political from the administrative aspects of the President's everyday functions. Hence, the assistants have rather been political 'trouble-shooters' for the President, each in a different sector : one in relations with Congress, another regarding Negro affairs, a third concerning general policy and the strategic facts on which it might be based, and another has acted as a general political handyman.   These have been extremely, indeed, indispensably, helpful; but not as the Committee foreshadowed, that is, in the co-ordinating conduct of administration.

In peaceful, normal times, if ever such can come again in this grinding age of critical economic transition, they may come into their own ; time alone will show.   If the Committee intended to secure a major co-ordination of administrative action, through the White House Staff, the hope, we think, was doomed.   For though co-ordination on the administrative side depends in the first place on the proper departmental assignments of duties, so that they dovetail from the beginning, it rests, above all, upon a real collective cabinet with corporate responsibility.   In the second place, major co-ordination of administrative action depends on a parliament which watches the Administration continuously and assiduously, and calls out promptly against any signs of marching in different directions, and the voice which calls out must have an effective threat of discipline in it.   But, in the American system there is no collective cabinet with collective responsibility, even during World War II.[49]   And, as for Congress, it is not in the position to exercise the co-ordinating influence of the British Parliament, because it is not organized to do so (it has, for instance, no Question Hour at all), because, and this is the crux of the matter, the Executive as Executive is independent of Congress, which, therefore, cannot mete out any punishment to the Executive, or compel correction, or even administer an effective rebuke.

Presidential Leadership, etc.

It is already clear that the conception and the fulfilment of the New Deal must have had broader political consequences than the legislative and administrative phases already sketched.   The governmental leadership of the United States Presidency, already well pronounced by 1932 (Vol. II, pp. 1016 ff., *Theory and Practice*) was very considerably enhanced by the strategy needed to defeat the depression and to wrestle with the more radical causes of the political maladies it revealed.   Leadership, that is, initiative, striving, inspiration, and the marshalling of all forces auxiliary to action, was needed, if the task were to be carried through.   Any political party in opposition to the Republican was necessarily obliged to offer something like this.   President Roosevelt's personality and experience designated him alone as the leader, and this in a sense even more emphatic than many of his supporters among the Democrats relished. The President's statesmanship, and his imprint on the Presidency as an institution, his handling of precedents and men, were, then, the consequences of a grievous emergency. But, in addition, they were the product of a party, and, above all, the offspring of a character. The breach of the third term tradition in 1940, was almost automatic as World War II approached America, and the attempt to make an issue out of it fell flat.[50]   So far as the American Constitution permits leadership, the Presidency has attained the major part of it.[51]   This is because Congress, composed of hundreds of members from distant districts, is divided into two Chambers, is divided by party membership, is divided in management through floor leaders and its scores of overlapping committees, is divided by the pressure groups, the lobbies—and division makes for confusion and distrust. The President, on the other hand, is one ; he is virtually directly elected by the single mass of voters in a single operation ; and he, therefore, symbolizes the unity of the American nation. While Congress makes the laws, he, not it, continuously guides the governmental machine in daily operation to convert the laws into effective social habits.

In the Presidency of the decade 1933–43, we see a vast social and economic programme, inspired by the presidential outlook and elaborated by a group of confidential advisers known in the early stages as the ' Brains Trust '. Changing in personnel with time, the Brains Trust began as a group of academic recruits from Columbia University, to prepare Roosevelt's first presidential campaign.[52] Others were then recruited from Harvard University (especially on the advice of Professor Felix Frankfurter, later Supreme Court Justice), with important assistance from the University of Chicago and the Public Administration Clearing House in the same city, and its net of recruitment was cast still further afield. Here was a group of devoted officials, unusually able, and devoted to the public welfare,[53] the product of American experimental boldness and exceptional readiness to entrust important responsibilities to young men.

Leadership showed itself in a series of magnificent presidential messages to Congress, the drafting of legislation in whole or in part in the Washington Departments (of course, informally, as Congress has its own drafting machinery [54]), but made acceptable by constant consultation of and operation through the Senate and House leaders of the President's party,[55] and especially through the Speaker of the House of Representatives and Alben Barkley of Kentucky,[56] the Senate floor leader. Since the President's party had a majority in both Houses, though after November 1942 a reduced one, presidential wishes were almost certain to be accepted in the main—in the first year of his administration very swiftly. Yet Congress was no rubber stamp, as was alleged by the Republican opposition, for to some presidential policies there were obstinate opponents, especially among the southern Democrats, whose diverse conservative tendencies began to be strongly felt in 1935.[57] For as a result of the poll-tax in eight Southern States only about 20 per cent. of the white population can vote. These conservatives fall roughly into two groups : a reactionary, anti-Yankee, anti-Negro, anti-Catholic, bigotted, spite-laden set, and a more advanced Southern reconstructionist class, but thinking of reconstruction in terms of *laissez-faire* for the in-dustrialization of the South. Congressmen from these States were unsympathetic to government assistance to share-croppers, or liberal treatment of the Negroes, and especially hostile to the Fair Labour Standards Act, which would level wages in South and North, and to the President's promotion of the status of trade unions. The Presi-dent was obliged to make concessions ; and, if he could not avoid them altogether, to reduce their importance by the exploitation of patronage, the time-honoured method of holding the party to the President's line. But President Roosevelt's power in this respect, as that of any recent President, was hardly so potent as students have hitherto believed. For once the jobs have been distributed, and this happens early in the President's tenure, he can only appeal to party principle and cohesion. And both are weak.

It is not surprising, therefore, in view of the spirit behind the President's policy, that he should have sought to hold his party together by unusually strong appeals to party principles, finally interpreted as loyalty to himself and his own interpretation of the party's platform. He observed that these had succeeded in bringing victory to him and his supporters. There were, in fact, more jobs to be given in the years of the New Deal than before. This was not enough. Furthermore, the first Hatch Act, passed in 1939, prohibited ' pernicious political activities ' on the part not only of those in the classified service, but *also* those in the unclassified service, except the President, Vice-President, and certain other of the highest officers ![58] The Second Hatch Act, of 1940, enacted that active participation in political management or in political campaigns is incompatible not only with the holding of public office under the U.S. Government, but also—this was the innovation—full-time public activities in State and local government whenever the service and any persons whose principal employment is in a federally-aided activity, wholly or partly financed by Federal loans or grants. Both these Acts tended to weaken the political influence of office holders.

Hence, in the Congressional elections of 1938, the President did what British party leaders have done since Walpole, to secure coherence of party and principle : he entered the primary campaign of certain prominent Democratic dissidents. (Woodrow Wilson had done this in the fateful election of 1918.) He rebuked them for exploiting the party and his popularity to win office which they would afterwards use to demean the first and thwart the second. The electors seemed to resent presidential intrusion (not unprompted by Republican friends of purity in elections) : some called it a ' purge ', a delicate term indeed in an era of totalitarian parties in Germany, Italy and Russia. But all in vain. The local machines defeated the President. American political parties are far from the solidarity of British political parties, and the President continued to be plagued by party divisions. Such opposition springs not merely from disagreement with the President's policy, but from the pride of men who have a high estimate of themselves, or an inferiority complex. Jealousy for the legislative rights of Congress is unbelievably extreme, even among the President's friends ; where the true opposition is concerned, it rises to the margin of hatred.

It would be a mistake, therefore, to see in the presidential leadership of Mr. Roosevelt anything of permanent and irreversible significance for the Presidency as an office. The Presidency will always be more powerful, if a future incumbent intends it to be, as a result of the daring precedents set by Mr. Roosevelt. It will also have gained authority because, with the increase of governmental activity supported by the favourable breeze of the Supreme Court, all organs of American Government will inevitably be less negative than before. For when constitutional limitations on governmental power are removed by the Supreme Court's decisions or by constitutional amendment, the potentialities of the Presidency benefit no less than those of Congress. However, presidential leadership will still be limited by the firm constitutional powers assigned to Congress over legislation and financial appropriation, and by its immense jealousy for these. And it will be further limited by the want of integration of Congressmen into political parties which would be real communities based on principle, out of whose body the President would arise, and which would simultaneously formulate the policy and select and support the man. Presidents, therefore, will still be frustrated by dissension in their own party ; and may be seriously defeated by a change in party strength in mid-term elections. These contingencies were well exemplified by party dissension from 1933 onwards, and especially since November 1942, owing to a large increase in Republican strength in both Houses (in the House of Representatives almost wiping out the Democratic majority), more particularly as the presidential contest of 1944 loomed into view.

Indeed, in the 1944 campaign the Republican strategy against Mr. Roosevelt was partly based on the appeal that if he were returned he could not govern, because there would be a Republican House of Representatives, and therefore a Republican president was necessary.

And, some argued also, that though there would be a *Democratic Senate* (as only one-third were up for re-election), the majority would be 'anti-New Deal!' and the necessary two-thirds vote for any treaties on post-war reconstruction might not be available.

From January 1943 Congress became exceedingly restive and repeatedly clashed with the President on the principal issues of manpower mobilization, price control, taxation policies, inflation, the claims of the Farm Bloc to high prices.[59]   On all of these the President's proposals were more rigorous than those acceptable to Congress. Early in 1944, there was a serious rift between the President and Congress on the provision of ballots for the Congressional and Presidential elections of 1944.   The President proposed federal distribution and collection of the ballots to all Forces overseas ; Congress opposed, arguing this would interfere with the usual 'States' Rights' to organize elections for these offices.   Some Southern Democrats even argued that only if the States remained in full possession of their rights could the negro voters be 'properly' treated !   In a Message on the bill as passed and sent to him by Congress, the President threw all responsibility for the result on Congress, ruefully letting the bill pass without either approval or veto,[60] for it maintained state control unless a state Governor certified otherwise.   As predicted, it was a fiasco.

In war time, the leadership of the presidency becomes broader than ever ;   for the President, besides being responsible for the faithful execution of the laws, is also Commander-in-Chief, and is naturally looked to in a time of danger.   These powers are tremendous (Vol. II, p. 1019) ; they are, indeed, as incapable of definition as the emergencies they may have to meet.[61]   Hence, the powers of Mr. Roosevelt which had been on the wane just before the U.S.A. entered the war, suddenly assumed new and epic proportions.   What the President did in 1941, before Pearl Harbour, was greater than what he could do in 1939 and 1940 ; but what he could do after Pearl Harbour was gigantic, and the national spirit as well as the presidential determination could be felt palpably to have undergone a transformation.   Yet Congress repeatedly challenged and beset the Executive leadership, not always by any means with war measures and men as appropriate as the President's, and called for and received frequent presidential rebukes in messages and vetoes.[62]   Some indication of the quality of this tension may be gathered from a passage in the President's Message to Congress on Labour Day, 1942, requiring the repeal of a law that it had passed in February, that, for the benefit of the farmers, had allowed large increases in the price of food.   The President asked that Congress should put a ceiling on prices, and so reject the increases demanded by the Farm Bloc.

I ask Congress to take this action by the first of October.   Inaction on your part by that time till leave me with an inescapable responsibility towards my country to see to it that the war effort is no longer imperilled by the threat of economic chaos. In the event that Congress should fail to act and act adequately . . . the President has the power under the constitution and under the Congressional acts to take measures necessary to avert a disaster which would interfere with the winning of the war.

In the same Message, the President assured the people that he would use his powers for one and only one end, to defeat the national enemies, after which their privileges would revert to them where they belonged.

It is to be appreciated, then, that the Presidency is at once the office of a national and world statesman, of a party leader, and an administrative general manager. Each demands different qualities. The first requires policies which may benefit and blend all groups and interests steadily over long-term periods and add to the permanent wealth, prestige, culture and diverse capacities of a nation as a single social unit and its ability to fulfil the obligations of a world order. The second calls for shrewdness in the defeat of opposition in his own ranks and the rival parties, and combining the group egoisms of the many sections to their respective satisfactions and the general good. The third requires a few additional observations.

The Federal Government of the United States is a mighty machine with nearly one million employees in time of peace, and its actions and influence extend powerfully to the States and the municipal governments.[63] The President is the centre, and properly the driving centre, of the articulating apparatus of the American nation. This implies the duty to see that of alternative operations those may be implemented which are in harmony with the policies of administration and Party, and without inner contradictions ; to co-ordinate collateral administrative departments ; to exercise a control over policy, and fulfil the function assigned to him by the Budget and Accounting Act of 1921 to submit a budget to Congress ; to give drive and pace and animation to the colossal code of laws that otherwise would remain a dead letter. The existence of departmental chiefs and cabinet officers and boards of directors and commissioners heading the many departments, and the hundreds of thousands of employees, only brings the task within the realm of feasibility. To come to grips at all seriously with it the President needs administrative ability of the first order, and a machinery of personal assistants. The latter, and other reforms to integrate and make more taut the pattern of administrative facilities, have already been discussed. The grave question, and it is anxious, not censorious, is whether in the American system, with a growing governmental responsibility for economic and social initiative, this is enough.

To judge by experience it almost certainly is not. For, though it is equipped administratively, and strongly supported by the electorate, the presidency suffers from a permanent weakness, namely, the unreliability of its support, co-operation and encouragement in Congress. This issues fundamentally from the Separation of Powers as organized by the Constitution, and especially the banishment of the Executive from attendance on the floor of Congress. This banishment is procedural and conventional; it is no part of the written constitution.[64] But even if, as has been suggested many times, and insistently during World War II, even if Cabinet Officers and others were brought into Congress to give information and be questioned, the object, a close correspondence between the two, their exchange of influence, would still hardly be achieved. Indeed, the arrangement might simply create additional friction and trouble for the Executive, by revealing differences, which because there was no power to cure them, might fester. For Congress has no authority over the President, and the President lacks authority over Congress. Congressional criticism could make a Cabinet Officer wince, but it could not make the President wilt. He could continue support of a Cabinet Officer disliked by Congress, and dismiss with impunity those who were its favourites. That is the harsh and skeletal truth about the government of the United States. While the powers remain separated, this form of government can never secure that steadiness of leadership, that clarity of Executive or legislative policy, that distinguishes the British Constitution. Yet legislators, nevertheless, may prefer the traditional separation of powers to better government. To them, it may be a gratification they are prepared to pay for. The resulting collisions and waste, even to the point of economic collapse, may be consciously risked and accepted. It certainly ought not to be risked otherwise than consciously. It may be thought that a land so rich as the U.S.A. can afford such risks. But, if it should happen that improvement is wanted, there is only one way, and it is ineluctable: to establish a true Cabinet system of the British type.[65] Nor should it be forgotten that one-third of the nation has been presidentially declared to be ill-housed, ill-fed, ill-clothed.

During World War II, the Administration was able to achieve much by use of the power of Commander-in-Chief, much again as legislative leader in the sense already presented, and very considerable advances, as the conductor of foreign relations. On the Executive side, remarkable prodigies of leadership and organization were performed, yet with an excessive expenditure of time, energy and funds. Authority in the major administrative conduct of the war was distributed, but the authority was ill-defined, and when disputes occurred, it was found that the authority, indeed, was not fully devolved. Sometimes, where the authority was clear, the men were not well-chosen. The failures were not always removed; but, instead, co-ordinating administrators were set above them and the other agencies with whom they had come into conflict. Again and again, this process occurred, and it was not until late in 1942 that anything like a War cabinet was set up.

Where, in essence, was the fault ? It may be in the good nature of the President, which prevents swift and summary change of policy and men.[66] But there is probably a deeper-seated cause, springing from the very nature of the constitutional responsibility of the President. In the American system all constitutional responsibility is concentrated uniquely in one man. It is an awful burden. If that man is sensitive to obligations, and conscientious in his wish to live up to the highest traditions of democratic public service, is it possible for so unique a responsibility to be distributed to others who may make mistakes, which, in the system, must necessarily ricochet to the person of the President ? In the British Cabinet system, a whole cabinet assumes corporate responsibility. The psychological and moral burden is carried not merely by the Prime Minister : it falls equally on every participant in Cabinet decisions. Each can fortify and encourage the other, and each knows that the rest also bear a responsibility for any initiative he or the whole Cabinet takes, and cannot disavow it in adversity. The distribution of both authority and responsibility occurs corporately ; the distribution of responsibility is actually decided by the whole body among whom the power is diffused. Therefore, there can be both tolerable certainty and definition in the sharing of power, and so there is a standing inducement not to concentrate it in, nor to refer it back to, a single person, but to spread it.

A Prime Minister finds particular comfort in this political brotherhood of the Cabinet, and during the present War, Mr. Churchill has taken pains to rest upon his colleagues, and to let it be known publicly that he does so, although he has acknowledged that he has the leading responsibility : ' I take constitutional responsibility for everything that is done or not done, and am quite ready to take the blame when things go wrong . . .' [67] Moreover, the moral assistance of the House of Commons is of profound importance : ' To try and carry on the War without the aid and guidance of the House of Commons would be a super-human task.' [68] All this, by the way, merely underlines the gravity of the mistake made by those critics of the British system who are enslaved by the fallacy that the House of Commons and the Cabinet are separate bodies. Their connexion is seamless.

Thus, the British system encourages the distribution and active exercise of authority, because it is founded on the sharing of responsibility. The American presidential system discourages the distribution of executive authority because it burdens one man with all the responsibility for everything and everybody. In this case, as in all aspects of social life, excessive responsibility is a depressant, and causes a paralysis of will accompanied by fitful and volatile interventions and feverish retreat.

The comparative weakness of the American presidential system and its Congressional organs becomes clear if we consider a claim made frequently during World War II by Congressmen, that they should be allowed to participate more closely in the conduct of the War— allowed, that is to say, by the President.[69] The British Parliament and the British Cabinet co-operate so intimately that it is difficult to discern their seam of separation, for in war as in peace they are parts of a single body. In Britain, it was possible to arrange a ' political truce ' between the opposed political parties, and to form a Cabinet by their coalition. And Parliament, being the sovereign political organ, can, if the national interest requires it, prolong its own existence beyond the legal term of five years.

But in the U.S.A. the Constitution prescribes the duration of the House and the Senate and the President ; it knows nothing of dissolutions of the assemblies, and therefore requires periodical elections. There is no way, excepting a constitutional amendment, of averting this difficulty. If, then, at every second year Congressional, and every fourth, Presidential, elections must be held, the parties are in a permanent state of irresoluble hostility. The institutions compel them to discover causes of opposition additional to the normal ones, and to expose to the public their infirmities. As is the way with those who wish to retain office, as well as those who wish to obtain it, exaggeration becomes the governor of conscience.

Congress has, indeed, attempted to participate in the war effort ; and in its *Special Committee Investigating the National Defence Programme* under Senator (now President) Henry S. Truman, accomplished a titanic work of investigation and remedial recommendations, of wider scope and deeper penetration than the British Select Committee on National Expenditure. But in its zeal Congress erred by setting up too many Committees on various aspects of war administration, for they numbered, with the usual standing and special ones, over forty in the Senate and fifty in the House, with a consequent overlapping and an exceedingly serious drain on the time of military and civil officials who must attend them to be interrogated.[70]

This disintegration itself frustrates the co-operation of Executive and Legislature, but there is a more fundamental institutional reason why collaboration is impossible. The President, not having a sure and certain following in each House, dare not inform all the members of those secrets without which the making of policy is illusory. There have been examples (Senator Borah's scornful rejection of the White House opinion that war was about to start in Europe, the Burton Wheeler disclosure of the occupation of Icelandic bases, and other leakages of official information, for example, from the State Department) which suggest grave doubt whether all Congressional members could be informed without a tangible risk to the nation. Is the

President to bear that risk ?   Suppose then, that, as has been proposed, there were either a Joint Committee of both Houses, or a small Committee of each, to co-operate with the Administration and to receive information. It is very doubtful whether Congressmen excluded from the Committee would tolerate its continued existence. They would ask of this Committee what the Committee had asked of the President ; and sooner or later they would obtain it. If information were not obtained directly, it would float about as rumour. This might be politically worse than the direct divulgence of the truth, as various episodes of Washington columnists demonstrate. The Chief Executive could never be sure that the engagement of confidence and full faith between the Committee and himself could ever be worth the poor risk of Congress's enactment of his policy. The President's responsibility, being already excessive, it would become further burdened by as many additional anxieties as there were Congressmen to whom information had been given. There is no coherent and continuous fellowship of trust between President and Congress. He cannot rely implicitly, as the British Prime Minister can, on permanent and assured support (while of good behaviour, of course), by one political party or a sound coalition of parties. For American parties are themselves split by sections, ideas, interests. It is not ignorance that keeps Congress from a deeper and more intimate part in the conduct of war. The amount of information at its disposal, for example, on manpower, rationing, and taxes, has indeed been overwhelming. It is the disintegration of policy in each party ; the cleavage and intensely bitter partisanship between the parties ; [71] the constitutional compulsion to divide the country in election years ; and the separation of powers ; that exclude Congress from the share that the legislature should take, and the moral elevation it would derive from such co-operation. And this also denies the Presidency the assistance and moral encouragement that he should receive from Congress. The fault lies deep in the system.

The Supreme Court and the New Deal

The President had declared his belief that his reforms could be fulfilled with the Constitution as it stood ; but he also suggested that if this proved wrong, then changes ought to be made in the revered document. Ample demonstration has been made (Vol. I, Chap. VII.) of Chief Justice Hughes's maxim that ' The constitution is what the judges say it is '. It was to be the nation's experience that if time were allowed the President, the Supreme Court would, as the philosopher Dooley observed, ' follow th' iliction returns '. It is possible that if all the New Deal legislation had been passed during the short period of intensest feeling in the year 1933, and if the Supreme Court had passed on measures like the N.I.R.A. and A.A.A. there and then, it would have been sufficiently affected by public opinion and overawed by the evidences of social catastrophe to validate it when challenged. But long intervals between legislation and adjudication are in fact, a distinctive feature of American judicial review. Furthermore, the Court could not be consulted beforehand, since unlike the Canadian Supreme Court it does not give advisory opinions. There were aged men on the Court who were not so easily to be coaxed out of their habits of mind in social matters. The principal New Deal legislation was brought before the Court in 1935 and 1936,[72] and with weak exceptions,[73] invalidated, and invalidated because it ' took away property ',[74] or infringed the rule that Congress could not give the Executive powers of administration which were not very closely defined in standards,[75] or used the power to tax as a means of regulating commerce which was not interstate,[76] or generally regulated powers which belonged to the States.[77] Passionate feeling was aroused by both the endeavour to legislate on the lines of the New Deal, and the judicial hostility to it. The small margins against the laws especially excited the public and Congressmen, while the better informed were dismayed by the divisions of opinion among majority and minority on the Court. The ' liberal ' dissenting judges, especially Justices Stone and Cardozo, seemed to express views reasonable, apt and appropriate to the economic system of the time. What they then argued became, only a little later, the opinion of the Court and the law of the land. (See Note 83.) How remote, how slender, how uncertain the ground of the majority for such sweeping social decisions ! Economic conservatives were, on the other hand, filled with triumph. At least one newspaper bore the Stars and Stripes on its shoulder, and thanked God heartily for the existence of the Court.

Many proposals had been advanced in the past for dethroning the Court from its sovereign position in the Constitution.[78] The President's determination to take action had been clearly implied in the Democratic platform of 1936 :

> We know that drought, dust-storms, floods, minimum wages, maximum hours, child labour and working conditions in industries, monopolistic and unfair business practices cannot be adequately handled exclusively by 48 separate state legislatures, 48 separate state administrations, and 48 separate state courts. Transactions and activities which inevitably overflow state boundaries call for both state and federal treatment. We have sought and will continue to seek to meet these problems through legislation within the constitution.

On 5 February 1937, the President produced a singular legislative project to deal with the Court. He proposed a bill to appoint an additional judge to the Court whenever a judge had reached the age of 70 and had failed to retire, but such appointments should not increase the number of the Court above 15. (The law would apply also to the whole federal judiciary, and the limit of numbers would be 50.)

This oblique policy of reform was probably chosen because the simplest popular appeal against the Court related to the age of its members : three of the conservatives (Von Devanter, McReynolds and Sutherland) were aged 78, 75 and 75 respectively. But Chief Justice Hughes was also 75 ; Justice Brandeis, 80 ; and Justice Butler, 71. The others were 65 and under. The intent, however, to pack the Court was so clear that the President aroused a fierce storm of feeling, evidently unexpected. It blew up not merely among the Republican opposition, but in his own party.[79]

In spite of the strenuous efforts by the Senate Democratic Party leader in the Judiciary Committee of the Senate, and the application of rewards and the strongest pressure, the proposal was rejected by ten to eight (seven Democrats being in the hostile majority) and by seventy to twenty in the Senate itself. The net result in legislation was two laws. The first, before the Report of the Senate Committee, permitted the retirement of Supreme Court Justices with ten years of service, at 70 with full pay. The second gave the Federal Government the opportunity to be heard through the Department of Justice on statutes attacked as unconstitutional in the District Courts, providing for speedy review thereof by the Supreme Court, for the transfer of judges to congested jurisdictions.

In the six volumes of Hearings [80] before the Judiciary Committee, witnesses, especially the most distinguished professors of constitutional law (who naturally disagreed on history, law, and policy), struck two clear notes. The first was, that it was open to Congress to form and reform the judiciary including the Supreme Court, exactly as it wished (though, of course, only a constitutional amendment could seriously change the character and spirit of the Court), yet that there existed something like a convention that the Court ought not to be subject to such manifest political interference. Secondly, the politicians distrusted themselves and their fellows : they could not believe in their own collective political virtue, reason, or self-control. Hence, it was necessary that the supreme political control which the Court exerts in the form of judicial power to invalidate be maintained. The alternative suggestion, of a constitutional amendment to include permission for the Congress to pass legislation of a broad economic and social nature, of the character of the New Deal, and suitable to the contemporary condition of mind and facts of the nation, was regarded as wildly impossible, given the difficulty of the amending process. And even if it could have been passed how could such an article be so worded as *not* to be susceptible of emasculating inter-pretation by the Court ?

The principal observations of the hostile Majority Report were that the bill did not banish age from the Bench, nor avoid divided decisions, nor affect the power of the Court to hold laws unconstitutional, nor withdraw from any judge the authority to grant injunctions. But, it did subjugate the Court to the will of Congress and the President, and therefore, destroyed the independence of the judiciary, the only certain shield of individual rights.

The President's bill was defeated after 168 days of struggle. But the Court, simultaneously with the struggle in Congress and the mounting public indignation, changed its attitude towards New Deal measures. Perhaps impressed by the election returns of November 1936, it made the 'switch in time that saved nine'. In March 1937 it upheld (5 to 4) the Washington State Minimum Wage Law; [81] in April, it upheld (5 to 4) the National Labour Relations Act; [82] in May, it upheld (5 to 4) the Social Security Act and attendant acts and cases which involved a federal tax for unemployment insurance purposes, allowing action which had previously been held to be only within State authority and financial assistance to this object, and also to provide old-age pensions, under the 'general welfare' clause. The decisions on this last set of cases, especially the 'general welfare' judgment, more than any other single decision, made the U.S.A. a dynamic nation-state as compared with its previous status of a rather negative federation of 48 states. The way was wide open for economic and social change : the Court henceforth could never again shut the open door : it could only see that Congress did not entirely tear it off the hinges.[83] These decisions weakened the argument for reform, as did the resignations of two conservative judges, one during the conflict and another soon afterwards, and the appointment in their place of men of different outlook. Thenceforth, all major cases of a New Deal nature were validated.

The net result of New Deal legislation, of the resolute spirit that went to its making and its public vindication, and the impact of political forces on the composition and outlook of the Supreme Court, was to expunge the principle of economic *laissez-faire* from the tables of interpretation hitherto applied by the Court (Vol. I, Chap. VII), in spite of its dissident members, and to recognize an authority in the Congress for the welfare of the whole country, the powers of the states and the reservations of the Tenth amendment, notwithstanding. The U.S.A. had acquired a new constitution. For in the generation since the turn of the 19th century, the economy of the United States had become a unified nation-wide web, and its national and international stresses and strains had impelled both industrialists and labour to solicit the benefits of governmental assistance. From the highest organization of all—the State—a contribution to planned progress, to take advantage of the great advances in science and invention, was in diverse ways universally demanded. America's experience was a new experience, beyond that of the judges whose education ended around 1885 ; and, as Justice Holmes said in his *Common*

Law : ' The life of the law has not been logic ; it has been experience.'

The Supreme Court exercises a negative function : for what it upsets it sets up no alternative as might a parliamentary opposition. But when it has stated the grounds of its decision clearly and comprehensively, it has enabled Congress and the Administration to devise an acceptable alternative, salvaging at least something, in a fresh law which takes note of the indicated permissions.   This was done in the case of the New Deal's agricultural policy, its encouragement of labour unions, and the regulation of the coal industry.

Since the Court has changed in composition, and therefore in mind, and is permeable by economic change as proposed by Congress, the clamour for reform or abolition of the Court has almost entirely died down.   The liberals are content ; the conservatives bide their time, making electoral capital out of the charge of ' packing ', since the Court does not, as usual, contain a recent Republican appointee (although Justice Roberts was appointed by President Hoover, and Chief Justice Stone, by President Coolidge !).

Although the Court has in the past been conservative as to economic and social reforms, it must be acknowledged to have three merits.

(*a*) In insisting on the reality of ' state's rights ', whether as a champion of them, or as an apparently reluctant but reasonable person who thinks they must be modified or overruled for better government, it has made it clear that if they are to be reduced, this should not be done by strained interpretations of ' interstate commerce ', but by constitutional amendment ; and, if that way towards an overdue adjustment of the claims of centralization and decentralization cannot be travelled, then the way of administrative re-adjustment between Federal Government and States must be sought.   *Helvering* v. *Davis* and the other Social Security Cases (see Note 83) are especially conscious of the problem of government involved.

(*b*) The Court has also (e.g. the *Schechter Case*) made it clear that if there is to be a delegation of sublegislative power to the Executive, it must be subject to standards stated by Congress and procedural safeguards in their administration.   This has called Congress and the Executive to an acknowledgment of their respective obligations.

(*c*) The Supreme Court has been a conservator of civil rights.[84] This is the beneficent aspect of its guardianship of the rights of persons and property, inadequately emphasized by non-American teachers to non-American students through the debris and dust and missiles of economic controversy.   To confine ourselves to recent years alone, in a long line of important cases, and in a firmness and elegance of language reinforcing respect for the rights so preserved, the Court has denied the right of a state to compel attendance at public elementary schools alone ; denied the right of another state to suppress newspapers on the ground that they were publishing malicious, scandalous or defamatory material; defended peaceful picketing; upheld participation in the public meetings or distributing the literature of radical groups, and distributing literature and holding meetings without permission of the public authorities; denied the right to exclude negroes from primary elections and from the law school of a state university; upheld trial by jury and meticulously fair and impartial criminal procedure (conspicuously in cases concerning negroes in southern states); quashed convictions secured by third-degree methods; denied the right of a public authority to subject the solicitation of money for religious or charitable purposes to public permit; declared invalid a state law requiring children in public schools to salute the American flag.[85]

Federalism

The U.S.A., it is manifest, is moving swiftly towards a unified economic and social system, co-extensive with its whole territory.[86] Economical administration requires large-scale operation. (Up to a point, if it is to be efficient.) The advancement of health, labour, manufactures, commerce, and morals in one state can be frustrated by the backwardness of its neighbours—an unchallengeable example is unemployment insurance systems. Higher taxes and better labour standards over the level of other states have been followed by the migration of employers and their industries to lesser-taxed places.[87] (See the acknowledgment of this by the Supreme Court in the Social Security cases.) Free mobility of labour and capital to their best prospects can be and has been obstructed by state and local differences of taxation, licensing, and, among other things, by an Employment Placement Service broken into forty-eight parts, each without any concept of the opportunities or deterrents to be encountered in distant states, which are yet part of a single country. Some states have even established barriers to migrants and commerce from other states, by imposing some sort of charge or the application of sanitary regulations for people and commodities or licences for transport vehicles, &c.[88]

Of course, whenever people and commodities are in ' interstate ' commerce the Federal Government may legislate and has legislated uniform conditions : or, where it has the power, it can formulate and has formulated different principles to suit different geographical and social conditions. But what is to be done where the popular desire for a higher standard of living, being as keen as it is, beats vainly against the poverty, the ungenerosity, or ignorance, or corruption of some state governments, yet where a uniform reasonable standard for all is a condition of the successful fulfilment of such demands ? Must children born in poorer states be doomed to inferior education ? [89] Must some states permanently suffer from inferior housing, corrupt

10

insurance inspection, business corporations whose charter has been obtained in complaisant states administered by officials of easy virtue ?   Must natural reserves, like water-power, remain in the hands of do-nothing state legislatures ?   Shall the utilities which are not interstate but which are still part and parcel of the national economy be immune from regulation by the Federal Power Commission ? How is a nation-wide market to be assured its uniformities of freedom or concerted regulation ?   What of market competition between meats and other foods and drink in interstate commerce, and so subject to the high standards of Federal inspection, with commodities displayed side by side but produced within the state, and possibly under the feeblest standards of cleanliness and purity ?   How can the moral interests of the states which prohibit or heavily regulate the alcoholic liquor traffic be defended ?   How can a national force assist the local agencies of crime control ?

Is the agriculture of the U.S.A. to be treated as one unit, and, accordingly, its policy of production and marketing to be uniformly regulated, especially in view of international agreements entered into by the Federal Government concerning the sale of certain primary farm commodities on the international market ?   Is the Federal authority to say that the marginal lands within a single state are to be abandoned in keeping with a *national* plan of soil conservation ?

New Deal legislation and the Supreme Court's attitude thereto, have clearly drawn attention to the rapid development of centralization, but they have also strongly emphasized the recognition of the need for the re-allocation of powers in a new balance, not excluding strong local organs of government.

The Constitution is, from this point of view, under tremendous strain, a strain even heavier than the similar pressures revealed by the Royal Commission on the Australian Constitution,[90] and the Rowell-Sirois Report on Canadian Dominion-Provincial Relationships.[91] Devices have, therefore, been sought, and some applied, whereby the Federal Government may assume the necessary additional authority. This has come about either by initiative where the states have not as yet used their own powers at all, or by the extension of the Federal sphere of ' general welfare ', or ' taxing ' or ' interstate ' commerce powers.   There has been a kind of transference of power from the states where these have used their authority, but inadequately, wherever the services which for full efficiency for the state no less than all its neighbours in the Republic, require large-scope treatment, most recently including insurance.[92]   Remedies for excessive state disintegration of the national economy and society are necessarily incomplete and indirect, for they have to pass the censorship of a Congress composed of representatives who hardly dare (at any rate openly and avowedly) to prefer the larger loyalty to the smaller, and of the Supreme Court.

It is impossible here to do more than merely indicate the chief methods used to bring about a higher degree of governmental integration.[93]   (1) There is a growing tendency to uniform State action fostered by the voluntary Council of State Governments and the National Conference of Commissioners on Uniform State Laws.[94] Yet action by the former is very slow, incomplete, admits of continued diversities, and is always uncertain, since it depends on subsequent action by the State legislatures.   Indeed, on the average, each of the uniform laws agreed upon (and it takes years to reach agreement) is adopted by only one-fourth of states, while in important matters the Council's work is altogether jilted.   (2) There is some slight influence exerted by the Conference of (State) Governors, sometimes meeting with Federal officials.

(3) A much more important mechanism of the re-adjustment of Federal-State powers is the Federal Grant-in-Aid.[95]   The Federal Government pays funds to the states, and sometimes directly to the cities and the counties, to implement a Federal statute.[96]   The grants are given providing Federal standards are fulfilled by the state governments, in respect of the purposes and principles of the service in question, the structure and procedure of administration, the recruitment and management of personnel, the furnishing of reports, and submission to Federal inspection.   Either or all of these conditions are applied in varying measure according to the nature of the service to be administered by this developing and peculiar partnership between national and state governments, and according to the quality of feeling in each case about the independence of the states as against the advantages to be derived from Federal assistance.   (4) Sometimes free skilled assistance in terms of advice or collaboration is rendered by the Federal Government to the states.   Here the action of the states is supplemented without obligation on their part, as for instance, by expert advice from the (now defunct) National Resources Planning Board, or the Federal Bureau of Investigation, or by the training of local officers at the same Bureau's police school.

(5) There is the growing practice by the Federal Government of conducting its own administrative agencies (e.g. the Farm Security Administration) and those in which it collaborates with the states through grants-in-aid (e.g. the Social Security Administration) in large regions, which include several states, with more or less of a common economic and social character imprinted by their geographical and production character or their contiguity.[97]   But so far there is only one truly regional governmental agency of the Federal Government (perhaps two, if we add Boulder Dam, the product of a compact made by seven states regarding the uses of the Colorado River).   It is the Tennessee Valley Authority.[98]   Yet these regional arrangements are by themselves no substantial modifiers of state powers or of the

divergencies in their use.   The states are the weak links in the American
system of government, so much so that the Federal Government has
been tempted to by-pass them and co-operate directly with the great
cities, or has sought, but hitherto not substantially found, a regional
solution.   It is improbable that the T.V.A. can be a model for the rest
of the country, for it came into existence to solve a precise local problem
based upon more than usually specific features.   Other Valley regions,
for example, the Missouri and Arkansas, have been proposed, and they
will certainly be of benefit in the solution of the two or three peculiar
local problems of their area.   But it is surely impossible to envisage
American Government conducted through a congeries of very diverse
Valley regions, or of regions on any other geographical basis pure
and simple.   The way of the grant-in-aid to the states and the cities
is at present discernible as the line of maximum progress in the
readjustment of Federal-State powers in an age which cries out for
government yet understands the need not only for administrative
decentralization but considerable local autonomy.

*   *   *   *   *   *   *

Since the death of Franklin Delano Roosevelt, on 12 April 1945, it has been impossible
not to appreciate even more acutely the significance of character and moral stature
for the functioning of the American Presidency. Though people spoke bravely about
governing themselves, it took hardly more than three months to show that such an
idea was too simple. It was soon demonstrated that effective democratic government
requires the interplay of the general body of citizens and the statesman ; that democracy
does not mean the exclusion of eminence but its contributive uses ; that the unity of
a dynamic society is a product not simply of mass, but of representative creativeness at
a responsible centre ; that the fellowship which marks a nation in its progress is in part
the product of men at the responsible summit who can relate the needs of whole social
situation to the fragmentary contending wants of millions of aggressive individuals.   No
man can rise to the ideal, and it would be perhaps too harsh for the world if he did.
But Rousseau's description of the Legislator implies the qualities at any rate which
pertain to democratic leadership.   ' A superior intelligence is needed, which perceives
all the passions of men and which for itself feels none of them ; which has no relationship with our nature, but which understands it through and through ; the happiness of
which is independent of us yet which nevertheless is anxious to serve ours ; finally,
which, as time goes on, raising up for itself a distant glory, can work in one century and
enjoy in a later.'
     In that enormously wide sub-continent, the U.S.A.—with its teeming and multi-
farious groups and regions, each robustly certain that it is good and right—the President
is in a position to see for the contenders consequences that each cannot see for himself
beyond his self-regarding horizon. He can be supreme mediator and conciliator. He
may establish a tableau of the ' national ' good sufficiently painless to all claimants to
induce agreement and relieve anger.
     Brain, energy, devotion, vision—F. D. R. possessed these qualities in the imponderable
but influential measure we call ' great '.   Soon after his passing, there being at the centre
neither a body of unifying and moving political and social principle, nor a Cabinet em-
bodying or creative of such, to continue the organizing of the ever-embattled groups, the
U.S.A. felt to its marrow the lack of that instant ' considerableness ' in the Chief Executive
which of itself and without argument enlists allegiance and trust.   Voice, style, appearance, demeanour, constitute political meaning and give meaning to argument.   Its
absence is palpable.   Things politic fall apart.   Even those who had most hated the
President—and they hated !—cried out for a rule to live by.
     When we think of the Presidency it is not a governing Man we should think of, but
a contributing Mind. For a democratic society is nothing if not a continuing many-
dimensional network of mind and mind.   It is the spiritual and psychological qualities
of the statesman rather than his formal authority that keep that network always mended,
coherent and purposeful.   In the absence of such Mind, the social fabric sags and stretches
until, embracing everything, it holds nothing.

CHAPTER VII

THE FUTURE TASK

THE principal, indeed the desperate, task of democracy is to maintain itself; its second, to improve and refine itself.

Since for centuries it has been the declared and persistent driving force of great mass movements, why should there be question of democracy's need to maintain itself?

Our own days, like those of Hobbes, have thrust upon us an awful opportunity of gazing into the deep cauldron of the social passions. In the light this has thrown, especially from 1914 down to this day, we must confess what a remarkable thing it is that so many countries still have democratic government and so many more seek it. In the world so luridly revealed, of animal forces and apostolic pretensions that variously divide men, and of ambitions and tempers that tear them apart and set them murderously against each other, the existence of even a seriously imperfect democracy, so long as it is recognizable, is a tremendous spiritual and technical victory of part of the human race. That is the primordial fact: that with all the potentialities of disruption from their darker depths to their active and flashing surface, men within and among the nations can be persuaded to stand and consult together in the same peaceful assembly, and then fulfil the accepted obligations without violence or even the show of it. It is not war, yet it is more magnificent. It is not perfect, but it is so grand a gain that men of true benevolence will widely teach its governing virtue. They will not practise the self-indulgence of not disavowing civil war, however strong and genuine their passion for social improvement.

However, the strain of democratic government is tremendous, even among the most experienced and temperate peoples, and democracy is temperance. For democratic government represents only one good among many others that men and women want and are able to choose. Many material temptations seduce from democracy. Ideas, too, can drive men mad, if we like to call it 'mad'. At least, ideas will make them precipitate and hard, and compel others to live dangerously. Also democratic government, like every human contrivance, has its costs of production and maintenance, direct costs in taxation, indirect ones in forbearance, some self-abnegation, in personal duties, in foregone material opportunities. When the democratic system seems to be secure, we are habituated to its incalculable benefits as compared with its relatively small costs; and habit is, by

N.B.—The Notes to this Chapter being on page 191.

definition, thoughtless.   We do not realize the extent of our spiritual and material assets, often bitterly paid for by others in the past ; nor the need for a continuing price which, by the way, fluctuates according to the social forces pressing on government from within and without for fulfilment.

Now, it used to be said, before society was swamped with the opinion that moral values are merely reflections of methods of economic production, that everything depends upon whether you put Truth in the first place.   The world's political future depends on whether democracy occupies the first place in our loyalties.   Nor is it important by what a short distance it wins the race over so many other competing values so long as it does win by a margin.   The fundamental condition of the maintenance and improvement of democracy is the universal and intense realization of what it signifies and entails.   The primary element in this, so elementary that it is easily forgotten, is how much superior it is for the maximum number, and in the long-run, than any other system.   It is normally superior in the short-run also ; but its justification is overwhelmingly strong as a continuing long-run principle.   No bickering about short-run economic, social, or electoral grievances or discrepancies, justifiable or indispensable as it may be to agitate these, can stand or ought to be pressed so as to eclipse the recognition of this elementary victory of human reason and self-control.   Furthermore, the use of ' long-run ' here is not such as to put the succession of short-run reforms out of mind.   Nor is the criterion ' perfect ' democracy.   The present argument is tenable in relation to the imperfect democracies we know, even the Third Republic, even the Weimar Republic, even the U.S.A. and its political bosses, even Great Britain and its still disproportionate power in the hands of a minority.   Democracy ought not to be equated with perfection, for it is not an exercise in perfectionism.   It is a painful attempt, one in a very long and forbidding series of tantalizing and bloody experiments, by imperfect mankind labouring to govern itself.   To confuse it with perfection is even to introduce an undemocratic temper into the discussion, to court unreasonable disappointment which may vent itself in a brutal reaction of impatience, and to risk falling victim to dictatorial siren songs.   But, of course, there is no reason whatsoever why any individual should postpone his own perfection until he has made absolutely sure that the machinery of government is entirely perfect.   Nor need men who declare that they are bent on an unrelenting quest for social justice be dispensed from doing justice for the benefit of their fellow-men while *en route*.

If it is to function, democracy requires sacrifices.   It is the most difficult and delicate form of government, as it is based on the accommodation of both similar and different tastes making diverse claims on a limited amount of goods.   And it is hard to say which of these—

the similarity or the difference of claims—causes the greater strain. For democratic government there is no regular or easy recourse to the bludgeon, the revolver, or the chloroform of propaganda. There is no democracy without a price : some to curb their over-mighty impulses, some to suffer patiently until a majority can be persuaded. Of all the items in the cost of democracy, vigilance, the old prescription, is in our time by far the least exacting. To avoid servitude, there are others far more complex and imperative and onerous. Yet, undemocratic forms of government require and will exact a far heavier sacrifice in the long run. For in them, though there may be a temporary consonance between government and people, and all may, for a time, seem happy and smooth and even exhilarating, yet the people are totally without the guarantee of restoring governmental wholesomeness and sanity if the government deviates from their spiritual and material needs ; and, as time passes, government cannot avoid doing this. And this is also to take no account of the values which have been surrendered by the people or seized from them, such as freedom of person, of speech, of opinion, of association, of equal treatment before the law, and the rest.

If it were argued that, after all, revolution is always available as the major corrective, it is not true that it is available in modern conditions of inquisition and automatic weapons ; but should it be, it would still by no means be a certain or durable relief. Perhaps the principal virtue of a democratic system is precisely the power it gives to citizens to repair errors made by governments when acting in their behalf, and so to repair their own mistakes of initiative or negligence. Regarded in the perspective of the millenial history of government it is a most amazing virtue. What folly to risk its abandonment as the price of some other transient value ! It is a bad habit to ask what wonders democracy will achieve ; democracy itself is the wonderful achievement.

But what is defective in western political society ? What is the malaise in democracy ? The malaise is essentially the neglect of the above-mentioned truths. But this is a fault not of the truths, but of ignorance of them. For their understanding would exercise at once a sedative and a quickening influence, whichever of these reactions were appropriate to a political situation. We may refer also to the activities of some shiny smart boys in democracies, smart as Goebbels in dictatorships, who irresponsibly play ducks and drakes with a supreme social inheritance—activities on the whole conducted more by those who have done rather well out of democracy's magnanimous protections than by the miserable who suffer from its defects.

But the preceding analysis of events in the different countries shows all too clearly that existing democracies have not yet solved certain pressing problems, of which two are cardinal—the economic, and the abolition of war. Some also complain that democracy does not give men a sense of a noble mission or scope for adventure. Others that it does not give opportunities to the abnormally able. In France, it was accused of inefficiency, that is, wastefulness in the efforts it undertook as well as the paucity of its social reforms. We may learn the value of the criticisms by asking who were the critics. Some are genuinely self-centred men whose ruling desire is to dominate others for economic or other reasons. They dislike democracy because it is an obstruction to their economic monopolies, privileges, inherited benefits, status or power. Yet it is rare that persons of marked ability and social goodwill need lack a share in government, fully proportionate to their qualities, whether by direct or by literary influence. Those, on the other hand, who ask for more than this are quite properly curbed ; indeed, they usually get less curbing than would be desirable. There are, however, many critics of sincere social goodwill whose honest motive is the improvement of the situation and opportunities of the poor masses. To them, democratic government is such that it will not answer this question at all, or at best will only answer it so slowly and incompletely that other measures ought to be adopted, even revolution.

Before we consider the answer which the people must give to these questions, let us recall and never forget what remarkable gifts democracies already provide. First, practically all men and women are entitled to choose their own government at periodical elections. Nothing but their own reparable ignorance, laziness, apathy and self-centred pettiness stand between their political ideas and wishes (if any, and some have none) and the kind of government which would fulfil them, except the obstructive interests of certain minorities. But even such monopolies and privileges, and even cunning election and economic tactics, could not hope to prevail against the clear mind and resolution of the majority. Wherever there is free access to books there is the prospect of justice. Wherever any two men may talk together freely, political and economic dictators are doomed. Time may unite the majority divided against itself by ignorance or egoism, and democracy offers the guarantee of free persuasion in time. Second, and with the same reservations as the first, it is open to the people to throw out incompetent legislators, and even, by pressure through the executive, to cast out administrators in the subordinate parts of government. Third, there is the wide-open opportunity, so wide that opportunity assumes the aspect of an obligation, to participate actively in the government. Fourth, there is a set of rights, implicit, explicit and guaranteed—rights to self-development, to think, read, speak, write, publish, to hear and choose what best suits the listener, to be tranquil under orderly processes, to equal treatment by the law and before the law courts, and therefore the rights to resist and defeat stupidity, tyranny, greed and cruelty. Such rights as these are essential to the exercise of political power : but without political power, that is the power to elect and cashier legislators and the executive at will, these rights are merely held on sufferance. Fifthly, democracy allows that amount of political unity which assists the dynamic operation of all the processes of society without expensive interruption and destructive force. I am only too acutely aware of all the little holes and some big ones that can be gnawed in each of these mighty pillars : but the pillars stand, are stout and constitute a titanic human achievement. *We* can look down on forty centuries ! Democracy, understood in this sense, will almost certainly lead to progress, and, so far as it is wanted and is generally regarded as just, towards economic equality ; it has done so already and very considerably, though its task is by no means complete. But economic equality is, in itself, not a guarantee of democracy, and therefore in itself is no guarantee of its own continuation. Yet, if we may truly count our democratic assets, and especially if we wish to preserve them, there are remedial tasks that must be performed, and the sooner the better.

Democracies, as we have seen, have been shaken and some have been shattered by foreign shocks and by war. Democracy can only securely exist in each country if it exists securely everywhere. More especially is this true of the larger and powerful countries ; powerful, and therefore capable of doing more harm if their polity permits it. In democratic lands, foreign shocks produce self-preservative reactions either of defence or of submissiveness to anti-democratic leaders. Democracy becomes second to other things. There is a danger to all democracies in the possibility of the emergence of a dictatorial policy, economic or military, but especially the latter, anywhere. Therefore, there must be established a world convention, arranging, and guaranteeing by sanctions if necessary, the basic features of democratic government—the legislature and the executive formed and reformed periodically by universal franchise. The tired idea that in this age any nation may freely build or maintain a system of government which tends to war or to domestic brutality and brutalization is still held by many people and statesmen. But it is at least as untenable as allowing diphtheric and tuberculous patients freely to circulate and ride in a bus.

Far graver than the foregoing observations (and in fact a condition of solving the problem they reflect) is the lack of comprehension among the masses of their political responsibilities to their nation and the world. Never were so many people so conscious of their political power as to-day. This result was the basic intention of the democratic pioneers, and in this respect they have indeed triumphed. And even more millions are becoming more profoundly conscious of social processes and the cares of government.

During the First World War, an irreparable shock was administered to the authority of the traditional governing classes in the western world. It was caused by the wide and almost immediate publicity regarding governmental incompetence in the conduct of the War. Where there was victory the cost was excessive ; where there was defeat there was accusation. Together with this discovery, which itself was a political education, formal education was everywhere extended. The issues of the day brought men and women into politics. The influence of Soviet Russia was colossal, since its declared theory was that the State wholly belongs to all the people, and even at its weakest moment it defeated foreign armies. With more rationality there was less authority ; with less authority, more questions ; yet there was insufficient political cultivation on which, confidently because wisely, that rationality could be grounded. The new citizens were not equipped to survey the whole process of society and history, and within this, the place and conditions of their self-government. The economic distress of the inter-war years, whether due to domestic or international causes, in deepening their anxiety widened men's horizons, and awakened persistent questioning. Above all, the dreadful sufferings of the Second World War, the dispersion of families, the mass transfer of men and women from their usual occupations, homes and neighbourhoods, compel them to inquire into the causes of these upheavals, and seek to locate responsibility.

Millions upon millions of ordinary men and women have eaten of the tree of political knowledge, and they can no longer be the same innocents, nor can their governments be the same guilty. But the many conscious and, therefore, restive millions are becoming harder to manage, and, what is far more important, and indeed, decisive, they find it harder to manage themselves. For while they sense the importance and opportunities of power and the right of political self-determination, they are still deficient in an informed and cultivated consciousness, whether of the fullness of their rights, or, most certainly, of the duties of a political sovereign. And that they are sovereigns is sure : for collectively they have replaced irresponsible autocrats. They are far from fully understanding the processes of government ; indeed, too many are without an inkling of these. More importantly, they are unconscious of the inter-connexions, invisible, complex yet inexorable between governments, and all the social and economic processes, and themselves. They do not regard themselves as the government with all the active responsibilities this implies, but rather as passive subjects or neutrals or as a crowd of carefree and inert, gum-chewing supers, content with the right of murmuring, until like a thunder-clap they are overtaken by unemployment or ordered to march off to war. The footlights lie between them and their government, though they themselves are indeed the true actors.

' They ' is not confined to the under-privileged or poor, but to people in all levels of society, all occupations, to rich and poor alike. At moments of decision, there is a want of political composure and judgment, and dynamic self-control ; sometimes there is an interjection of violence on a petty or large scale into a process which should be one of steady, if anxiously contested, accommodation among disputing individuals and groups. Especially is there a faulty choice between present goods and the long-run good. ' Short views we take, nor see the lengths behind,' says Pope.

The trouble and the task is not primarily in classes ; but primarily in the individuals who constitute them, and who can and will and do abandon them wholly or partly at their own whim. It is very easy to gloss over this very tough problem of individuals and ride away on the class dynamics of government. It is, indeed, simple and tempting to sum up the past in a Marxian sentence, and the present and all the future in a single, short, apocalyptic phrase, much as the dictators have done or their sophists have done for them. It is astounding, indeed, that some even repeat the Marxian idea that individual differences cancel out, except that they wish they could be cancelled, since this certainly simplifies thinking and governing. For if government is founded on opinion, and if revolutions begin in the mind, are not we, who wish men well through government, ourselves governed by individual men's eternal anxieties regarding death, self-sacrifice, reward and punishment, race, children, dominion over others, the validity of force and the uses of cruelty, other people's rights, glory and ambition, national greatness and patriotic duty, work and vocation, economic security, the burden and priority of economic effort relative to other satisfactions, the ways of God to man ? Especially in a time of domestic and world-wide crisis is it impossible to ignore these questions, because the answer to them for each individual determines the strength and the direction of his loyalties, even to groups, even to classes, and of course to the nation ! They are at the base of all politics and government. The task for our time is to relate millions upon millions of individuals to the whole of society, to their classes and to other classes, and traversing any particular class, and through and beyond it to the nation and the great globe itself. Each social group is the centre and prey of complex and contradictory wishes and so is each individual. Their state of mind is not simple. Over and above these collective or individual units, their clarification and interlacing are necessary. The unity of each nation and the unity of the world are the primary quests of democracy, and the first thing democracy somehow has to serve. In extreme cases of disunity there may be civil war ; or, as we have seen, nations may be subjugated by an oppressor and have their self-determination altogether destroyed. But not reaching these bitter extremes, it is urgent to secure the least friction and discontent compatible with the fullest production and the most favourable distribution of economic wealth and the maintenance of the moral bases of democratic society, that is, the whole range of civil rights.

This is not possible unless each individual can learn to abandon the self-satisfaction of disruptive egoism. With enlightened individuals the group egoisms of our time could never have had the power they have exerted in some cases, as in France, to their own destruction, and in all countries very close thereto.

It is impossible and dangerous to ignore that one of John Stuart Mill's wisest observations about democracy is neglected :

In any political election, even by universal suffrage . . . the voter is under an absolute moral obligation to consider the interest of the public, not his private advantage, and give his vote to the best of his judgment, exactly as he would be bound to do if he were the sole voter, and the election depended upon him alone. . . . His vote is not a thing in which he has an option ; it has no more to do with his personal wishes than the verdict of a juryman. It is strictly a matter of duty ; he is bound to give it according to his best and most conscientious opinion of the public good. Whoever has any other idea of it is unfit to have the suffrage. . . . Instead of opening his heart to exalted patriotism and the obligation of public duty, it awakens and nourishes in him the disposition to use a public function for his own interest, pleasure or caprice : the same feelings and purposes, on a humbler scale, which actuate a despot and oppressor.

There are group interests, and since we necessarily live in a democratic world, this is the age of government by bargaining and adjustment among interests. But what is the alternative to their reconciliation ? Forcible repression of some by others, or by a prepotent interest ? Reconciliation of a durable, and therefore peaceful and orderly kind, cannot occur simply at the level of group representation, for by that stage contentious dispositions are likely to be hardened, not only against other groups but even in the group leaders in relation to their own membership. That is shown by the short, brutish record of the Italian Corporate system ; it is shown in the relationship of economic groups and interested parties in all democratic countries. Reconciliation is durably to be discovered only in the pattern of the State that commends itself to the individuals, the pattern that is laid up in the heaven of the individual's own consciousness, in the individuals who are at once members of the lesser groups and members of the all-inclusive group. The operation of the Corporate State in Italy, so far as we can argue from that immature and truncated experience, destroyed unity ; the Guild Socialist nostrum has always been justly vulnerable to the criticism that though (even because) it would bind men in the many smaller Guild publics, it would blind them to the major unity of the national and international public. The conclusion is ineluctable : ' Back to the individual, he who makes, unmakes, enters and leaves classes, who makes and unmakes nations and their government.' The individual is a much graver and more difficult problem for democracy than classes ; and perhaps that is why there has been a flight from the individual to the class in explaining the nature and problems of government.[1] There is a shocking fatalism in the ascription of dynamic force to classes ; it leads to government not by responsible insight but by armed cliché.

There are two problems to be solved in the relationship of individual egoism to the nation and the world : the problems of knowledge and feeling. Some citizens know and do not care ; some care but do not know ; some neither know nor care ; and some, worse still, are not interested in either knowing or caring. Is it possible to get the facts and teach the facts of the individual's visible bonds to government— still more, the viewless network binding them in regular association with their fellows in their own great society which is but fragmentary and incomplete unless the dovetailed projections of world society are taken into consideration also ? For, at any moment, a critical situation may require that the average man shall act as a supreme statesman by supporting or repudiating the course taken by his government—so, for example, in the years before Munich, so in coping with the economic crisis of 1929 to 1939, so in the successive crises of the Second World War, and so, it is to be expected, in the coming years when it is ended. All may depend on time, perhaps, indeed, on critical hours. The decisive millions crowded away from their classes and rushed in droves to the Swastika ! They had not been taught to recognize a danger signal and that in a crisis only readiness to die may purchase a good life. It is true that the many must rely on leaders ; but to support, follow or reject them is itself a kind of leadership, and it is required from average men and women. We rely on leaders instead of being leaders ourselves because our democratic governments are still imperfect and immature, being in their infancy only. The facts of government can be discovered and taught ; they can be simplified to the point where they can be easily apprehended without losing their veracity. The stumbling which is due to confusion is remediable. The instruments of research, the radio, the film, whether documentary or fictional, and television have given us this power, and even old-fashioned schools can assist where they have able teachers and vivid accurate textbooks and a proper time-table. On this side of the problem the richest contributions have been made by H. G. Wells : one may consult *World Brain* and *The End of Homo Sapiens* and *The Shape of Things to Come*. Army education in civic affairs offers much encouragement and instruction in method.

Yet, the crucial problem is not facts and knowledge : it is feeling. Can we feel the feelings of others, and can we feel for them ? Yes ; on three conditions : if they are close to us geographically, if they are present to us constantly, and above all, *if they matter*. Is not this the essence of Aristotle's discussion on the proper size of a city, ' the largest number which suffices for the purposes of life, *and can be taken in at a single view* '. Is this not also the distillation of Rousseau's doubts about large States and his idea that between them and the individual to be represented, worms in the form of group interests get into the intestines of the State ? Let us insist again on the nature of the problem : that there must be some deliberate contrivance by government and people to secure that the facts are so presented as to bring the things and people they represent close to us geographically, to make them present constantly, and to make us realize that these matter. The Platonic Republic was founded on the supposition that the affairs of any one in the community could be made to matter to all others. He says :

> And is not that the best ordered State . . . which most nearly approaches to the condition of the individual—as in the body when a finger of one of us is hurt, the whole frame, drawn towards the soul as a centre, and forming one kingdom under the ruling power therein, feels the hurt and sympathizes all together with the part affected, and we say that the man has a pain in his finger ; and the same expression is used about any other part of the body which has a sensation of pain at suffering or of pleasure at the alleviation of suffering . . . then when any one of the citizens experiences any good or evil, the whole State will make his case their own, and will either rejoice or sorrow with him.

Thus the Platonic Republic is founded on the assumption that all will make any individual's case their own. But the problem of the twentieth century is that each individual shall make the community's case his own. In our discussion we do not assume, as Plato does, the soul as a centre already existent : our problem is precisely how, through the individual, to contribute to its creation. As Plato says a little earlier, in the best ordered State ' the greatest number of persons will apply the terms " mine " and " not mine " in the same way to the same thing '. That is the problem of modern democracy— to supply that understanding, to inculcate it in order that individuals may through their unforced choice approach the Platonic criterion. Here, however, we would be careful to observe that we neither believe in the desirability of this Platonic coalescence nor in its possibility. On its possibility something more must be said presently. The desirability of such a unity as Plato presents is denied by Aristotle who extols the plurality of life in the State. He, too, however, looks to unification, but he looks to unification not in what he calls the ' false notion of unity ' from which Socrates starts, and not to an equalization of mankind's possessions, but rather to the equalization of men's desires, and, for that, he proposes ' a sufficient education provided by the State '.

Plato's unification cannot be, because his device to secure it was not practical but metaphysical. It depended upon citizens coming back into the Republic from Heaven, reborn after having passed through certain heavenly experiences—almost an examination in political science !—and a process of selection which assured that those who did return to the mundane Republic possessed a soul in harmony with all others.

On 20 June 1940, as the dusk of prostration descended on the Third Republic, Marshal Pétain broadcast a message, the concluding words of which were : ' Stand by me. The fight goes on. It is for France, the soil of her sons.' But neither France, nor any other country, is the soil of each of her sons with that degree of felt identity which will cause men to fight for all the soil of all the other sons as though their soil were his own—unless the identity of interest is of purpose brought home to each individual. The soil of France's sons or of any other country is the soil, if there is any, of each son, not of ' her sons '. Each would fight, work, sacrifice for his. As Locke observed, his labour, his person, is mixed with his soil : it preserves him and makes him prosper : it nourishes his mate and his progeny. This, his own soil, is close, closer, Machiavelli thought, than a relative's life : for he believed that a man would rather forgive the murder of a relative than the confiscation of the relative's fortune. It seems to be true ; and if it is, why is it true ? Because the fortune secures its possessor, defends him, guarantees his development : his brother's life, not.

A sanctified command has for 2,000 years prayed, ' Love thy neighbour as thyself '. Who is my neighbour ; and how shall a distant phantom be brought close enough to matter ? Who will have regard for his fellow Frenchman, Englishman, German or American as himself ?—next door, over the street, beyond the hills and seas, away throughout the tremendous expanse of countries and continents, and, in our world, in distant time, also, for we plan. The question is why should he ? That is chiefly and ultimately a spiritual question. The other question is, can the distant citizen, the citizen on the frontier, the shadow on the horizon, be so represented as to affect the everyday feelings of the rest ? The primary question—the condition of all else—is why does it matter that it should ? For if that could be answered, then there would be the steady stimulus to the search for knowledge of the situation and the men we should know about, and the determination to establish and use those instruments of communication which would make other people's affairs and fate continuously and closely present to us. If it is true, as Burke said, that ' a man's circumstances are the preceptor of his duty ', then we can appreciate his compulsions only if we know his circumstances.

Who will find the answer to this question which will make us anxiously want to see the image of all France and England, America, Germany and all other countries, and the whole globe itself ? What

will prick our thick skins and make our teeth ache like the distant
other man's, or arouse in us the same intensity of his joys and experiences ?   How can we think of the distant millions, as Elizabeth
Browning said, and experience the same feeling of running to the
help of them as we feel when seeing a red-haired fever-stricken child ?
'. . . but a million sick . . .   You could as soon weep for the rule
of three, Or compound fractions.'   How can we overcome what André
Malraux has called ' the crevasse that separates us from universal
life ' ?   How can we burst out of the gates of the simple five senses
to the rescue of the Great Society ?   William James has said :

> Our judgments concerning the worth of things big or little depend on the
> feelings the things arouse in us . . . if we were radically feelingless and if ideas
> were the only things our mind could entertain, we should lose all our likes and
> dislikes at a stroke and be unable to point to any situation or experience in life
> more significant than any other . . . each is bound to feel intensely the import-
> ance of his own duties and the significance of the situations that call this forth.
> But this feeling is in each of us a vital secret for sympathy with which we vainly
> look to others.   The others are too much absorbed in their own vital secrets to
> take an interest in ours, hence the stupidity and injustice of our opinions, so far
> as they deal with the significance of alien lives.   Hence, the falsity of our judg-
> ments so far as they presume to decide in an absolute way on the value of other
> persons, conditions or ideals.

Yet this problem of communication and unity must be solved, in
so far as it concerns those things without which a breakdown of
domestic and international society must occur.   What persuasion can
make us care about others and so learn about others sufficiently to
care about others which means to control ourselves and make concessions ?   Is there a principle upon which such persuasion can be
founded ?

There were ages, we are told, when a principle was a faith, and
taught men their duty to men, and unified the known world.   So in
the Christian era of medieval Europe.   (Can we be sure of this, as we
anxiously scan the evidence ?)   The body of Christ was one, and all
men were its members.   (But horrible sanctions lay behind the faith,
and the works of Troeltsch and Niebuhr have demonstrated that
Christianity has always been a torn tissue of sects.)   In our own day,
however, there are profound inveterate disagreements regarding the
principle or principles of society.   In an age when patriotism was
said not to be enough, even patriotism has failed, for in most countries
there has been too little of it.   And Progress is a little tarnished.

Can a single unifying faith be found for our rationalist age ?   The
only thinkable one is that which is least vulnerable to argument.
This can only be the position itself that it is the historically demonstrable nature of man that no single transcendent principle of the
supreme good and truth exists that can carry an unchallengeable
conviction founded on revelation or scientific proof.   For the Lord

no longer says. The good and the true inhere in all of us together, and we come to their fuller recognition in ourselves and in others in the unfolding experience of society. No external and objective cosmic pattern is set above all. The pattern, if it becomes one, springs from the internal and contributory portions we each give, even in our passivity. Thus, men are thrown back on their own resources. Then, what have they to discover ? A way by which they may steadily, durably, tranquilly and with the least coercion, develop and externalize the truth in themselves, the truth of the spirit, of beauty, of economic desire and activity. At the same time they must offer, create, and defend the open way for others, because the truth is as inherent in others, and may be more important when it is expressed ; and also, out of reciprocity, to get their own claim defended. Neither revelation nor scientific proof points unchallengeably to any man or a few who possess the truth infallibly for all time and for all of us. That is the faith, pallid and cool as it may be, that may make the way to unification possible.

This defines our duty to secure and guarantee to others (who would therefore guarantee to us) the social and governmental arrangements which will constitute the maximum resistance to force and repression, give the maximum latitude for spontaneity of ideal and action to all, that is, which will keep the way open for diverse loyalties and interests, and give the least ground for any person to sacrifice another. That is the fundamental we seek. We may put it in Marx's words : ' An association . . . in which the free development of each is the condition for the free development of all.' And, therefore, when the free development of all must be supported by each, at the minimum for his own sake.

Other persuasions, of course, have been and can be advanced, why men should be concerned for each other's fate though the whole world lies between them. They may sound nobler, they may be warmer. Every man has his own passionate ideal or charity. Appeal could be made to the universal feebleness of even the mightiest, and certainly of ordinary men, praying humbly for their daily bread, before the vast undiscriminating forces of Nature. It might be pleaded that it matters to all of us to avoid the misery of any man, in the great alien world of men, where that misery is not inevitable ; for when it comes, as it must, it comes as a tribulation. Ethical and metaphysical arguments of the noblest classical and religious descent, might persuade each man that all men matter, such as the dignity of man, the brotherhood of man, the partnership of men in toil and disaster, the magnificence of mercy, the splendour of justice, the glory of compassion. Or some offer Socialism as the faith-making substitute for a faith-losing Christianity to recapture the dynamic of the martyrs. Yet all of these, it seems to us, lead back too soon to a cosmic question-mark, which finds men still divided instead of suggesting an answer which is a lasting and universal thread able to hold them together in the same easy social texture.

We need that fundamental which assumes the least of belief and effort and sustained height of enthusiasm, not that which demands too much for too long. Too high a temperature spells the dissolution of the body politic. This is a cool, a Stoic, and a stumbling creed. It is, to repeat, the tenet that a single unifying indisputable ideal cannot be found either in revelation or by scientific test. We are, therefore, driven to embrace the faith that there is none, and therefore to draw the social conclusions of this. The chief consequence is the principle of supporting everybody everywhere in the maintenance of those institutions which grant men the freedom and latitude to fit themselves, their qualities, and desires, where they can best fit themselves, with the maximum permissions and allowances of the right to dwell elsewhere in thought, opinion, occupation and place, with abundant grounds of appeal and the chance of mercy and redemption over and above the assurance of justice. That is the frame of a universal freedom, defensible by each for all because the defence of freedom for all is the maintenance of freedom for each. Inside this frame of freedom, and not transgressing or throwing it over, all faiths and minds and characters should find an initiative, limited, but avenues of development, and a not too oppressive haven from harm. This is, perhaps, the principle which will find the maximum, though not universal, acceptance ; and, therefore, will require government to exercise only the sad reluctant minimum of coercion. That is, at the least, why it matters whether the individual shall seek to identify himself with the aspirations and interests of all others, no matter of what land, race, and creed, and cast down all intermediate barriers and loyalties which obstruct it, and defend all institutions, procedures, policies and activities which promote it. The persuasion of this is possible as an ultimate faith of very many, perhaps the majority ; and, as for the rest, who still cannot find in this an adequate identifying and unifying bond, the persuasion may be accepted on the basis of expediency, that is, as empirical reciprocity and mutuality, the everyday working arrangement of live and let live.

When Rousseau's *Emile* had so far progressed with his education, the Savoyard Vicar had to confess a faith. It could have been that there was none, and that it was necessary therefore to throw one's self on the reciprocity of freedom as the principle to which reference could always be made, because every other appeal had been tried in the experience of the world of government, in all climes and all centuries, and had collapsed. If the Vicar had accepted this as his principle, he would then have taught his pupil to apply that criterion on the different occasions and in different vicissitudes. *Emile* would have had to ask how far does this particular action or policy promote the continuance of the reign of the fundamental, how much does it restrict it, how much does this new commodity or desire or compulsion bind our hands and our power to move forward or retrace our steps as we freely will. And all would have had to make their peace with this civil religion, as Rousseau, the parent of *Emile*, would have had them to do in the ' civil ' religion, as proposed in the Social Contract. All men could steadily and enthusiastically progress as they desired until this voice said ' No '—a voice which would sternly condemn any impulse to be suicidal about democracy. That is the ultimate.

How produce the conditions of proximity and permanent presence so that the test ' that it matters ' may be applied, provided the principle has been so inculcated as to make other men's fate matter ? If it is achieved, it makes the argument that it matters easier to commend with success. The task is performable, but for technical reasons it is as difficult to accomplish as it is, for pedagogical reasons, to make historical analysis the instrument of moral conviction. ' My country 'tis of *me*,' they sing. The bombs that fell in the next block might almost as well have been a thousand miles away for their effect on the social mentality. Only a few miles away the comfortable ones hold fast to their empty rooms and deny billeting space to their own national refugees from horror ! The workers who remained in civilian occupations during two world wars of the acutest ideal import have never in any country insisted that their wages be reduced to a point where they were not a bit better off than their fellow-men on the battlefield ; even if the simultaneous abolition of all profits were proposed, they could not get into the other men's skins. In our own time it was possible for a British Prime Minister (27 September 1938) to refer to ' a quarrel in a far-away country between people of whom we know nothing '. ' Of whom we know nothing ! ' Nor did a single country fighting Germany or Japan begin until self-defence was unavoidable ; and even then many reluctantly ; and again even then, in the midst of war, there are standers-by and black markets. ' *Lisbonne est abimée ; et l'on danse à Paris*,' lamented Voltaire. We never will and never ought completely attain Plato's postulate of the unified soul and body of the State, but that is the direction.

It is no shame to confess that this all ends in a prescription which is commonplace and simple, even if its metaphysical basis is not : that a doctrine is needed to teach what matters, that organization is required to secure by education, by agitation, especially through the talents of men and women who are specially sensitive, the presence and permanence of facts and people that matter. As the Physiocrats said, where men are to be liberated, and yet not to injure each other by their spontaneous activity, its minimum requirement is the provision of ' public evidence ' of the ' natural order ' of things. We must draw an inference from Hume : we must find a doctrine and a method by which ' the mind is so enlarged, and so replete with friendship and generosity, that every man has the utmost tenderness for every man '. There must be a mass, concerted, and continuous ventilation of knowledge and ideas, to show that the soil of all France is the soil of each of her sons, whether near or far from his own property ; that an integral part of the product and character and value of that soil is its distant consumers or suppliers or first defenders or legislators, and that for good or ill the connexion is held by invisible but demonstrable bonds—essentially of ideas and loyalties—operating in good faith towards that son of France and his own soil, that his home cannot be built and cannot stand unless there is a defence of the homes far-away. And it would show that where these moral associations and fellowships have not yet reached or cannot reach, then institutions of regulation and coercion are unavoidable, and if these go too far or not far enough, social cohesion is disrupted, and horrible remedies will be sought in war or dictatorship. World economy and world peace and their democratic conduct without world-minded citizens cannot be.

The criterion is the grant of all freedom to act and develop except to destroy or indubitably endanger that freedom. In the light of this, there are bounds to all forms of expression and action, for individuals, groups, classes, parties, and occupations, and a doctrine would elaborate and illuminate this. The Nazis and the Fascists produced such a doctrine for their devilish purposes. Its intent, not its content, is relevant. It was to serve to clarify the relationship between the kaleidoscope of hundreds of diverse events in the common man's environment and experience, the many everyday seemingly eccentric and arbitrary happenings and their civic relevance to him. It was to replace the chaos of the city streets by a world's meaning. It was on the way to achievement by the establishment of a doctrine of human destiny and duty, drawn in part from history and in part from reason, to serve as the thread and signal of direction. All things that the common man saw, and heard, and surmised, but could not co-relate or draw meaning from, the Nazis and the Fascists suffused with coherence by relating to the focus of meaning which they had created. The Russian Communist Party, concerned to secure continuous and dynamic loyalty, was forced to seek an answer to the problem whether its members could be reliable unless they had absorbed the Marxian historical analysis and logic.

There is no doubt at all that the like can be achieved and made acceptable for and by democratic man, by relating the events of his society to an essential democratic doctrine.

Can such a doctrine be spread, the education be successful, the remnant of coercion be tolerable, without certain social changes ?

Hardly. The delicate bases of belief, however strong these bases in reason, will not bear a heavy strain. The example of crass egoism, especially economic, is no persuasion to self-control. Short views produce short views. But the most difficult problem of the political leader is to induce self-control and the fulfilment of duty in the light of very long views.

So far what has been said amounts to this. In the maintenance and conduct of democratic government the modern world cannot rely on an identity of basic conviction universally acceptable because it comes by spontaneous revelation or can be proven beyond the shadow of a doubt. If such a universality ever were to arise, the problem of the system of government would be solved, or would cease to be. If there is spontaneous consensus or an important degree of it, it is so much to the benefit of people and governments. But it cannot be relied upon, for there is a perpetual falling away and renewal of generations, and the composition of the public mind is therefore ever-changing. For purposes of the science and art of government it is unwise to assume that there is or can be a universal revelation or scientifically demonstrable principle of the supreme good, and that it can evoke the same responsive action. Therefore we are forced back to the problem : what substitute for this, which will exact the least of our passions and reason, what edifice of theory and what pattern of government will be likely to be least controvertible and vulnerable, what demands the least credulity, what can be least gainsaid ? Our purpose is to secure, maintain and perfect democratic government, which means law and order established by a freely operating people with the majority eventually making decisions. The purpose is to show that it *matters* to everybody for himself that this system shall prevail, and that it cannot persist for himself unless he helps it to persist for all others who live in its orbit. That orbit is as wide flung as the whole world, but it is especially important in some crucial fields ; geographically, economically, and morally ; it concerns the long-run as well as to-day and to-morrow. When it is declared that a thing *matters* to us the term may have either of three meanings. It may mean that it can be ideally justified. The present argument does not rely on this meaning. To *matter* may, secondly, mean that there are practical gains to us if we follow out the precepts, and loss to us if we do not. It is difficult, but by no means impossible, to employ this approach. Thus, it can be clearly shown in convincing, specific, and causal details, that all men are held in a network of mutually determined fate in their villages, their nations and in the whole world ; and that the advent or prevention of plague, pestilence, famine, battle, murder, sudden death and unemployment depends upon a recognition of the real and inexorable elements which bind men together even although they are invisible until they are, like

bacteria, submitted to minute observation. The third implication of
the phrase that 'it matters' is the one that is of supreme and dominant
importance—that all are interested in democracy for all, because
this offers in the long-term sweep of history the maximum opportunity,
for the maximum number, of latitude, and security for spontaneous
development, and mutual social influence upon each other, and than
this mankind has not yet so far discovered a superior rule of living.
The three aspects of the phrase 'that it matters' can be illustrated,
and the present author believes demonstrated, and conveyed by
modern methods of instruction, by the history of the last two thousand
years of government; the second and the third more forcefully than
the first.

*   *   *   *   *   *   *

Now, there are injustices of ancient or modern creation which fly
in the face of this argument (in all brevity, that men are their brothers'
keepers, but not their masters). Men are prone to narrow and short-
run views, which by reason of their intensity (and perhaps the unconscious prompting of the instinct that life is short), usually prevail
over long-term and distant good. Substantial differences in wealth
divide men: for, apart from anything else, men are disposed to
regard any differences which exist in their favour, even if the result of
pure chance, and even of infamy, as a title of superiority and a claim
for privilege. Therefore democracy, on the basis postulated, must be
made noble and credible by concrete social improvement, itself one
of the most vivid parts of education. This, in our own time, implies
very substantial social and economic adjustment, national and
international.

The Philadelphia Charter of the I.L.O., unanimously adopted on
10 May 1944, by 41 nations, is a major common pattern. It declares
a war against want; and affirms that all human beings, irrespective
of race, creed or sex, have the right to the pursuit of both their material
well-being and their spiritual development in conditions of freedom
and dignity, of economic security and equal opportunity. These are
the governing principles. For our own time they involve certain
practical and early tasks, and it may be said at once that these tasks
are not simply derivations of the principles, but both they and the
principles issue from certain imperative passionate demands from the
vast majority of politically and economically conscious citizens, stimulated, nourished, intensified by the miseries of the inter-war years and
the tribulations and awful sacrifices of the World War. They issue
also from the substantially justifiable conviction that our present-day
possession of science and technology, economic science, the available
industrial and distributive managerial ability, public and private, can,
if it is willed, and if the organization of resources obeys the rules indi-

cated by the will, offer a comfortable and secure, if steady and laborious, livelihood in most nations in a not very distant future, and that that is progressively obtainable in substantial stages soon.[2] Indeed, the restlessness of the world in recent years has not been caused by ' capitalism in a phase of contraction ', but a widespread surmise of the expansionist potentialities of modern resources. First and foremost, then, is ' full employment and the raising of standards of living ', which means jobs for all and good jobs. Then follow :

The employment of workers in the occupations in which they can have the satisfaction of giving the fullest measure of their skill and attainments and make their greatest contribution to the common well-being.

The provision, as a means to the attainment of this end and under adequate guarantees for all concerned, of facilities for training and the transfer of labour, including migration for employment and settlement.

Policies in regard to wages and earnings, hours and other conditions of work calculated to insure a just share of the fruits of progress to all, and a minimum living wage to all employed and in need of such protection.

The effective recognition of the right of collective bargaining, the co-operation of management and labour in the continuous improvement of productive efficiency, and the collaboration of workers and employers in the preparation and application of social and economic measures.

The extension of social security measures to provide a basic income to all in need of such protection and comprehensive medical care.

Adequate protection for the life and health of workers in all occupations.

Provision for child welfare and maternity protection.

The provision of adequate nutrition, housing and facilities for recreation and culture.

The assurance of equality of educational and vocational opportunity.

Along with these are the promises of the Atlantic Charter,[3] President Roosevelt's Four Freedoms in January 1941, and the Bill of Rights proposed by the President of the U.S.A. in January 1944.[4]

* * * * * * *

These economic and social proposals are advanced here for themselves, and as the answer to some plain inequities and certain palpable inefficiencies or organization ; and as a basis for making credible and appealing the democratic doctrine that other people matter, that unity in freedom matters. This is a commitment in principle, and not a commitment to the extreme programme that can be imagined on its basis, or the speed with which it can be completed. It is *ad referendum*. It is a policy whose final shape still depends on acceptance, rejection or variation by democratic processes in each country. And what its concrete shape would be in another ten or twenty years no man exactly knows. Such reforms would be a support to the maintenance and improvement of democratic government. But fulfilment would certainly be an extremely exacting problem in democratic government itself ; because they constitute a very tall and insistent order for solution by democratic processes. Moreover they have to be so instituted that the freedom, latitude, choices, appeals, and the independence of fate of each individual are not essentially subverted, or an unfair and intolerable responsibility for the fate of others loaded on some, and some relieved of their proper obligations of self-sustenance, self-development and self-control. The prospect is not easy : for the execution of considerable economic and social reforms democratically, properly implies that those who have an interest in opposing them are guaranteed their freedom to oppose. Further, after the reforms are successfully achieved, there must still remain a continuing anxiety whether the basic liberties to freedom, that is to say, freedom of expression, free debate, free change of government, freedom of association, impartial judgment before the courts, can stand up against the high degree of organization, of self-control and the external controls involved in national and international economic planning.

Will the inhibitions be permanently tolerable ? Those who declare the problem to be insoluble, those who claim that in the pursuit of social justice the world is about to fall into slavery,[5] forget two essential saving conditions. The first is that people can be instructed regarding the price they must pay for the goods they grasp at, that the process and the terms of change are voluntary. The second saving condition is that men and women are not likely so to diminish their own liberties that, if, perchance, the surrender is excessive, they cannot recede. Society, after all, is always proceeding and receding by making, repealing, amending and nullifying its laws. The economic analysts tend to confront the logical conclusions of two absolutely opposed premises (which, of course, by hypothesis do not permit of compromise) rather than to look inside the political process of human development which includes, and has always included, not only contention among ideas held by different men, but conflict among desires *within* men on the same side, and the capacity of human beings for one-quarter, or one-half, or three-quarters measures. The problem, in other words, is not logical, it is quantitative ; a choice between degrees of interest and of different principles. This was pointed out over thirty years ago by Graham Wallas in his *Human Nature in Politics*. But the lesson seems not to have been learned. Extremes lend themselves best both to teaching and vilification.

I have no wish to minimize the difficulty of securing considerable reforms by democratic processes, and thereafter of keeping society democratic. But the travail of the Second World War has made the solution of both tasks easier. The first, by reason of the suffering, the sympathy it stirred and the mutual aid and comfort it brought forth, and the discrediting of the governing classes who were least sensitive of all. The second by reason of the increased knowledge of how to handle social and economic mechanism. And both, by the sacrificial reaffirmation of human freedom in a time of desperate troubles and mortal threat. The world to-day knows better how to use technicians and why to avoid technocrats; how to employ civil servants without instituting civil servantry; how to build administrative controls and yet safeguard so much of liberty and enterprise that the average man, with all the genius of mind and character that may perchance spring from him in a later, if not in this, generation, shall count no less than politicians and officials.

To the technocratic couplet of Pope,

> For forms of government let fools contest,
> What e'er is best administered is best;

we have validly learnt the answer (as the instrumental techniques are available):

> But what is best must free men still decide,
> Lest leaders gull them and officials ride.

Furthermore, the principles of decentralization are well enough known.

James Burnham may have persuaded some credulous persons that capitalism and democracy are no longer maintainable since they cannot solve the problem of mass employment (arguing *en route* that capitalism and democracy are one thing), yet that the alternative of socialism is impossible, because, he alleges, the Soviet Union shows that class rule cannot be abolished, and socialism is supposed to abolish class government. And consequently, he contends that the only alternative to capitalistic democracy, or democracy-capitalism, is 'Managerial Revolution'; that this is already on the way, that is to say, that self-appointed industrial and commercial managers possess, in our society where ownership is highly concentrated, the actual power of decision regarding production and the uses to which property shall be put in the economic process. Soon, he suggests, this revolution will be fully consummated, at which time the managers, self-perpetuating, will find a single political party to support their rule, and yet give the plebs the illusion of democracy. His history is false; his terms are strained; his analysis is dissolute; and not all the alternatives are brought before the bar. Why can there not be a democratic socialism? Burnham does not validly say. But Schumpeter has solidly and brilliantly shown its feasibility; and, as regards the measured and temperate socialist side of such a system, its probable indispensability for the restoration of the shaken social self-discipline of our time.

The social fundamental is democracy, not economic equality, for the first will always guarantee the eventual possibility and maintenance of the just degree of the second. But economic equality, desirable and necessary as it is, is no guarantee at all of freedom in government.

Both are necessary, but the first is of prior indispensability, being the balance wheel of society itself. In the light of this, it is unfortunate that some social critics in our own time make play with the dramatic word 'revolution' as the way to a social democratic state. It has been, for example, pretended in relation to the government of Great Britain, that is to say, the government of some 45,000,000 people, that the 'fundamental' is economic equality, and that social privilege will not be surrendered without a civil war. It is argued that the democratic political parties of Great Britain—that is, democracy— will function only where they are based on a common acceptance of the fundamentals. And it is then argued that the only tenable fundamental is not democracy (that is forgotten), but social reconstruction, and failing this, that men will turn to violence. But what is in the critic's mind as worthy of violence may not be in the minds of the workers and lower middle-class who make up that party in Britain that would most profit from some social and economic changes. This is only one respect in which the theory is inappropriate to the situation. The problems to be solved are not soluble in terms of a critic's categories, but of the nature of the actual men and women who follow the existing political parties.

Hitherto, the fundamental principle in Britain has been a conviction that social progress shall be possible, and social reaction also possible, by the democratic method. There is abundant authority in British history and political philosophy for the simple truth that there is more than intelligent agreement, that there is even deep-seated conviction, upon this fundamental. Moreover, the vague historical generalization on which the alleged existence of an irreconcilable cleavage among parties is sometimes founded, namely that throughout the nineteenth century and to World War I, the political parties which dominated the English scene were agreed upon fundamentals, needs thorough re-examination for its terminological and factual strength. What 'fundamentals'? were they social policy or democracy? and when? There were mighty cleavages in 1829, 1832, 1835, 1845, 1867, 1884, 1892, 1906, 1908–14, and 1926. In all cases the cause of progress won, peacefully, although there were 'fundamental' differences. And social progress between 1919 and 1939 was very substantial. And no one stopped the formation of the Labour Party !

Democratic accommodation is the fundamental principle, and the real parties in existence (see for example the Labour Party's pamphlet, *The New Society and the Old World*) as distinguished from the furious phantoms of introspection, consider that democratic accommodation is the fundamental principle. That is why the masses of British mankind remain their obdurate, pedestrian, sceptical, and democratic selves. It ought never to be forgotten that in each Englishman there is a touch of Edmund Burke. They believe with him ' the people have no interest in disorder '. And the spirit of the reform party, that is the Labour Party, was never in singing the ' Internationale ', but rather in ' Abide with Me '.

That democratic accommodation is and should be the fundamental of the State can be seen upon reflection on the nature of Equality (chiefly economic). When people ask for Equality (and the demand is by no means universal), is it Equality they want, or something else ? The concrete demands are principally (a) the abolition of hereditary privileges, especially those which have no recognized contemporary social utility ; (b) the levelling upwards of their social and economic condition ; and (c) importunately the opportunity to acquire wealth, or bluntly, wealth itself.

First, then, would claimants admit the general social utility as a ground for special gifts of power, status, dignity, or wealth ? There would, at any rate, be much dispute about the nature of social utility, and the price in terms of inequality to be paid for it. That is, there is not a simple and universal formula of Equality to which all mankind is loyal, and which makes a simple choice between the two absolutes, Equality and Democracy, an automatic and foregone conclusion. Next, the privileges which in our own day are condemned, are those that obstruct the development of the discontented and their offspring. To test the significance of Equality to-day, there is a question that may be asked. Can we be sure that when present-day privileges have been swept away, the discontented and many, perhaps even the vast majority, of citizens, will not continually strive to secure privileges for themselves, whatever régime society may adopt ? Common observation of all government shows that people try resolutely and persistently to escape from rules of equality, to become exceptions, even at the most anxious moments in the life of their country, and that among those who so act, are to be found some of the most highly cultivated who teach, even professionally, others the duty of Equality and Justice. There is always some reputable excuse for *not* sending one's own children to the people's schools, and for sending them to private schools. There is always some reason, with a noble face, for helping one's self, one's friends, and especially one's children into nice jobs. When, therefore, men offer Equality to others, or demand it for themselves, they must ask themselves how far they would be prepared to go ; and then *how far* makes the question, not one of principle, but of quantity and expediency.

Above all, is Equality's obligation accepted, that, in the competition of talent and character that never slackens in any society, men are in this equal society prepared to sink, with their posterity, to the place they therein deserve, whether it is a free or a planned society that has the function of placing them ? All may be ready to rise. Who is prepared to fall ? The answer is *not* determined by class : it is a remorseless question for individuals and 'Class' gives no answer. Yet this is a fundamental problem of government—ask Stalin!— and many generations will sweat to answer it. Many people who demand Equality are only asking for a different order of inequality ; and it is not denied that many, indeed, who ask this, may have justice on their side. Will men accept the obligation to fall as well as the opportunity to rise as Equality's consequence ? It must not be forgotten that at some time all those who are not now in the lower categories of power and wealth once (more recently than when Adam delved and Eve span) sprang from the body of the people. Manifestly, they did not choose to loiter at the starting point, or oscillate at the average level. This argument is not obstructive of Equality or, indeed, of benevolence : it is an appeal that a passionate ideal may be soberly considered before it reduces Democracy to a second place.

In most societies Inequalities are being reduced by many measured and practical arrangements, such as very heavy inheritance taxes, the broadening of social provision of education, health, housing and food, and such social control of business in various forms as may open the doors to talent, whatever its origin. Yet, when the cruder inequalities have been swept away, will society legislate Equality regardless of the natural differences among men ? Will it, ought it, go beyond the grant of charity, and how abundant will charity itself be ? Must the mentally, aesthetically, and physically able bear the responsibility of assisting the less able to perpetuate themselves ? Thus, Equality cannot mean unqualified Equality. And since, in order to be just, it is to be qualified, how much better than by the steady process of democratic decision, can the qualifications and proportions be defined and authorized ? A time may come, it may be even not far distant, when abundance will make inequality a problem in political philosophy which is *passé*. That time has not yet come : and those who write about Equality on the unconscious assumption of abundance are not facing the question.

Now, it must be reluctantly acknowledged that the cry for Equality by some, even by many, is nothing but a disguised cry for wealth. They want to be rich, though they ask to be equal. It is no answer to claim that most people are intrinsically modest. Appetite wedded to opportunity has produced remarkable effects in plain people ; enough, indeed, to encourage the strong suspicion that, without distinction of class, many demands for Equality are nothing but outcries for wealth.

These reflections warrant some conclusions. The first is that most people who ask for Equality do not know exactly what they would find acceptable at the time of fulfilment. They are misled or unclear as to the nature and consequences of their plea. If their discontent is not with inequality but with poverty, they may expect, or may have been persuaded to expect, a standard of acceptable wealth so far beyond present or probable future resources, and technical and managerial capacity, as to open the way for social troubles.

No one knows to-day the degree of Equality that people will tolerate in face of the physical, intellectual and spiritual deficiencies of many of his fellow citizens. That degree is not yet fixed. It is in the making, and is by nature always changing and changeable. Labour's demand for ' the right to the whole produce of labour ', was a cry with a double note : the exclusion of privilege, but also an insistence by the individual on the equivalent of what *he* produced. Those who forget that British Trade Unions practised a ' means test ' before the British Government did, ignore a most important contribution to the theory of social equality. Account must also be taken of the Soviet Union's deliberate and very substantial departure from the principle of equal economic reward regardless of output, for this proved unavoidable even where class differences had been absolutely crushed. Stalin came upon the truth that most people did not wish to work for the good of others all the time. Nor did he rely upon patriotism alone, not even in the Soviet's most ghastly hours. The political issue is not whether people will work only for gain, but how hard and for how long they will work knowing that it is for other people. Therefore, the quantitative approach to the subject of feasible Equality, is essential if it is thought advisable to avoid later disappointments. The problem of government—to be just to each, and therefore to discover what justice is, and, therefore, to reward and encourage the desirable talents and discourage the unwanted—still remains.

Thus, the dependence of Equality upon Democracy becomes manifest, for the latter is the method by which the former may be built to stand wear and tear. It is the supreme merit of David Hume that he showed that our notion of justice never arrived complete in the heads of primitive men and societies, nor in ourselves when born, but, that what justice is, or ought to be, results from a long and gradual process of trial and error. ' It is only from the selfishness and confined generosity of man, along with the scanty provision nature has made for his wants, that justice derives its origin.' And Hume underlines this observation. He then affirms : ' . . . The sense of justice is not founded on reason, or on the discovery of certain connexions or relations of ideas, which are eternal, immutable and universally obligatory. . . . It was therefore a concern for our own and the public interest which made us establish the laws of justice . . . those impressions, which give rise to this sense of justice are not natural to the mind of man, but arise from artifice and human conventions.' And this last phrase also is underlined by Hume. Now Hume's view of the nature of justice applies to the notion of Equality. Indeed, it is difficult to distinguish between justice and Equality, and Hume himself (in *The Principles of Morals*) uses the latter as a synonym for the former. Equality is a formula growing out of public interest and individual interest, and arises from artifice and human conventions.

There is no original God-given pattern, level, or lineament, still less a programme, of Equality. Equality, its meaning, no less than its practical social and economic objectives, is in the making by the as yet unfinished political process. A livable convention implies its progressive establishment by democracy in spite of all shortcomings. The democratic process offers the most trustworthy, assured, steady, propitious, and guaranteeing procedure and temper, by which a formula of Equality may be discovered and realized by its instrumental duties. In this sense, Democracy is fundamental, and prior to the principle of Equality. By this means the price may be discovered, and weighed, and enacted for durable fulfilment.

Thus, we return to Democracy, and the grinding necessity of securing loyalty to it by conviction. It can be founded in the knowledge that no other faith has or can be discovered to unify mankind to its degree and so durably. For it is the mediation of all the freedoms which men ask for themselves. It requires the interweaving of mind and mind in the national and international communities, so that all may feel the presence of others closely, incessantly, and may be so touched with democratic significance that they care. To maintain balance, men in society must throw into the scales of everyday trafficking, not a sword as was done by the sovereign in ancient days, but the weight and force of a principle.

Where then shall we look for the binding together of the world-wide network of mind and mind, to the end that the principles of democratic unity shall be applied and defended ? Who can bind the cluster of the social Pleiades ? The labours are, of course, divided among the exceptionally gifted, and the universal body of men and women everywhere. The latter depend for the earliest intimations of vision and feeling upon the gifted, but must always have the last word, should they still want it, after having heard and considered the first. And one of the unending tasks of government it to protect the open way for the communications of the gifted, and equally to maintain the proper conditions by which the multitude's reflection upon them is promoted. Those with exceptional gifts are not divinely appointed ; for all men are divinely appointed, or none ; they spring from the common body of the people. There are men and women of peculiar talent who can see across distances of social space inaccessible to the senses of ordinary men. Some have minds fitted by nature to comprehend the distant experience of humanity in time, that is in history ; or are geniuses of intellectual co-ordination, of immense span, who sense connexions, correlations, and causality, and can predict the shape of coming things ; such as an Aristotle, a Montesquieu, a Hegel, a Marx, a Toynbee, or an H. G. Wells. Others are geniuses of psychological and spiritual insight : the unuttered secrets of individual capacity and aspiration yield to them, and the hopes and fears of salvation dwelling in the labyrinth of each person emerge at their scrutiny : Socrates, Aquinas, Machiavelli, Spinoza, Rousseau, Bentham, Goethe, Shaw. There are geniuses of feeling and sensitivity, of justice and mercy : they feel more vividly and more painfully than others with St. Thomas that ' it is no part of Christian perfection to endure with equanimity the wrongs inflicted on other people '. Often, therefore, they can express these feelings more vividly, and under their impulse sacrificially dedicate their lives to the establishment of remedies and opportunities for human society by preaching, teaching, or politically and socially building ; for instance, Tom Paine, Thomas Jefferson, Elizabeth Fry, Abraham Lincoln, Robert Owen, Florence Nightingale, Lord Shaftesbury, Jane Adams, Mrs. Sidney Webb. These are on the summit, but close to them are many thousands, themselves able critics, thinkers, and intermediaries and popularizers, and some are practical political and social leaders. All such people think and feel earlier and differently from the general body of their fellow citizens, so much so that they may be repugnant to the latter. Yet these are the men and women who will in the long run advance the freedom and happiness of all if they are tolerated for long enough to impress their message. For the sake of the general freedom, their special freedom is necessary above all, and its defence is an obligation of the masses, returning incalculable benefits. The nation is blessed that cherishes its heretics.

To this it may well be responded, even by the naturally tolerant and audacious, that the allegedly gifted may be insane, or unwholesome, or charlatans. They may echo Hobbes and declare : ' So that God Almighty can speak to a man by dreams, visions, voice and inspiration, yet he obliges no man to believe he hath so done to him who pretends it ; who, being a man, may err, and (which is more) may lie.' And, indeed, there are natural exaggerators. For, dazzled by an inward light or feverish with inborn heat, they cannot see the facts staring at them from the document or the manifest succession of events. There are some who are perpetually incandescent, and for whom even the most placid time wears the aspect of an immediate and acute crisis. They confound the promptings of habitual, untested introspection with political science or social goodwill.

The task of the plain man in a democracy is, then, not easy. The continuance and operation of this system of government requires that he tolerate and listen to innovation and adequately reflect so that he may distinguish between the sincere and the insincere, the well-wishers and the misguided, and to decide how much of the contribution of each is not only for his own good now but for his own good in the long run, and not only for his own good in the long run, but for that of his neighbours all over the world.

There is no doubt that the central, though by no means the only, sieve for this purpose in democracies is Political Parties. For good or ill these are the instruments of twentieth century democracy. Much attention was given them in the first edition of the present work (see Vol. I, Chaps. XI–XV). These nation-wide fellowships of interest, these communities of principles and ideas, these bridges between the individual and the nation and beyond it to the world, these selectors of leaders, controllers of governments and conductors of the vitality of the masses to the heart and mind of the state—these require the closest attention to their deficiencies. For the political parties govern, but they are in need of government. They require custodians to purify them of abuses of function and to cast out the adulteration in their power as collective bodies, to remove temptations and set straight their faulty organization. If decentralization is required in the state, as it desperately is, it is no less required in the parties in the sense of local participation of the electorate, especially at the stage of the nomination of candidates for leadership and the formulation of policy.

So, inevitably, the cycle of argument returns again to the individual citizen who is the component and should be the master of political parties. He has sought, or there has been sought for him, certainly for his long-run good, the reversion to the political sovereignty formerly monopolized by kings or dictators. It is still open to him to subject himself to either; and he may do so, involuntarily, from sheer ignorance. For it is easier to lose than to gain an empire in a fit of absence of mind. But, as history shows, such a choice or such negligence is hardly for his benefit, for he then loses any guarantees of being his own master, even if for a time an autocrat employs him as the master of others, which dubious dignity is for some men a snare.

Now dictators claim that their power is built on concern for three basic duties on which political power of any kind depends : knowledge, interest, and the overcoming of social divisions. That is to say, the dictators have commended the effectiveness of their government by reason of (1) their superior knowledge of contemporary and historical facts, (2) their superior interest in the task of government, with the twenty-four-hour day of unremitting application and engagement of mind and energy to this, to the exclusion of other pleasures, activities, and interests, and (3) their recognition that unity among men was necessary as a continuing basis of a continuing state, and that the institution of unity required deliberate enlightenment by a doctrine based on a rationale designed to link men in the State to men in Nature, History, and Spirit.

Whoever, then, wishes permanently to defeat dictatorial government can only do so by fulfilling the three governmental obligations mentioned. The degree to which they are fulfilled, in intensity of application, and the proportion of the population which so applies itself, will determine the degree to which dictatorships as such or the dictatorial elements which still lurk and work in all democratic systems shall be replaced by democratic government. There is every reason to repeat that democratic men and women can remain democratic only if they successfully carry the burden of mastering the relevant Knowledge needed for leadership, direction, and decision ; if they show an unflagging Interest in public affairs and due participation in them ; and, since as Hume observes, all government is founded on opinion, if they progressively formulate a liberal doctrine and develop institutions which will in liberty, modesty, and stoical sincerity (and not as in dictatorships by fanatical gospels, coercion and lies), foster the spirit of Fraternity. It was suggested earlier that the ancient prescription, vigilance, was by no means enough to preserve twentieth century democracy, for that assumed that a government to some degree removed from the people should be merely watched, to be followed, no doubt, by the application of remedies at the crucial time. But now the unrelaxing positive collaboration of all has become indispensable. For in this age, government is involved deeply in the life of all with unprecedented scope, profundity, detail and authority ; no single government can fulfil its essential and solicited tasks in isolation, but must fit its operation into a world pattern that is in constant movement ; errors are more than ever possible and the consequences more drastic and less reparable ; but the opportunity for beneficent activity is by the same token more generous. The division of labour in democratic leaderships, the hierarchy of responsibility, in legislature, executive, in the political parties, from the powerful summit and centre through the whole body politic are visible and necessary. But the responsibility of each individual, of each fragment, is undeniable, inescapable and imprescriptible.

Democracy cannot afford to plan or act in terms of its cheaper members, though it may recognize and yet not worry that there will always be some, and for a long time many. Nor can it disavow the need for government and the use of power. Acton's saying that ' power corrupts, and absolute power corrupts absolutely ' has in recent years again been put into vehement circulation, strangely enough by those who more than others propose policies which inherently necessitate its more massive use. But the cases where men have been ennobled by the possession of power are just as numerous as those where they have been corrupted. Power corrupts

12

only those who were already corrupted. Government is power : democratic government is democratic power : whether it shall be corrupt or noble depends not on a more or less sincerely wry-faced disavowal of power, but on a universal and responsible intervention in the daily process of its exertion.

One hundred and fifty years ago, in the midst of the French Revolution, the Abbé Siéyès asked, What was the Third Estate ? and answered that it was Nothing ! And further, What did it want to be ? and replied, Something ! And finally, What ought it be ? and declared, Everything ! To-day, the Third Estate is Everything, for the People hold the plenitude of power. This new era bursts with new questions, forthright, and not to be denied. What do the People demand ? Equality ! What do they want ? Plenty ! What do they need, and what ought they give ? Mercy ! And of all the polities known to us, democratic government is Mercy's most assured and durable instrument, and the best tempered.

*   *   *   *   *   *   *

The brusque arrival of atomic power, especially the destructive, dreadfully emphasizes the theme of the foregoing chapter. Indeed, these pages might have been a deliberate preface to Hiroshima and beyond. Other types of weapon, including the bacterial, also rank with the Bomb in their danger to man. Are we to descend into a Hobbesian era, or can the genius of Thomas Paine carry the weight of uranium ? A few brief observations are offered.

If political science, studying historic and contemporary man, has any axioms at all, then this is one : that any increase in the power possessed by an individual or group must, when its gravity is appreciated, be followed by an increase in social control, or, in other words, the power of Government. Scattered agricultural, weak, groupings do not produce or require intense central control of power. Densely populated areas, with powerful groups jostling each other, cannot avoid it. The social control of individual power means the assumption of a controlling or counteracting power by the central authority. The history of legislation in surprisingly varied phases of social life attests this axiom.

Power means the ability to do others harm or withhold what is for their good. The power may consist in *material* form : for example, explosives, disease germs, or swiftly-moving, and therefore lethal, mechanical vehicles. Or it may be *intellectual* : knowledge, for example, of the technique of government ; or of mathematics ; or the secrets of personal relationships or activities inside one's own or foreign groups. Clever people are held in distrust. Or, thirdly, power may consist in a *spiritual* form, such as ritual, charms, incantations, doctrines about human destiny and salvation. Power to influence destiny and salvation has been claimed by various orders of priesthood. Government has finally stepped in to subordinate such power. In whatever form, if others can be frightened, influenced, coerced, or signally rewarded by gift or immunity from harm, so long as it is recognized as a substantial influence, the struggle arises to control it. Consider the history of monopolies of all kinds.

In the long run, the alternatives are that the possessor of power subjects society to his own will; or that he exercises self-control, limiting or suppressing his power in a measure that is tolerated by society; or that society domesticates him and his power to its purposes and will. In bygone ages the subjection of the masses was possible. For the future it is always a menace, but becomes less and less a possibility. It must suffer defeat by the combined effect of the diffusion of knowledge, the consciousness of the collective power of the majority, and the deep-rooted faith in the right of the majority to rule. As for the exercise of self-limitation, an appropriate illustration is the possession of the world by coercion: a Genghiz Khan, an Alexander, perhaps a Napoleon, would not hesitate. But that solution to international insecurity is excluded by the democratic scruples of the Bomb-owner.

The imminence of power's effects in *time*, that is, the rapidity between its exertion and its consequences, is of the essence of the problem of control, that is, of government. The speed of its deadliness must cause a tightening of controls over the Bomb, in the sense of Justice Holmes's phrase in *Abrams* v. *United States*, that the action of government is proper where there is 'a clear and imminent danger that it will bring about forthwith certain substantive evils'. The emphasis is upon immediacy. The area threatened defines the size of the society urgently interested in control, and the area is defined by the range and speed of modern vehicles.

Two aspects of atomic control can be foreseen. One is the sharpening of control by each nation over its own scientists and technical workers, by means of instruments like the Official Secrets Act. It will matter little that the nuclear expert may claim his liberty to investigate the beneficent peaceful uses of nuclear energy, for its fateful destructiveness will always be paramount in society's mind until it is conquered. There can never be a retreat to the innocent state of mind before its advent. Like all experts, the nuclear physicist will certainly and properly be brought under 'civilian' control, and subordinated to a responsibility to society through government. It can be taken for granted that the impulses which mastered theocracies, plutocracies, bureaucracies, will not suffer domination by technocracies. Those who put government by priests in the second place will not let government pass to the laboratories; the repositories of test-tubes will not be allowed to house the *arcana imperii*, any more than the temples were.

The greater his power for weal or woe, the more will the technologist be controlled—and all industry ancillary to his awful magic will also be governed by society.

The international implication is the certainty of national controls over industrial establishments in order to implement each government's pledge to the international organization to allow an inspectorate full access to all plants. The effectiveness of the International Labour Organization would be heightened if it could employ such an inspectorate : but its scope of authority—to abate bad labour conditions—has not been regarded by the nations as important or as urgent as the menace of the new weapons.

If international engagements and organization are not invoked to control the weapons of mass slaughter, then the alternative to war with them is national self-control. Perhaps universal national self-control is not feasible except in a world of democracies. This is, in part, because a régime of free political parties and publicity is a régime of moderation and predictable governmental action. But, above all, it is in such politics that there inheres the most reliable prospect of fashioning policy upon a basis of Mercy.

Some of the authorities cited may bear a date of publication later than the events referred to; but they either offer relevant evidence or they exemplify or continue, the evaluation, sometimes both, of ideas and tendencies discussed in the text.

NOTES TO CHAPTER I

[1] *Mussolini's Italy*, p. 501, by the present author.

[2] Cf. Beveridge, *The Pillars of Security*, 1942; *National Resources Planning Board Report*, 'Security, Relief, and Public Works', 1943; Cole, *The Means to Full Employment*, 1943; and *White Paper on Employment Policy*, Cmd. 6527; 1944, H.M. Stationery Office, London.

[3] Ludendorff, *Total War* (London): Lauterbach, *Economics in Uniform*, Princeton, 1944.

[4] Cf. annual *World Economic Surveys*, from 1929, League of Nations publication.

[5] Cf. E. W. Bakke, *The Unemployed Man*, 1933; Pilgrim Trust, *Men without Work*, Cambridge, 1938.

[6] Rowe, *Markets and Men*, 1936.

[7] Brookings Institute, L. S. Lyon *et al.*, *The National Recovery Administration*, 1935; A. S. J. Baster, *The Twilight of Capitalism*, 1937.

[8] E. M. Burns, *British Unemployment Policies*, 1929–38.

[9] M. Dobb, *Soviet Planning and Labour in Peace and War*, 1942, and *Soviet Economy and War*, 1942; series on Russian economic life by E. L. Hubbard, especially *Soviet Labour and Industry*, 1942.

[10] W. Guillebaud, *The Economic Recovery of Germany*, 1933–38.

[11] L. Gordon, *The Public Corporation in Great Britain*, 1939; Robson *et al.*, *Public Enterprise*, 1937; Van Dorn, *Government Corporations*, 1924.

[12] For Italy, Finer, op. cit., and Rosenstock-Franck, *Les Etapes de l'Economie Fasciste*, Paris, 1938. For Germany, Neumann, *Behemoth*, 1942; M. N. Sweezy, *Structure of Nazi Economy* (Harvard, 1941); Singer in *Economic Journal*, 1940, p. 534, and 1941, pp. 19 and 193.

[13] Stuart Chase, *Technocracy, an Interpretation*, New York, 1933; J. G. Frederick, For and against Technocracy: a symposium, New York, 1933: Technocracy, Inc.: *Total Conscription*, 1942.

[14] Mannheim, *Man and Society in an Age of Change*, Chap. V.; F. Zweig, *The Planning of Free Societies*, 245 ff. Hayek, *The Road to Serfdom*, 1944, who totally rejects the idea that freedom can subsist with planning. Cf. Note 1, to Chap. VII.

[15] Cf. discussion on the reform of the constitution, 1936. *Moscow News*, May and June, *passim*, especially the passages concerning the 'rejection of the principle of socialism. . . . From each according to his ability, to each according to his need,' and the enactment of the same phrase, but with the word 'work' replacing 'need'. And there was added in Art. 12, 'Work in the U.S.S.R. is the obligation and matter of honour of each citizen capable of working, according to the principle: "He who does not work shall not eat."'

[16] M. Murphy, *The British War Economy*, New York, 1943.

[17] Cf. F. P. Chambers, *The War behind the War*, 1939.

[18] Cf. House of Commons Debates during 1942 regarding Equality of Sacrifice.

[19] Cf. International Labour Office, *Survey of Social Security*; and *Approaches to Social Security*, 1943.

[20] The German Economic Council was abolished by the Nazi Government, which had its own much more integrated and coercive machinery for controlling the economic life of Germany. The German Economic Council had been a consultative organ co-operating with but not overruling the Reichstag. But in their planning based on military aims the Nazis had no use for consultation, which implied the balancing and compromise of interests, still less for that of a parliamentary body with sovereign power. Cf. for an obituary article, Rogers and Dittmar, 'The RWR, de Mortuis', *Political Science Quarterly*, Dec. 1935.

[21] Mansergh and others, *Advisory Bodies in Great Britain*, 1941.

[22] Cf. short survey in Sir Henry Bunbury, *Governmental Planning Machinery*, Chicago, 1937. For recent suggestions for improving the British Cabinet machinery of planning cf. *PEP*, Nos. 173 and 214.

[23] Cf. Jennings, *Cabinet Government*, 1937, pp. 247–9.

[24] Cf. articles by the present author in *Journal of the Institute of Municipal Treasurers and Accountants*, London, England, January–February 1936.

[25] Pennock, *Administration and the Rule of Law*, 1940 ; Hart, *An Introduction to Administrative Law*, 1940 ; Gellhorn, *Cases in Administrative Law*, 1940. See, also, the extremely important *Report and Monographs of the Attorney General's Committee on Administrative Procedure*, 77th Congress, 1st sess., Doc. No. 8, U.S. Govt. Printing Office, 1941, and *Hearings*, June and July 1940. 'This Committee is concerned with the procedures and the procedural practices of the administrative agencies, and the general methods provided for judicial review of their proceedings' (*Report*, p. 1), in a sense the committee parallels the British Committee on Ministers' Powers of 1932.

[26] Cf. Lord Perry, *House of Lords Debates*, 18 February 1941 ; and Lord Reith, *House of Lords Deb.*, 17 June 1942 ; and C. T. Carr, *Concerning Administrative Law*, 1940, Chap. IV, and J. M. Jackson, *The Machinery of English Justice*, 1940, Chap. 6.

[27] Cf. Sixteenth Report, Select Committee on National Expenditure, No. 120 ; 1942, *Organization of the Civil Service and Control* ; also *Report of the Committee on Training of Civil Servants*, Cmd. 6525 of 1944. But another report is necessary to go beyond these, namely, on the methods of recruitment and previous education of the Civil Service.

[28] *Economist*, 23 October 1943, 'An Economic Civil Service' ; and 'Public Service', 12 February 1944. See also, Cole, *The Means to Full Employment*, pp. 168–9, and Cole, Beveridge and Laski in *Plan for Britain*, 1943.

[29] Less than one out of five of the two million children between the ages of 14 and 17 were being educated in State-maintained or State-grant-aided schools. In U.S.A. considerably more than one in two of the children attend high school, the proportion being much lower in the Southern states, especially for negro children. Only one out of twenty leaving the public secondary schools in England went to a University, and rather less than one in twenty went to Training Schools or Colleges. Altogether some 40,000 are students at such institutions. In U.S.A., with a population only three times that of Great Britain, there are over one million students at this, the highest, level of education.

[30] Cf. for U.S.A. *Report* of the President's Committee on Administrative Management, 1937 ; with Special Studies ; White, *Public Administration*, (ed. 1939) ; and Lewis Meriam, *Personnel Administration in Federal Government*, 1937. Recent works on bureaucracy in U.S.A. are mentioned in the notes to Chap. 6.

[31] Cf. *Report*, President's Advisory Committee on Education, Govt. Printing Office, 1938.

[32] Stafford Cripps, *Democracy Up to Date*, 1936.

[33] Cf. the observations of Cole, in *Plan for Britain*.

[34] Cf. the reasonable and penetrating analysis in Schumpeter, *Capitalism, Socialism and Democracy*, 1942.

[35] Lenin, *The State and Revolution*, can be seen in Emile Burns, *Handbook to Marxism*.

NOTES TO CHAPTER II

[1] Cf. discussion in Koelreutter, *Allgemeine Staatslehre*, 1934 and later editions.

[2] The authority is E. R. Huber, *Verfassungsrecht des grossdeutschen Reiches*, Hamburg, 1937, p. 230.

[3] *Mussolini's Italy*, p. 207.

[4] Webbs, *Soviet Communism, A New Civilization*, pp. 443 ff., and Sloan, *Soviet Democracy*.

[5] *Moscow News*, May and June, 1936, *passim*.

[6] For the making of the Plan cf. Hubbard's studies; Webb, op. cit. Part II, Chaps. VIII and IX; Dobb, op. cit.

[7] Cf. the interesting essay by Sidney Hook, *The Hero in History*, New York, 1943.

[8] Cf. Mannheim, *Diagnosis of our Time*, 1944, Chap. I.

[9] *Kolnische Zeitung*, 26 September 1942.

[10] *Organizationsbuch der N.S.D.A.P.*, 1940, Para. 1.

[11] Ibid.

[12] Cf. *World News and Views*, 31 March 1939.

[13] *Short History of the Communist Party of the Soviet Union*, Moscow, 1939, especially pp. 264–346.

[14] O. P. Giles, *The Gestapo* (Oxford Pamphlets on World Affairs), No. 36.

[15] Finer, *Mussolini's Italy*, p. 246

[16] Boris Souvarine, *Stalin*, 1939.

[17] L. W. Doob, *Propaganda : Its Psychology and Technique*, New York, 1935 ; H. L. Childs, *Propaganda and Dictatorship*, Princeton, 1936.

NOTES TO CHAPTER III

[1] Books written before September 1939 : Adolf Hitler, *Mein Kampf*, (edn. London, and Reynal Hitchcock, New York). I have made my own translations from the German edition of 1925–6. F. L. Schuman, *The Nazi Dictatorship*, 1935 ; R. T. Clark, *The Fall of the German Republic*, 1935—excellent analysis of strengths and failures of the Weimar system ; Rosenberg, *A History of the German Republic*, 1936 ; Mowrer, *Germany Puts the Clock Back*, 1933 and 1939 ; Heiden, *History of National Socialism*, 1931 ; R. Olden, *Hitler*, London, 1936. Since the beginning of World War II : J. Braunthal, *Need Germany Survive ?* ; Heiden, *Der Führer*, New York, 1944 ; Fraenkel, *The Dual State*, Oxford, 1941 ; F. Neumann, *Behemoth*, 1942 ; Loewenstein, *Hitler's Germany*, 1940.

[2] Cf. also Norman H. Baynes (the Roman historian), *Collected Speeches of Hitler*, August 1922–August 1939 (Oxford 1942).

[3] E. Banse, *Germany Prepares for War*, New York, 1941 ; Haushofer, *Weltpolitik von Heute*, Berlin, 1934 ; Ludendorff, *The Nation at War*, 1936.

[4] F. Thyssen, *I Paid Hitler*, New York, 1941.

[5] Heiden, *History of National Socialism*, early chapters.

[6] Abundant material will be found in the novels, plays and prefaces of Bernard Shaw.

[7] Aurel Kolnai, *War against the West*, London, 1938 ; R. D. Butler, *The Roots of National Socialism*, London, 1941. Butler's work traces back the ancestry through the nineteenth century ; Kolnai reviews the ideas developed since 1918. See also F. W. Foerster, *Europe and the German Question*, 1940.

[8] Rauschning, *Hitler Speaks*, p. 247, 1939.

[9] Cf. Butler, *The Tyranny of Greece over Germany*, Cambridge, which is not ' political ', but is a study of German aesthetics based on Greek art and culture. See also, G. R. Halkett, *The Dear Monster*, London, 1939, an extremely important autobiography of a scion of a Prussian-Scottish family, who went through the usual Junker-boy education of our own time.

[10] *Begriff des politischen*, in *Archiv. fur Sozialwissenschaften und Sozialpolitik*, Band. 58, 1927, pp. 1–35.

[11] Gooch, *Germany and the French Revolution*.

[12] On the conversion of revolutionary feeling into wars, see H. E. Fried, *Political Science Quarterly*, January, 1944. But the problem is still not solved, for *if* the Germans have always been cuckolded by their rulers, what is it in them which makes them dupes ?

[13] *The Guilt of the German Army*, New York, 1942.

[14] Cf. E. J. Gumbel, *Vier Jahre Politischer Mord*, Berlin, 1922, and *Lässt Köpfe Rollen*, Berlin, 1931.

[15] Cf. Otto Strasser, *Hitler and I*, London, 1941 ; K. G. W. Lüdecke, *I Knew Hitler*, New York, 1937 ; Goebbels, *My Part in Germany's Fight*, 1935 ; Goering, *Germany Reborn*, 1934.

[16] This is especially well brought out in Mowrer, op. cit.

[17] *Der Angriff*, Munich, 1936, pp. 71–3.

[18] This generalization from the *Reichstagwahlergebnisse* is amply confirmed by S. L. W. Mellen, *Am. Pol. Sci. Rev.*, August 1943, pp. 601–25.

[19] Cf. also Pollock, *An Areal Study of the German Electorate 1930–33, Am. Pol. Sci. Rev.*, February 1944. It was not within the scope of this very valuable article to consider the effect of Nazi anti-Russian propaganda on the Marches, and perhaps, Silesia. These were closest to the colossus, whether as a fat *Lebensraum* of the future or an enemy to be feared.

[20] Cf. Hans Gerth, ' The Nazi Party : Its Leadership and Composition,' in *American Journal of Sociology*, January 1941.

[21] Professor Arnold Brecht's, *Prelude to Silence* (1944) gives a close eye-witness's testimony on this score in an admirably cogent and economical narrative.

[22] Cf. A. Sturmthal, *The Tragedy of European Labour*, 1942, Part II ; also F. Borkenau, *The Communist International*, 1938.

[23] H. J. Heneman, *Growth of Executive Power in Germany*, 1934 ; F. M. Watkins, *The Failure of Constitutional Emergency Powers under the German Republic*, Cambridge, 1939.

[24] F. K. Süren, *Die Deutsche Gemeindeordnung*, 30 January 1935 ; *Kommentar*, 2 vols., Berlin, 1935.

[25] Jesserich, *Zeitschrift für die gesammte Staatswissenschaften*, 1938, p. 92.

[26] Cf. Lepawsky, *Am. Pol. Sci. Rev*, 1936, pp. 324 ff. ; Wells, ibid, pp. 350 ff.

[27] Cf. Fraenkel, op. cit. This, I believe, was the first of the commentaries in the English language. Several subsequent works have drawn much from this eminently perspicuous treatment of the subject. It is superior to most of its successors.

[28] Cf. Stödter, *Archiv. für öffentliches Recht*, N.F.Bd.27, p. 166 *et seq.* and especially p. 178. Cf. also, Poetsch-Heffter, *Jahrbuch des öffentlichen Rechts*, 1935, p. 210.

[29] There is a nice essay on this subject in Brooks Adams, *Theory of Social Revolution*, originally published 1898 ; new edition by Beard, 1943.

[30] Hitler's Reichstag speech, 26 April 1942, a denunciation of judicial independence.

[31] Neumann, op. cit., L. Hamburger, *How Nazi Germany Controlled Business*, Washington, 1943; Guillebeaud, *Social Policy of Nazi Germany*, 1941; M. Sweezy, op. cit.

[32] Of the Prussian members of the Higher Civil Service in field positions (1663 members) 28 per cent. were dismissed as ' unreliable ', Jewish, etc. (12·5 per cent.), or dismissed or demoted for ' administrative reasons '. In the middle groups of the Service, especially the Clerical Class, only 3·46 per cent. were dismissed or demoted. Cf. Brecht, op. cit., pp. 110–11.

[33] Cf. Law regarding German Officials, 26 January 1937 : trans. Pollock and Heineman, *The German Civil Service Act*.

[34] See a very interesting lecture by A. Rowan Robinson, relating the results of a tour of these schools, in *International Affairs*, March–April 1938 : ' The Training of the Nazi Leaders of the Future '. ' What, we may ask, will be the final results of this education ? Will it be a man, a superman, or a machine ', p. 246, and p. 250 : ' People were not encouraged to think for themselves. If people thought they might think differently, and the whole point in Germany was— and this had been echoed by a member of the Board of Education visiting one of the Schools—that it did not matter what people thought as long as they thought the same thing.'

The first graduates of the Adolf Hitler Schools, in February 1942, chose as professions : 67·23 per cent., political leadership ; 10·92, officers ; 7·15, technical and scientific ; 4·62, teaching ; 3·36, medical ; 2·94, business ; 2·10, forests and agriculture ; 1·68, liberal professions. *Nazional Zeitung*, 20 February 1942.

NOTES TO CHAPTER IV

[1] Before 1940 : Alexander Werth, *France in Ferment*, 1934 ; *Destiny of France*, 1937 ; *France and Munich*, 1939 ; M. Belgion, *News of the French*, 1938 ; D. W. Brogan, *Modern France*, 1940 ; Ralph Fox, *The Future of France*.

After 1940 : Louis Lévy, *The Truth about France*, 1941 ; Elie J. Bois, *Truth on the Tragedy of France*, 1942 ; J. Rosan, *La Fin d'un Régime*, Paris, 1941 ; Pertinax (André Géraud), *Les Fossoyeurs*, New York, 1943, translated as *The Gravediggers*, New York, 1944 ; Pierre Cot, *Triumph of Treason*, New York, 1944 ; Marchal, *De Pétain à Laval*, Montreal, 1943.

[2] J. C. Fernand Laurent, *Gallic Charter*, Boston, 1944.

[3] Vol. I, 147.

[4] *Discorsi*, III, 8, and I, 18 ; and cf. III, 30.

[5] In May, 1940, the French Army in North-Eastern France had 91 divisions, and there were 10 British and one Polish. There were 22 Belgian divisions. The German Armies in the attack in May counted some 140 divisions and were rapidly increasing.

[6] D. V. Glass, *The Struggle for Population*, 1936.

[7] Cf. Battestini, *L'Industrie Française du gros matériel mécanique et electrique*, 1937.

[8] Blum, *L'Experience Blum*, Paris, 1937 ; Kalecki, ' The Lesson of the Blum Experiment,' *Economic Journal*, March 1938 ; and Paul Lombard, *Quatorze Mois de Démence*, Paris, 1937 ; International Affairs, July–August 1937 ; Rosentock-Franck, ' Démocraties en Crise Roosevelt ; Vanzeeland, Léon Blum,' Paris, 1937.

[9] The works by Pertinax and Elie Bois may be consulted ; also L. Guerdan, *Je les ai tous connus*, New York, 1942, and Mme Genviève Tabouis, *They called me Cassandra*.

It is possible to name a Ministry of all the Talents. For example, Mandel, Tardieu, Marin, Blum, de Gaulle, Herriot, Reynaud, Daladier. But as soon as they are mentioned, one realizes how impossible it would have been for these men to collaborate ; and even to say this, is still to leave out of account obstruction and disavowal by their own groups.

[10] In 1934, de Gaulle had published his *Army of the Future* (*L'Armée de Métier*) ; on 31 March 1934, Paul Reynaud introduced into the Chamber of Deputies a de Gaulle inspired proposal for an armoured corps. In 1935 de Gaulle revised the military chapter of M. Reynaud's book *The Political Future of France*, Paris, 1935, once again emphasizing their military theory. See also Pierre Tissier, *Riom Trial*, pp. 110–26.

[11] The Superior Council was composed of the Prime Minister, the Minister for Foreign Affairs, three Defence Ministers, the Commander in Chief, and their Chiefs of Staff. It was rather like the British Committee of Imperial Defence. A smaller Committee of the same kind, a permanent Committee of National Defence, met only twice, and then under Léon Blum. The War Committee, set up in June 1938 to assist the Prime Minister in the conduct of the war, rarely met as a whole under Daladier. Its meetings were regular only under Reynaud.

[12] Cf. Elie Bois, Chap. XVIII.

[13] Cf. Marcel Privat, *Pierre Laval*, Paris, 1931, for a work of ignorant ingratiation ; Tissier, *I worked with Laval*, London, 1942.

[14] Henri Torrès, *Pierre Laval*, London, 1941. And yet even M. Torrès acknowledges that though he suspected Laval, he was too busy with his profession to undo him.

[15] The pact was ratified by the Chamber of Deputies on 27 February 1936, by 353 to 164 ; and in the Senate by 226, with 48 Senators of the Right voting against and 34 abstaining, on 12 March 1936, after Germany's reoccupation of the Rhineland and the denunciation of Locarno.

[16] It is impossible in this scant space to characterize all those, even the principals, who contributed to the state of mind which eventuated in capitulation. Among the many may be simply cited Georges Bonnet, Pierre Etienne Flandin, Fernand de Brinon, Marcel Deat, Jacques Doriot.

[17] Cf. Werth, *Destiny of France*, for proposals to regulate the scandalous press.

[18] Cf. Brogan, op. cit., for a description and setting of them in the perspective of the period 1870–1939.

[19] Adapted from Georges Lachappelle, *Elections Legislatives*, 1 and 8 May 1932, and 26 April and 3 May 1936, and *Le Temps*, for groupings.

[20] Louis Lévy, *Truth about France*. M. Lévy was a member of the Executive of the French Socialist Party from 1926 to 1939, and very close to M. Blum.

[21] I refer literally to the French practice of using officially-stamped forms for many diverse applications to government authorities, for complaints and petitions ; and, figuratively, to the whole cranking official apparatus where public employees and even institutions like the banks and utilities could only be persuaded to take the simplest decisions and perform the most ordinary transactions after the furnishing of multifarious forms, receipts, warrants, and identifications. W. R. Sharp's, *The French Civil Service*, 1935, gives indications of this administrative malady.

[22] Emmanuel Berl, *La Politique et les Partis*, Paris, 1932.

[23] Cf. J. G. Heinberg, *Am. Pol. Sci. Rev.*, April 1939.

[24] Cf. Tardieu, *L'Heure de la Décision*, January 1934, is a short treatise on the proposals submitted to the Chambers in 1933. See also *Le Temps*, September 1934, report of Doumergue's broadcast on the need for power to dissolve the Chamber.

[25] For the Civil Servants, see my *British Civil Service*, 1937, pp. 173 ff. The politician was Mr. J. H. Thomas; cf. *Report, Budget Disclosure Inquiry*, 1936, and Minutes of Evidence.

[26] The case for the civilian control of the conduct of war had been argued with relentless cogency by the British statesmen (Lloyd George, *War Memoirs*, *passim*, and especially the ninetieth chapter; and in Winston Churchill's, *The World Crisis*). But, in the vital years, M. Daladier was in the hands of Gamelin, and could not be induced to consider alternative military policies. Yet many have testified that the General was no warrior, but only an administrative prefect. But the French Navy was efficient, due to the professional gifts of Darlan, who, however, lacked compass and chart in politics.

[27] The General Staff failed even to assure itself of a fighting moral in its troops by proper training between the outbreak of war and May 1940. It tolerated quiescence, stagnation and boredom. It misunderstood the offensive power of the bomber, of parachute troops, and the State-crashing technique of the tank. Gamelin, Weygand, and Pétain, instead, sponsored Maginotism.

[28] Harold Butler, *The Lost Peace*, Chap. on France.

[29] Cf. Hon. George Peel, *The Financial Crisis of France*, 1926; and *The Economic Policy of France*, 1937.

[30] Cf. an excellent article by K. R. Bopp, 'The Government and the Bank of France', in *Public Policy*, pp. 1–35, 1941 (Harvard).

[31] It was suggested at the Riom Trial, that out of resentment at the semi-nationalization of certain armament works, M. Schneider of Le Creusot, and perhaps other industrialists, had hampered the manufacture of arms. *Vide* Tissier, *Riom Trial*, p. 89.

[32] Cf. Charles Maurras, *Mes Idées Politiques*, Paris, 1937, and *La Seule France : chronique des jours d'épreuve*, Lyon, 1941; and Maritain, *A Travers le désastre*, New York, 1941.

[33] Belgion, op. cit. *passim*, and the excellent concise study by C. A. Michaud, *The French Right and Nazi Germany*, Duke University Press, 1943.

NOTES ON CHAPTER V

[1] A. Hutt, *Post-war History of the British Working Classes*, 1937; W. A. Rudlin, *Growth of Fascism in Great Britain*, 1935.

[2] Cole, *The People's Front ; Annual Reports*, Labour Party Conference, 1932–39; Estorick, *Sir Stafford Cripps*, 1941, and Labour Party pamphlet, *Unity, True or Sham*, 1939.

[3] Toynbee, *Survey of International Affairs* (for the Spanish Civil War). See also *Vigilantes* (K. Zilliacus): *The Dying Peace ; Inquest on Peace ; The Road to War* (preface by C. R. Attlee).

[4] Cf. Burns, British Unemployment Policies, 1920–38; Eli Ginzberg, *Grass on the Slag Heaps*, New York, 1942; *Reports of Commissioners for the Special Areas*, 1935–38. Most of the objectionable features of the Means Test were abolished by the *Determination of Means Act*, 1942, when World War II had chastened the hard of heart, and many defeats had put them on public trial. In any case, the Beveridge Social Security Plan of January 1943 opened a new era in social security administration, the Bill of 1944–45 following it closely. Cf. paper by the present author in *Annual Report*, 'American National Conference of Social Work,' 1943.

[5] Cf. Cannan, *An Economist Protests*.

[6] Cf. Hugh Dalton, *et al.*, *Unbalanced Budgets*, 1934, and League of Nations Intelligence Service, *Public Finance*, 1928–35, Geneva, 1936.

[7] The central Executive of the Labour Party consists, since 1937, of 23 members : 12 are nominated by the Trade Unions, one by socialist co-operative and professional organizations, five are nominated by constituency labour parties, and five women members nominated by all affiliated organizations. They are elected by the Party's Annual Conference, which is the supreme authority of the Party. It will be seen that the Trade Unions dominate the Party, or if one likes to put it that way, that the Party is a Trade Union Party. But that is not all. Voting at the Conference is apportioned according to the numbers of members of the affiliated organizations duly represented at it, and the organizations receive one voting card for each 1,000 members. The Trade Unions in 1937 outnumbered other membership in the proportion of four to one. During the War, owing to the increase in Trade Union membership and the fall-off in constituency membership, the proportion became something like eight to one. Furthermore, the Trade Unions supply about 75 per cent. of the annual income of the Party. It is a little difficult to discover exactly what a vote on a resolution at the Annual Conference means, because delegates cast their votes *en bloc*, the minority view within each set of cards not being represented, though it has expressed itself and voted at the meeting of its organization which chose the delegates.

[8] Cf. Reports of the Trade Union Congress for 1932, 1933, and 1934.

[9] Cf. Walter Greenwood, *Love on the Dole* ; George Orwell, *The Road to Wigan Pier* ; Ellen Wilkinson, *The Town that was Murdered*, 1939, and Wal Hannington, *The Distressed Areas*, 1937.

[10] Its 287 seats compared with, say, 304, required as a bare majority, not to speak of a working majority.

[11] Committee on National Expenditure, headed by Sir George May, Cmd. 3920 ; 1931.

[12] On the whole episode consider MacNeill Weir, *The Tragedy of Ramsay MacDonald*, 1938.

[13] Cf. Sidney Webb, *What Happened in 1931* ; Philip Snowden, *Autobiography*, II, pp. 929–62 and 1003–1085 ; Laski, *The Constitutional Crisis*, 1932 ; Jennings, *Cabinet Government*, pp. 28 ff.

[14] Thus, Bowley and Stamp, *National Income*, p. 78, show that the percentage of the occupied population increased from 19 per cent. in 1881, to 26·9 per cent. in 1921, and 29·11 per cent. in 1931. The 'middle-classing' of Great Britain and U.S.A. has very important implications for non-radical courses in politics. For U.S.A. cf. E. P. Herring, *The Politics of Democracy*, 1940 ; and A. N. Holcombe, *The Middle Class in Politics*, 1933 ; Lewis Corey, *The Crisis of the Middle Class*, and F. C. Palm, *The Middle Classes then and now*. For Great Britain, E. M. Durbin, *The Politics of Democratic Socialism*, 1939.

[15] Mr. MacDonald's action caused the Labour Party Executive to frame rules to control the action of the Leader of the Party regarding the formation of a Cabinet. In future, the Labour Prime Minister would be required to consult regarding such a matter with a committee of three persons to be appointed by the Parliamentary Labour Party ; he would be subject to majority decisions of the Cabinet ; and he should recommend a dissolution of Parliament only on a decision of the Cabinet confirmed by a meeting of the Parliamentary Labour Party. Cf. *Annual Report*, Labour Party Conference, 1932 and 1933.

[16] Disraeli in 1873. Cf. Jennings, *Cabinet Government*, pp. 42–5. Does the Labour Party disclaimer apply to a minority as compared with two other parties just emergent from an election, or to some parliamentary situation leaving choice of office open ?

[17] *The Times*, 23 January 1932.

[18] Cf. Debates, 8 February 1932.

[19] *Autobiography*, II.

[20] *Manchester Guardian*, 29 September 1932.

[21] Besides the parliamentary debates, see L. Woolf (ed.), *The Intelligent Man's Way to Prevent War*, 1936.

[22] D. W. Brogan, *Is Innocence Enough*, 1941.

[23] The individual membership of the Party, through the constituency organization, appeals to vast numbers of persons with the most diverse opinions. For Mr. Lansbury's outlook see George Lansbury, *Looking Backwards and Forwards*.

[24] Cf. Estorick, op. cit., Chaps. V and VII.

[25] Cf. Report, 1934 and App. II, *On War and Peace*. The Appendix says, categorically, ' The responsibility for stopping war ought not to be placed upon the Trade Union movement alone '. The T.U.C. had in earlier years adopted the Standing Order, 8(h) that required a Special Congress in the event of danger of international war ' to decide on the question of industrial action, which is guarded language '. But in the proceedings in 1934, Mr. Henderson said, '. . . we have not abandoned the idea of the general strike ', but argued that such an issue required unanimity for acceptance.

[26] Cf. Report of the Royal Commission on the Private Manufacture of Arms, and Minutes of Evidence, and Philip Noel Baker, *The Private Manufacture of Armaments*, Vol. I, 1936.

[27] Consider the terrifying candour of Lord Maugham, then Lord Chancellor, in all his defences of the Munich Agreement, nearer to absolute than those of any other person, e.g. *House of Lords Debates*, 3 and 4 October 1938 ; also speech at the Assoc. British Chambers of Commerce, Glasgow (*The Times*, 7 October 1938, p. 11), it was forcefully argued that the loss of real wages and inflation and the discontinuance of the social services must be the consequences of a war of prolonged hostilities. Above all, see speech to the Constitutional Club, 14 December 1938 (*The Times*, 15th, p. 18) :

' A person who claimed to be a statesman and made war against another country without having counted the cost ought to be impeached. Conditions since the last war had wholly changed. The power of bombing had entirely altered the position. The Germans had it in their power to let loose 3,000 bombs in a single day. . . . It was not an unfair calculation that in the first week or two of war the Germans might do an amount of damage in London and other great cities which would amount in money to £500,000,000.'

He thought that men who undertook war without considering all sides of the matter in this way ought to be shot. It was denied, that if there were any obligation to Czechoslovakia, that it merited military action.

[28] Cf. E. Charles, *The Effect of Present Trends in Fertility and Mortality upon the Future Population of England and Wales*, &c., London and Cambridge Economic Service, 1935. In 1944, a Royal Commission was set up to consider the whole problem of population in Great Britain.

[29] House of Commons, reply of Mr. Duff Cooper, First Lord, to the Duchess of Atholl.

[30] Cf. Neville Henderson, *Failure of a Mission*, for his account of his instructions ; also Vansittart, *Lessons of My Life*, for the Government's pressure on him. Cf. also Government's *Proposals for the Reform of the Foreign Service*, Cmd. 6420 (1943).

[31] Cf. quotations in S.Haxey, *Tory M.P.*, 1939 ; and *Your M.P.*, by ' Gracchus,' (Gollancz, 1944).

[32] On the Public Schools see *Report* (Fleming) Committee, *The Public Schools and the General Educational System*, July 1944, Nos. 27–258 ; and R. H. Tawney, *The Public Schools*, W.E.A., 1944.

[33] Gray and Moshinsky, in *Political Arithmetic*, ed. L. Hogben, 1938 ; for other data see Year Book of Education. Changes enacted in the Education Act, 1944 (mainly raising free education to the age of 16) will produce a very considerable improvement in educational opportunity, particularly in the long run and cumulatively, especially when account is taken of the supplementary

legislative and administrative reforms based on *Reports* (April 1943) *on the Abolition of Fees in Grant aided Secondary Schools* (Nos. 27–258) ; *Curriculum in Secondary Schools* (Nos. 27–257) ; and *Teacher and Youth Leaders* (May 1944, Nos. 27–360).

[34] Webb, *What Happened in 1931* ; Arthur Greenwood, ibid., 1941 ; Herbert Morrison, *Annual Report*, Labour Party Conference, 1942.

[35] Cf. J. F. S. Ross, *Parliamentary Representation*, 1943, far more valuable for its statistics than for its theories of remedy.

[36] Figures calculated from *Return Election Expenses to Home Office*. In 1944, *The Speaker's Conference on Electoral Reform*, &c. (Report, Cmd. 6543, July), proposed a very drastic lowering of the legal maximum expenditure. For Boroughs there was to be a basic maximum of £450 plus 1*d*. per elector. In Counties it would be £450 plus 1½*d*. per elector. Thus, with 60,000 electors the maximum in a borough would be £700 instead of the present £1,300 ; in a county, £825 instead of £1,575. It may be added that it is recommended that where there are four or more candidates, unsuccessful candidates will forfeit their deposit only on failure to secure *one-tenth* (now one-eighth) of the votes cast. Expenses incurred by party or other organizations and individuals in elections should be reported to an office of the Crown. By 15 to 14 a limitation on the use of cars additional to the existing ones was rejected.

[37] Cf. Ian Harvey (a would-be candidate), *Evening Standard*, 4 January 1939.

[38] *The Speaker's Report* referred to, in note 36, deprecated ' that a prospective or adopted Parliamentary candidate or a Member of Parliament should give any substantial donation or contribution to any charitable, social or sporting organization in the constituency or to any charitable fund specifically benefiting the constituents '. Also, the Conference, ' regarded with disapproval the direct or indirect payment of substantial contributions or annual subscriptions to party organizations (including local party organizations), designed to influence the action of such organizations in selecting any particular individual as a Parliamentary candidate '.

If these reforms were carried out, together with the equalization of electoral districts as recommended in an earlier *Speaker's Letter*, May 1944, Cmd. 6534, considerable advance would be made to truer representation of the people in Parliament. But the business premises (' plural vote ') was recommended to be retained ; and both P.R. and the Alternative Vote were rejected. The Conference had, of course, a Conservative Party majority. The Conference rejected a proposal that the State should afford direct financial assistance to candidates—a wise decision, for though the proposal is superficially attractive, it raises more serious problems than it solves.

[39] House of Commons, 17 November 1938.

[40] G. Mander, *We Told You So*, London, 1944.

[41] Cf. *The Peace Ballot, The Official History* : by D. A. Livingstone and M. S. Johnston, London, 1935. Lord Robert Cecil makes it clear that the purpose was to support the League of Nations and collective security—that is, *Lord Robert's* aim was that.

The Ballot illustrates the ambiguities and dangers of a Referendum on such complicated though, apparently, simple issues, of war and peace. What could be easier, what more apt, for the average man to decide ? The voters were strongly in favour of the League of Nations—but to what extent and on what issues ? They were in favour of all-round disarmament. But did they mean that all should start disarming at the same time, or only after agreement had been reached by an international conference ; and did they mean that, in any circumstances, Great Britain should scrap its Navy ? The vote favoured abolishing the private manufacture of arms, but was it in favour of energetic rearmament by the Government ? The vote was strongly in favour of military action against an aggressor nation if economic pressure did not suffice (but how much economic pressure ?), yet nearly 86 per cent. were in favour of abolishing naval and military aircraft. What does such a Referendum prove ? The Conservatives pretended a pacifist conclusion was to be drawn from the vote. Labour denies that. But it must be admitted that the results are not war-like. Nor did the Referendum propose alternatives for Government prosecution should the courses voted for prove unsuccessful.

[42] ' The League of Nations will remain *as heretofore*, the keystone of British foreign policy. . . . We shall therefore continue to do *all in our power* to uphold the Covenant and to maintain and increase the efficiency of the League. In the present unhappy dispute between Italy and Abyssinia there will be *no wavering in the policy we have hitherto pursued*.' I have italicized the phrases that leave a most uncertain feeling.

[43] On Proportional Representation, see Vol. II, Chap. XXI. The Conservative Party is hostile to P.R. The Labour Party is also hostile. The Liberal Party is favourable. The Communist Party, like all minority parties (e.g. the Liberal Party), which wish to utilize every vote for itself wherever it may be cast in the nation as a whole, advocates P.R. Some alleviation of the degree of non-proportional representation may be produced by the equalization of electoral districts already referred to.

As may be appreciated from the closeness of the Labour and Conservative popular vote, in the event of a swing over of perhaps less than a million votes from the latter to the former, or a substantial participation of the 25 per cent. of the electorate which does not vote, Labour might have a sound working majority in Parliament. The contingency keeps both parties alternately hoping and fearing, and therefore stimulates political keenness. In July 1945, the swing over occurred.

Here reference may be made to the most recent general treatise on proportional representation, scientifically hostile to it. F. H. Hermens, *Democracy or Anarchy ?* (University of Notre Dame, Indiana), 1941.

[44] Debates, 12 November 1936.

[45] Finer, ' Cabinet and Commons under the Impact of War ', *Political Science Quarterly*, September 1941.

[46] Debates, 10 December 1935.

[47] Cf. Debates, 5 March 1936, for discussion of the Fascists' provocation and police action. The Fascists contrived in some places to give the police force the impression that they were the supporters of law and order, while other organizations, making street demonstrations, were somehow subversive. The police became very restive under the strain. Cf. the Thurloe Square procession case, 22 March 1936.

[48] *The Public Order Act*, 1937, passed after much agitation and public debate about civil liberties, and the means of compassing the end, made it an offence for any person to wear a uniform signifying association with any political organization in any public place or meeting. Sir John (now Lord) Simon deserves great credit for introducing and carrying this measure through Parliament. It produced a notable sedative effect.

[49] *Incitement to Disaffection Act*, 1934. The Bill was bitterly fought by the Labour and Liberal Opposition, since the Government proposed, among other things, to permit the police to obtain a warrant for search for material which might cause disaffection in the armed forces from two Justices of the Peace. The Government were compelled to yield, substituting a High Court judge for the two Justices.

[50] In *Rex* v. *Cattle*, 1938, the issue was the demand by the police of a journalist that he acknowledge whence he had procured certain police information which appeared to be the basis of an article he had written. Did the Official Secrets

Act, 1920, para. 6, apply ?   It was held that a police official could give such information lawfully as had been given.   An Act was passed in 1939 amending the original Act, which required that the police must obtain the assent of the Secretary of State to conduct such an inquiry, except in case of grave emergency.

[51] Mr. Sandys sent the Secretary of State for War a note to ask whether there would be objection to his asking a question in the House regarding the inadequacy of the anti-aircraft defences of London.   The Attorney-General was apprised of this, and he told Mr. Sandys that he was liable to prosecution under the Official Secrets Act, para. 6, if he did not disclose the name of his informant. The issue of Parliamentary privilege was raised, especially when, as Junior officer in the Territorial Army, Mr. Sandys was summoned to answer before a military court of inquiry.   The strong reaction of the House of Commons and the vindication of privilege, as well as the narrative of events, may be read in House of Commons Debates, 28, 29, 30 June, 11, 19 July, 28 September, 5 December 1939.   The Select Committee of the House on the Official Secrets Acts and their applicability to Members of Parliament, reported on 25 April 1939, that disclosures by M.P.'s in debate could not be made the subject of proceedings and any other disclosure which though not in the House might be held to form part of the business of the House should have the same immunity.   The House itself had the power to discipline its errant Members.

[52] House of Commons, 12 November 1940.

[53] Cf. House of Lords Debate, 18 February 1941, for the discussion of the *Black Record* broadcasts and the problem of anonymity.

[54] Cf. Vansittart, *Lessons of my Life*, for discussion of his own position, and the principle which seems to forbid the resignation of a Civil Servant when such resignation would signalize disagreement with the Government's policy, and thus show a cleft between Cabinet and Civil Service advisers.

[55] House of Commons, Questions, 17 November 1938.

[56] Cf. A. B. Keith, *The King and the Imperial Crown*, Oxford, 1936 ; and *The King, the Constitution, the Empire and Foreign Affairs*, 1938.   Also, Kingsley Martin, *The Magic of Monarchy*, 1937.

[57] Graham Wallas, *Our Social Heritage*, Chap. ' Constitutional Monarchy '.

[58] His Majesty's Declaration of Abdication Act, 1936 ; the Regency Act, 1937.

[59] Edward VIII and George VI, cap. 39.

[60] Cf. Second Reading Debate, House of Commons, 27 February 1941.

[61] No. 120 ; 1941.

[62] Debates, col. 745, April 1937.   Cf. especially Sir John Simon's masterly survey of the constitutional background and arguments at the opening of the proceedings on the Bill, 12 April 1937.

[63] Cf. *Report on Mr. Speaker's Constituency*, No. 98, 1939.

NOTES TO CHAPTER VI

[1] Cf. generally, Beard, *America in Mid-passage*, 1938 ; *The Republic*, 1943 ; and Morrison and Commager, *Growth of the American Republic*, II, Chaps. XXII–XXV.

[2] For various calculations of the unemployed, see C. Gill, *Wasted Manpower*, New York, 1939, and Labour Statistics in Yearbook of I.L.O.

[3] Cf. Corey, *The Truth about Hoover*, 1932 ; and Herbert Hoover, *American Ideals* v. *the New Deal*, New York, 1936.

[4] The messages of the President may be seen, together with other campaign and public papers, annotated, in *The Public Papers and Addresses of Franklin Delano Roosevelt*.   They commence with the campaign for the Governorship of the State of New York and go to 1940.   For the present reference see Vol. II.

[5] For the origin of the phrase, see Raymond Moley, *After Seven Years*, New York, 1939, p. 23.

[6] Inaugural, New York, 4 March 1933, *Papers*, II, p. 11.

[7] Theodore Roosevelt, *Autobiography*, Chap. XII, 'The Big Stick and the Square Deal'; 'They realized that the Government must now interfere to protect labour, to subordinate the big corporations to the public welfare, and to shackle the cunning and fraud exactly as centuries before it had interfered to shackle the physical force which does wrong by violence.' The *Autobiography* demands re-reading to-day.

[8] Cf. speeches published under this title by J. M. Dent, London; W. Diamond, *Economic Thought of Woodrow Wilson*, 1943; and William Allen White's, *Woodrow Wilson*, 1924.

[9] E. K. Lindley, *The Roosevelt Revolution, First Phase*, New York, 1933.

[10] Beard, *America in Mid-passage*, p. 249.

[11] Cf. Pecora, *Wall Street under Oath*, New York, 1939; and *Hearings of the Senate Committee* (1933–4) *on Banking and Currency and Stock Exchange Practices*. Judge Pecora was counsel to the Senate Committee.

[12] There is an interesting account in *Fortune*, May 1940.

[13] Cf. E. W. Kemmerer, *The ABC of the Federal System*, Princeton, 1938, (especially pp. 167 ff.).

[14] The reader is recommended to consult *Security, Work, and Relief Policies*, Report of the National Resources Planning Board, 1943; MacMahon and others, *The Administration of Federal Work Relief*, Chicago, 1941; E. M. Burns, *British Unemployment Programmes*, 1920–38, Washington, 1941; Howard, the W.P.A. and Federal Relief Policy, New York, 1943.

[15] Here is a partial list of tangible accomplishments: Up to 30 June 1940, the W.P.A. had built 454,606 miles of rural roads, principally of a low-type surface or unsurfaced. In urban areas 12,797 miles of high-type surface streets and 32,248 miles of low-type surface streets had been built. The W.P.A. had newly constructed 4,383 school buildings while making improvements and additions to 30,511 existing school buildings. It had built 132 hospitals and made improvements for 1,670 others. It had constructed 1,799 stadiums, bleachers, and grandstands, reconstructed 639, and made additions to 91 others, all with a seating capacity for some 6,000,000 persons. The W.P.A. had laid 17,977 miles of new storm and sanitary sewers, while improving 3,242 miles of sewers. It had built 197 aviation landing fields, improved 317, and made additions to 50 others. In order to protect community water supplies, the W.P.A. had sealed 211,000 abandoned mine openings. Thirty-nine electric power plants had been built and 144 others improved.

Moreover, by 1 January 1940, the W.P.A. had sewed over 222,000,000 garments of all kinds for men, women, and children on relief; it had canned over 42,000,000 quarts of food; it had renovated over 67,000,000 books for school and public libraries. In a two-week period in January 1940 more than 119,000 persons were examined and treated in W.P.A. medical clinics. During March 1940 nearly 23,000,000 lunches were served in some 13,720 schools. In June 1940 more than 850,000 persons were enrolled in adult education classes, and more than 4,500 musical performances were given.

The Administration of Federal Work Relief, MacMahon, Millett, Ogden, Public Administration Service, Chicago, 1941, pp. 5–6.

[16] Wesley McCune, *The Farm Bloc*, Chap. II, 1943; this work is an intelligent appreciation of the complex and interwoven interests which together compose the 'farm' bloc—although the term 'bloc' too often gives the impression of a unified and undifferentiated interest. Cf. also E. G. Nourse and others, *Three Years of the Agricultural Adjustment Administration*, 1937; also Blaisdell, *Government and Agriculture*, 1940.

[17] For their situation see John Steinbeck's novel, *The Grapes of Wrath*, and Cary McWilliams, *Factories in the Field*.

13

[18] *Towards Farm Security*, published by the Farm Security Administration.

[19] *Report*, President's Committee on Farm Tenancy, 1936.

[20] L. S. Lyon and others, *The National Recovery Administration*, Brookings, 1935; C. F. Roos, *N.R.A. Economic Planning*, 1937.

[21] Cf. *Recent Social Trends*, I, 93 ff. This work, published by McGraw-Hill in 1932, was instituted by President Hoover to provide a scientific survey, by distinguished scholars, of the nation's most difficult problems.

[22] Cf. Finer, *T.V.A.: Lessons for International Application*, Montreal, International Labour Office, 1944.

[23] Cf. Bonbright, *The Public Utilities and the National Power Policies*, New York, 1940; and Monograph of the Attorney General's Committee on Administrative Procedure, 1941 (Govt. Printing Office), No. 25, *The Federal Power Commission*.

[24] See Huey Long's own book, *Every Man a King*, New Orleans, 1933; T. O. Harris, *The Kingfish : Huey P. Long, Dictator*, New Orleans, 1938; Forrest Davis, *Huey Long : a candid biography*, New York, 1935.

[25] Lee and Lee, *Fine Art of Propaganda*, 1939; and such a sample as, C. E. Coughlin, *Eight Lectures on Labour, Capital and Justice*, the Radio League of the Little Flower, 1934.

[26] Cf. V. O. Key, Federal Grants-in-Aid, Chicago, 1939.

[27] Cf. survey in Higgins and Musgrave, *Deficit Finance—The Case Examined*, at pp. 136–207, *Public Policy*, Harvard, 1941, and in the same volume, pp. 37–62, *Budgetary Symbolism and Fiscal Planning*, by H. S. Perloff.

[28] Cf. *World Almanac*, for platform.

[29] Cf. *World Almanac*, 1937; for acceptance speech, *Papers*, IV.

[30] Madison Square Garden, 31 October 1936, *Papers*, IV.

[31] Cf. C. J. Friedrich, *The New Belief in the Common Man*, Chap. 3, p. 114.

[32] *Report*, President's Committee on Administrative Management in the Federal Government, 1937, Government Printing Office—see edition with Special Studies.

See also, Schuyler Wallace, *Federal Departmentalization*, 1941, New York, for a most illuminating analysis of theory of departmental division of duties.

[33] J. A. Farley, *Behind the Ballots*, especially pp. 223–38, and Chap. V. Thus : ' I frankly said I believed in the patronage system and intended to follow it, something which they (the Republicans) never did.'

[34] Cf. article by the present author on the Commission on Public Service Personnel, *Political Science Quarterly*, January 1936.

[35] L. D. White, *Government Career Service*, Chicago, 1935.

[36] For another view compare *Public Administration Review*, II, 2 : *The Making of Administrators*, Spring, 1942.

[37] J. M. Beck's *Our Wonderland of Bureaucracy*, appeared in 1932—before the New Deal started ; for a review of public fallacies about the public service, see *Better Government Personnel*, 1935. Retrospects of New Deal ' bureaucracy ', appear in J. H. Crider, *The Bureaucrat*, New York, 1944, and L. Sullivan, *Bureaucracy Runs Amuck*, Indianapolis, 1944. A more reasonable text is J. M. Juran, *Bureaucracy, A Challenge to Better Management*, New York, 1944.

[38] Eighty per cent. of those on relief favoured Roosevelt; sixty-eight per cent. of the voters under 25 supported him. *Vide* Report, Institute of Public Opinion, *American Political Science Review*, February 1941.

[39] *Theory and Practice*, Vol. II, Chap. XXXVI.

[40] Address before the American Law Institute, *New York Times*, 13 May 1938.

[41] Cf. Justice Stone's opinion in *U.S.* v. *Morgan*, 307 U.S. 183, 191 (1939), and opinion of Justice Frankfurter in *U.S.* v. *Morgan*, 313 U.S. 409, 422 (1941).

[42] Cf. President Roosevelt's Veto Message on the Walter-Logan Bill, 18 December 1940 ; and for the nature and development of the issues as a whole the literature recommended in footnote 25, to Chap. I.

[43] Compare *Manual of United States Government*, for 1933 and 1940 ; and Final Report, *Attorney General's Committee on Administrative Procedure*, pp. 8–18.

[44] Cf. Brecht, *Three Topics in Comparative Administration, Organization of Government Departments*, &c. in *Public Policy*, Harvard, 1941 ; and Brecht and Glaser, *The Art and Technique of Administration in German Ministries*, Harvard, 1940.

[45] L. Brownlow in *Public Administration Review*, I, No. 2, pp. 104–5. There follow important papers on other features of the reforms.

[46] Cf. especially article by Harold Smith, the Director of the U.S. Bureau of the Budget, loc. cit., and another in *Public Administration Review*, IV, No. 3, ' The Budget as an instrument of Legislative Control Executive Management'. Compare these observations with the similar objectives of the British Select Committee on National Expenditure, Report 16, No. 120 of 1942, *Organization and Control of the Civil Service*.

[47] Cf. Congressional Committee inquiries, *Hearings, Joint Committee on Government Organization*, Senate Document, No. 8, 1937 ; *Hearings, Select Committee on Government Organization*, U.S. Senate, Bill, S.2700, August 1937.

[48] Schmeckbier in various notes in *Am. Pol. Sci. Rev.*, 1937–39.

[49] Cf. David Lawrence, *Washington Diary*, a record to the middle of 1942 not excessively friendly to the Administration ; also Hearings and Reports of the Truman (Senate) *Special Committee to Investigate the National Defence Programme*, Senate Resolution 71. From April 1941 to date.

[50] Cf. C. W. Stein, *The Third Term Tradition*, 1942. Since 1880 there have been no less than 100 proposals to limit the Presidency to two terms ; of which not one was accepted even by Congress. The issue of re-eligibility was raised again by the Republican Party in 1944, and by publicists who expressed the fear that the President's health might collapse before 1948, amidst foreign and domestic crises. It was countered by the argument that the President was Commander-in-Chief, that it was inadvisable to change military horses in the Siegfried Line, and that *if* the President and his administration were rather older than their political opponents, they had the compensating merits of intense experience.

[51] Among the recent American accounts are, E. P. Herring, *Presidential Leadership*, 1940, a short penetrating account of political relationships ; E. S. Corwin, *The President : His Office and Powers*, 1939, a most illuminating treatise on all aspects, exhibiting realistically constitutional law in practice. G. J. Milton's historical essay, *The Use of Presidential Power*, New York, 1944, is illuminating.

[52] Cf. Moley, op. cit., Chap. I, especially p. 22.

[53] Alsop and Kintner, *Men around the President*, 1935.

[54] Cf. E. E. Witte in Report President's Committee, op. cit., Studies, No. V ; and *Public Administration Review*, Spring 1942, pp. 116 ff.

[55] Roland Young, *This is Congress*, 1943.

[56] This is subject to severe friction from time to time. It is always a difficult problem in personal relationships, the marriage of true minds at both ends of Pennsylvania Avenue, and the strategy of persuasion by argument and rewards. On 24 February 1944 Senator Barkley came to the end of his tether, when President Roosevelt had returned, with a veto, the Finance Bill for the year, since in the President's opinion it did not provide enough funds, was ' a relief not for the needy but for the greedy ', and was couched in language, written by Congress, which ' not even a dictionary or thesaurus can make clear '. The Senator, who had been Floor Leader for seven years, twice as long as any previous

occupant of the office, was stung to a mighty blast in the Senate, declaring his resignation. 'Mr. President,' he cried, 'for twelve years I have carried to the best of my ability the flag of Franklin D. Roosevelt. For the past seven years I have carried the flag of the Administration as majority leader of the Senate, and during these years I have borne that flag because I felt that President Roosevelt in himself constituted a dynamic leader in the great crisis in the history of our country and the world for whom the people yearned. I daresay that during the past seven years of tenure as majority leader I have carried that flag over rougher territory than was ever traversed by any previous majority leader. Sometimes I have carried it with little help here on the Senate floor and more frequently with little help from the other end of Pennsylvania Avenue. . . . I wish to say that I have disagreed many times with my colleagues here on both sides of the political aisle, but I have sought to earn their respect and their esteem '. The President then sent him an apologetic letter, explaining that he had made some changes in the message as the result of discussion with the Senator, and expressing his great grief were he to insist on resigning. But the Democrats would not let the Senator resign—unanimously they refused the tendered resignation. This touched him, and he agreed to stay, and in a letter to the President he said : ' I realize that in these terrific times you are burdened with a responsibility no American President has ever borne. Throughout this perilous period my heart has gone out to you in sympathetic understanding, not only of your great responsibility, but your high purpose in meeting that responsibility. . . . We have sometimes disagreed as to policies, and we have sometimes disagreed as to methods. Frequently I have submerged my own views in recognition of your more intimate knowledge and your greater responsibility. Sometimes you have yielded your views to mine. . . . But it seems to me that there is something broader and more fundamental than any personal acquiescence as between you and me over matters of public policy and fundamental principles. In this great crisis of our nation's history we must all seek some common ground upon which we can meet and have confidence in one another. That applies to all branches of our Government. If we cannot trust each other in this tragic period of the history of our nation and the world, how can the people trust us ? '

With this may be compared the Earl of Clarendon's description of Charles II's relationship with the House of Commons through his ministers, Clarendon and Southampton. *Life of Clarendon* (Oxford, 1843), p. 1093 ; 301 years earlier.

[57] Cf. *Rankin of Mississippi*, *American Mercury*, June 1944, and Volta Torrey, *You and Your Congress*, pp. 22–28, on Southern Congressmen.

[58] Cf. the extremely valuable article by Otto Kircheimer, *The Historical and Comparative Background of the Hatch Law*, in *Public Policy*, Harvard, 1941, pp. 341 ff. ; also article by V. O. Key in *The Future of Government*, Chicago, 1941.

[59] Cf. the annual articles in the *American Political Science Review* on Congress and the President, under the title, ' American Government in War-Time.'

[60] Cf. Letter to *New York Times*, Sunday, 1 October 1944, by Professor Kenneth Colegrove, protesting against the deliberate refusal by the Governors of 28 States (Republican) to act as permitted by the Federal Wartime Voters Act, 1944, so that the Federal Government could transmit ballots to soldiers and sailors overseas. Ostensibly they so acted to preserve States' rights to conduct Federal elections. Yet there were allegations that such behaviour was calculated to avert the casting of votes for the Democratic candidate.

[61] Berdahl, *The War Powers of the Executive in U.S.*, Illinois, 1921 ; and, Blanket, *The Powers of the Commander-in-Chief*, 1939–44.

[62] Cf. G. C. Robinson, ' Veto Record of Franklin D. Roosevelt,' *Am. Pol. Sci. Rev.*, February 1942.

[63] Cf. National Resources Committee, Kirkpatrick and staff, *Report Federal Relations to Urban Government*, 1939.

[64] Cf. Hazlitt, *A New Constitution Now*, New York, 1943.

[65] Some observations differing from this view are to be found in a robust and interesting article by Dr. Don K. Price in *Public Administration Review*, Autumn 1943, ' Presidential and Cabinet Government '. I find myself in firm disagreement with this analysis of the British system, since it is largely founded on the fallacy that Commons and Cabinet are separate and separable bodies.

[66] Cf. David Lawrence, op. cit.; Marquis Childs, *I Write from Washington*, New York, 1942, pp. 217 onwards, *passim*; also MacMahon, op. cit., offers evidence in the same sense; and James Hart, *Am. Pol. Sci. Rev.*, especially pp. 31 ff.

[67] House of Commons Debates, 24 February 1942. In relation to what is said about Presidential responsibility in the text, the following remarks in the House of Commons by Mr. Churchill, in debate on 2 July 1942, deserve careful reflection. ' This Parliament has a peculiar responsibility. It presided over the beginning of the evils which have come on the world. I owe much to the House, and it is my hope that it may see the end of them in triumph. This it can do only if, in the long period which may yet have to be travelled, the House affords a solid foundation to the responsible Executive Government, placed in power by its own choice. The House must be a steady, stabilizing factor in the State, and not an instrument by which the disaffected sections of the Press can attempt to promote one crisis after another. If democracy and Parliamentary institutions are to triumph in this war, it is absolutely necessary that Governments resting upon them shall be able to act and dare, that the servants of the Crown shall not be harassed by nagging and snarling, that enemy propaganda shall not be fed needlessly out of our own hands and our reputation disparaged and undermined throughout the world. On the contrary, the will of the House should be made manifest upon important occasions. . . . Sober and constructive criticism, or criticism in Secret Session has its high virtue; but the duty of the House of Commons is to sustain the Government or change the Government. . . . I work myself under the supervision and control of the War Cabinet to whom all important matters are referred and whom I have to carry with me in all major decisions. . . . I am your servant, and you have the right to dismiss when you please. What you have no right to do is to ask me to bear responsibilities without the power of effective action, and to bear the responsibilities of Prime Minister, but clamped on each side by strong men.' And a little earlier, ' You will not get a government to run risks unless they feel that they have behind them a loyal, solid majority . . .' Cols. 602 to 607.

[68] H. C. Debates, 22 January 1941.

[69] Vide *Coronet*, July 1943, article by Senator Vandenberg; cf. also J. H. Perkins, ' Congressional Self-Improvement,' in *American Political Science Review*, June 1944.

[70] Cf. Galloway *et al.*, *Am. Pol. Sci. Rev.*, December 1942, *Congress—Problem, Diagnosis, Proposals*.

[71] 1944 being a Presidential election year, the Congress, under Republican pressure, and by a rider slipped into Title V of the Soldiers' Vote Act by a very clever Senator, the Army and Navy Departments were prohibited from allowing the distribution of literature to the Forces which might influence the coming elections. This prevented the showing of a film of the career of Woodrow Wilson, the circulation of Professor Charles Beard's *The Republic*. On the repeal of the rider after much derision and agitation, the *New York Times* claimed that if Congress had become a laughing stock, the fault lay with Congress.

[72] Cf. E. S. Corwin, *The Constitutional Revolution, Ltd.*, 1941, and B. F. Wright, *The Growth of American Constitutional Law*, 1942, Chaps. IX and X.

[73] In *Perry* v. *United States*, 18 February 1935 (294 U.S. 330), the Court by a five to four decision only upheld the Congressional Resolution of June 1933, abrogating the right of holders of U.S. Bonds to payment in gold.   In *Ashwander* v. *Tennessee Valley Authority* (297 U.S. 288), 1936, there was an eight to one decision in favour of the validity of the activities in water-power generation and sale of the T.V.A.—but only so far as Wilson Dam was concerned.

[74] The Frazier-Lemke Act, under the power of Congress to deal with bankruptcy, allowed farmers to enter into a voluntary composition with their mortgagees, and if this could not be accomplished stayed proceedings for five years, during which the debtor could retain the property, paying a reasonable rent, under control of the court.   In *Louisville Joint Stock Land Bank* v. *William W. Radford* (295 U.S. 555), 27 May 1935, the Court by unanimous decision decided that the Act allowed ' the taking of substantive rights in specific property acquired by the bank prior to the act '—though Congress is not prohibited from impairing the obligation of contracts, the Fifth Amendment, ' due process ', forbade this kind of taking of property.

[75] The National Recovery Act had provided that to eliminate unfair business practices each industry should formulate a code of proper practices by a body representative of the industry, and this should be law on the approval of the President.   Among the very many codes made, one regulated the poultry trade. The Schechter Poultry Corporation of New York challenged indictment for violations of the code.   The Court (*Schechter Poultry Corporation, et al.* v. *United States*, reference (295 U.S. 495), 27 May 1935) then held unanimously that the delegation by Congress of legislative power to make codes violated the principle of the separation of powers since Congress had provided no standards or procedures to contain the discretion of the Executive.   But further, the chickens stopped in New York State, after having ' flowed ' (to use the sanctioned kind of commerce) from all over the United States—but they stopped, stopped dead, after having crossed the road.   Hence, they ceased to be in interstate commerce. Hence, Congress had no jurisdiction.   This is known as the ' sick chicken ' case. In the 'hot oil' case, *Panama Refining Co., et al.* v. *Ryan, et al.* (293 U.S. 388), 7 January 1935, the Court by eight to one (Cardozo) invalidated the Petroleum Code made under authority of the Act of 16 June 1933, authorizing the President to prohibit the interstate and foreign transportation of petroleum in excess of the amounts permitted to be produced and drawn from storage by State Laws. The intention was the limitation and regulation of production.   The Court held the principle of the non-delegability of the legislative power to the Executive to have been violated.

[76] The Railroad Retirement Act, 27 June 1934, established a compulsory system of retirement, with the purpose of providing for superannuation and so promoting efficiency and safety in interstate transportation.   The Fund would be drawn from employers' and employees' contributions.   The system was compulsory.   By five to four the Court invalidated the law because it was highly unreasonable and arbitrary in that it compelled solvent railroads to contribute to insolvent carriers.

[77] The Agricultural Adjustment Act of 12 May 1933 was designed to regulate agricultural production so as to maintain prices which would give farmers a purchasing power equivalent to that during the period 1909–14.   Processing taxes could be raised by the Secretary of Agriculture to make a fund from which he would pay benefits to farmers who would enter into voluntary agreements with him for the reduction of acreage or of production, and to pay the administrative expenses.   In *United States* v. *Butler, et al.* (297 U.S. 1), 6 January, 1936, the Court by six to three invalidated the tax as being one which was an integral part of an unauthorized plan.   There was then raised the issue whether the Government could raise such a tax for ' the general welfare ', as in Constitution,

Art. I, Sect. 8. The Government contended that agricultural relief was general welfare, and while not arguing that this term had an unlimited meaning, believed that it could properly apply here. The Court held that the power of appropriation could fall within the ' general welfare ' clause, and need not be limited by the enumerated grants of power, but it would not then decide whether agricultural relief was or was not within the scope of the term. But rather, it held that agriculture was within the reserved powers of the States. This was an invasion of the area. In the case of *Carter* v. *Carter Coal Co.*, 298 U.S. 238, 18 May 1936, the Guffey Coal Act of 30 August 1935, was invalidated on similar grounds. This Act provided for a Code for the coal mining industry, including labour conditions, to regulate production and prices. This was to be sanctioned through a sale tax on coal at the mine, with a rebate to the producers who practised the Code. The Court's attitude was more than usually eclectic : it invalidated the law by five to four, with various dissents. But the majority invalidated it because the promotion of general welfare was not a power granted in itself by the Constitution. Was it to be discovered in the enumerated powers ? The only one applicable was the interstate commerce clause. But the ' production ' of coal was not ' commerce ' in coal. The regulation of labour conditions was too remote in its effect on commerce to count in this case.

Note 83, below, has more to say on the ' general welfare ' provision of the Constitution. It was finally given a very liberal interpretation.

[78] Warren, *Congress, the Constitution and the Supreme Court*, 1925.

[79] Alsop and Catledge, *The 168 Days*, New York, 1938.

[80] In these Hearings, a Senator, confused and nettled by frequent references to the ' non-existence ' of the British Constitution, cried out : ' File me a copy of the British Constitution ! '

[81] In this case, *West Coast Hotel Company* v. *Parrish* (300 U.S. 379), involving state laws fixing minimum wages for women, one justice, Mr. Roberts, changed his attitude of a year before on a similar case, abandoned the conservatives, and thus the Chief Justice was able to overrule the Adkins case which had stood since 1923 (cf. Vol. I, p. 220). The Chief Justice denied that the Constitution, in protecting liberty, recognized an absolute and uncontrollable liberty. It was in the public interest to protect the welfare of women, furthermore, ' What these workers lose in wages the taxpayers are called upon to pay. The bare cost of living must be met. . . . The community is not bound to provide what is in effect a subsidy for unconscionable employers.'

[82] Here the Court decided that the effect of unfair labour practices of the Jones and Laughlin Steel Corporation (301 U.S. 1), was to obstruct interstate commerce in the commodity which it manufactured and sold. For the Court held the power to regulate commerce was the power to legislate for its protection and advancement. The argument that a ' flow ' of commerce was necessary, as in the Schechter case, was not essential. If, as in this case, the activities were intrastate in character when separately considered, but yet had such a close and substantial relationship to interstate commerce, then Congress could not be denied the power to protect it from burdens and obstructions.

[83] In *Carmichael* v. *Southern Coal Company*, the Unemployment Compensation Act of the State of Alabama was in issue. Justice Stone, speaking for the majority, drew attention to the permanent incidence of unemployment in America's industrial system ; observed that its economic and social wastage permeated the entire social structure ; and that *local agencies were unable to cope* with the task. Alabama itself had only been able to provide five per cent. of the relief money spent in the State from 1933 to 1935. The Social Security Act did not coerce the State into establishing unemployment compensation schemes, by taxing employers. The Alabama and the Federal statutes constituted a co-operative effort to carry out a public purpose common to both, which neither

could fulfil alone ; and the Constitution did not prohibit such co-operation, assisted by the Federal taxing power.   Then, the same day, the Court upheld the federal tax on employers for this purpose (*Steward Machine Co*. v. *Davis*). Finally (in *Helvering* v. *Davis*), (301 U.S. 495), the levying of a tax to provide funds to be paid out in old-age pensions was validated as constitutional under Article I, Sect. 8 of the Constitution which reads : ' The Congress shall have Power : To lay and collect Taxes, Duties, Imposts, and Excises, to pay the Debts and provide for the common Defence and general Welfare of the United States ; but all Duties, Imposts, and Excises shall be uniform throughout the United States . . .'

This issue, whether Congress is limited to the specific list of powers in the Article, or whether ' General welfare ' gives Congress a general power to act for the good of the nation, and so to tax and spend for it, has been in debate since the Constitutional Convention.   In this case, said Justice Cardozo, ' it is now settled '.   But the line must be drawn between particular and general.   ' The discretion, however, is not confided to the Courts.   The discretion belongs to Congress, unless the choice is clearly wrong, a display of arbitrary power, not an exercise of judgment. . . .   Nor is the concept of general welfare static.   Needs that were narrow or parochial a century ago may be interwoven in our day with the well-being of the Nation.   What is critical or urgent changes with the times. The purge of the nation-wide calamity that began in 1929 has taught us many lessons.   Not the least, of the solidarity of interests that once may have seemed to be divided. . . .'

This was the first time the significance of general welfare had been passed upon by the Court.   But it had been the subject of political and lawyers' controversies since the founding of the Constitution.   Cf. J. F. Lawson, *The General Welfare Clause*, 1934.

[84] Cf. especially H. W. Edgerton, ' The Incidence of Judicial Control over Congress ' in *Cornell Law Quarterly*, XXII, April 1937, pp. 299 ff. ;   Swisher *American Constitutional Development*, Chap. 32 and pp. 978–82 ; and B. F. Wright, op. cit. ; and Warren, *Congress, the Constitution and the Supreme Court*.

[85] See *W. Virginia State Board of Education, et al.* v. *Walter Barnette and others*, 14 June 1943.   Known as the second Gobitis Case.

[86] James Hart, ' A Unified Economy and States' Rights ', *Annals, Am. Acad. Pol. Sci.*, May 1936.

[87] H. N. Groves, *Tax Differentials and Relocation of Industry*, 31st Annual Conf. on Taxation of National Tax Association, 1935, pp. 557–61.

Temporary National Economic Committee, Govt. Printing Office, Monograph on Interstate Economic Barriers.

[88] F. E. Melder, *Agricultural Quarantine as Trade Barrier*, Chicago, Council of State Governments, 1939.

[89] *Report*, President's Advisory Committee on Education, 1938.   Tables 1 and 2, pp. 225–6, on the differences in educational expenditure per child in the various States.

[90] *Royal Commission on the Australian Constitution*, 1929.   Cf. also defeat by referendum of attempt to increase Commonwealth powers, August 1944.

[91] *Reports of Royal Commission on Dominion-Provincial Relations* (The Sirois Report), 3 Vols., 1940, and the series of Studies in Appendices, 8 Vols., 1938–9.

[92] *U.S.* v. *South Eastern Underwriters Association* ; decision given in a Court of seven by a majority of one.   Cf. Thomas Reed Powell, ' Insurance in Commerce ', *Harvard Law Review*, September 1944.

[93] For recent surveys of the problem and the growing solution, see J. P. Clark, ' The Rise of the New Federalism ', Columbia, 1938 ; G. S. S. Benson, ' The New Centralization ', New York, 1941 ; and A. W. MacMahon, ' Taking Stock of

Federalism in the U.S.A.', *Canadian Journal of Economic and Political Science,* May 1941 ; also Senate Document 69, 1943 ; *Federal, State and Local Government Fiscal Relations.*

[94] W. B. Graves, *Uniform State Action,* North Carolina, 1934, and W. B. Graves (editor), 'Intergovernmental Relations', *Annals, American Academy Political Science,* January 1940.

[95] Cf. V. O. Key, op. cit.

[96] Report, National Resources Planning Board, *Federal Relations to Urban Government,* I, Pt. II.

[97] Report, National Resources Committee, *Regional Factors in National Planning and Development,* 1935.

[98] Cf. Finer, op. cit., Pritchett, *T.V.A. : A Study in Public Administration,* 1943, and Lilienthal, *T.V.A. : Democracy Marches On,* 1944.

NOTES TO CHAPTER VII

[1] Cf. Harold Lasswell, *World Politics and Personal Insecurity,* New York, 1935.

[2] Cf. Reports I and II of the International Labour Office to the Conference, May 1944, entitled, respectively, *Constitution, Future Status and Policy, I.L.O.,* and *Economic Aspects of Social Policy.* Also Eugene Staley, *World Economic Development,* I.L.O., 1944.

[3] Art. 5 runs : ' They desire to bring about the fullest collaboration between all nations in the economic field with the object of securing, for all, improved labour standards, economic advancement and social security.' Art. 6 looks to a peace which will give all nations safety and ' which will afford assurance that all the men in all the lands may live out their lives in freedom from fear and want '.

[4] ' The right of a useful and remunerative job in the industries or shops or farms or mines of the nation ;

' The right to earn enough to provide adequate food and clothing and recreation ;

' The right of every farmer to raise and sell his products at a return which will give him and his family a decent living ;

' The right of every business man, large and small, to trade in an atmosphere of freedom from unfair competition and domination by monopolies at home or abroad ;

' The right of every family to a decent home ;

' The right to adequate medical care and the opportunity to achieve and enjoy good health ;

' The right to adequate protection from the economic fears of old age, sickness, accident and unemployment ;

' The right to a good education.'

[5] I refer to von Hayek's *Road to Serfdom,* 1944, and to Ludwig von Mises' *Omnipotent Government,* and *Bureaucracy,* Yale, 1944.

The works mentioned are very stimulating and offer serious questions for theoretical answer, and for solution in the practice of government and administration. Von Hayek's chief points are : (1) The diversity of human desires is so great that no planner can even imagine the good of others. (2) Even if the planner only plans a part of the field of human existence, the rest is affected, and affected possibly in a way that is not deliberately wished : so there is regimentation everywhere, yet some at least escape desire and control. (3) As there are such great diversities of desire Parliament can never agree on a plan, so that its making is left to the arbitrary action of the administrative authorities, and this, as well as the continuing need for constant adjustment in time to meet all the usual dynamic contingencies of a modern economic system, must mean arbitrary action and therefore the discarding of the Rule of Law. (4) That the plans cannot therefore be justified by reason, and therefore will be made and executed by force ; and since this is so, the worst elements of the population will come to the top.   Planning in the sense and by the means suggested is already dominant in the climate of opinion in Great Britain, and is identical with the situation in Germany twenty years ago ; and even as that produced the Nazi dictatorship in Germany, so the same trend will, if not stopped, produce dictatorship in Great Britain.   Von Hayek saw the former at first-hand while in his native land of Austria.

There are cogent answers to these fears of von Hayek.   They are (1) Not all social life will be planned : Parliament and the common man have never followed the theoretical extremists, on whichever side they may be.   (2) It is possible to plan, and limit and measure your planning, to secure what Parliament, representing the whole people, wants, and not to overlap into what it does not want.   Men have been making laws, that is planning, for centuries, and they are even cleverer to-day than they were at an earlier stage in the State's existence. (3) Society can always stop short when its imagination tells it that there is something undesirable as an accompaniment of something that *is* desirable.   (4) Society is continually retracing its steps when it realizes that it has made a mistake in legislation or administration.   (5) It is highly possible that Professor von Hayek has not fully followed the development of governmental and administrative techniques, which enable society to avoid some of the minor pitfalls which form part of his inhibitory arguments.   The choice, too, is not between an entirely notional and abstract system of *laissez-faire*, and a system of administration by public authority which runs true to the horrid notional and abstract form provided for it by deductive reasoning from an untenable premiss, but between industry and commerce such as they are, and administration and government such as they are and such as they may easily be.   (Cf. Finer, *The Sense of Responsibility in Social Life*, pp. 152–250 of *Le Sens de la Responsabilité dans la Vie Sociale*, Université Libre, 1938, Brussels ; the Hearings of the Temporary National Economic Committee, U.S. Congress, especially the Monographs, and among these Marshall Dimock's *Bureaucracy in Large Enterprises*.)

Finally, it may be suggested for consideration that Germany is not Great Britain.   Professor Hayek goes back to the good old days in England, when Mill and others like him swayed economic and political opinion.   But can he quote the like in German from German authors ?   He compares two nations that cannot be compared, which is rather a weak kind of argument.   ' You cannot step into the same river twice,' said the classic ancient.   Do you believe it possible to step into the same country twice, still more to step into two very different countries and argue that their experience is sufficiently the same to found a structure of deduction ?   Englishmen are not Germans or Austrians. They may be worse or better, but they are not the same.   Whether a country can plan, and how much it will want to plan, to what degree, and by what machinery, will be decided not by observation from the outside of their theories and institutions, but only from the *inside* of the institutions and the *inside* of the men.   And it happens that in this case the peculiar qualities of British nature in politics and government are things decisive of the issues, not general concepts or particular Germans.

Cf. *The Road to Reaction*, by the present author, to be published November 1945 (Boston, *Atlantic Monthly* and Little, Brown).   A full answer to *The Road to Serfdom*.

INDEX

Printed in Great Britain by
Butler & Tanner Ltd.,
Frome and London